# BEYOND THE BRINK
# WITH INDIANA

# BEYOND THE BRINK WITH INDIANA

## By BOB HAMMEL

The Bloomington Herald-Telephone
&
Indiana University Press
Bloomington & Indianapolis

# Acknowledgments

| | |
|---|---|
| Editor | John Harrell |
| Art director | Steve Snyder |
| Production | John Matson |
| Graphic arts | Danny Wagoner |
| Photographers | Larry Crewell |
| | Phil Whitlow |
| | John Terhune |
| | Jim Rider |
| Cover photograph | Larry Crewell |
| Editorial assistance | Allan Murphy |
| Project director | Michael Hefron |

ISBN 0-253-33100-5
ISBN 0-253-28535-6 (pbk.)

# Contents

# Introduction

"The 'brink' of what, John? Fill in the blank."

John Feinstein, the nation's newest and most unexpected millionaire author, already was a veteran of talk shows and meet-the-author press sessions by the time the question came at a late-January stop in Indianapolis. It wasn't a new question, and the answer was glib, though not an answer.

"Anything you want," Feinstein said.

Whatever was in mind when Feinstein picked the title, *A Season on the Brink*, for his book on spending the 1985-86 season inside the Indiana University basketball inner sanctum, the 1986-87 Hoosier team

**For Bob Knight, his basketball team, and the state of Indiana, it definitely was not a season on the blink.**

John Terhune

surely went beyond it.

The Hoosiers won the national collegiate championship.

They did it with a flourish that had melodramatic overtones. They had to come back to win in their first real tournament test — against Auburn in a second-round game before a record crowd in the spacious Indianapolis Hoosier Dome. And their home-state darling, Steve Alford, led them through. They had to come back from the dead to win against Louisiana State in the Midwest Regional final at Cincinnati. And a son of Cincinnati, Rick Calloway, gave them the last-seconds rebound basket that won the game. They had to rally from eight points behind in the last eight minutes of the national championship game against Syracuse in the Louisiana Superdome. And a son of Louisiana, Keith Smart, hit the biggest jump shot in Indiana history to make them a last-seconds winner.

Their championship came on the night that Hollywood awarded its Oscars. A major film of the season was named *Hoosiers*. It didn't win an Oscar, but it won America. It had nothing to do with Indiana's 1986-87 season, and it had everything to do with it. Its story line was written by the Milan Indians of 1953-54, Indiana's all-time most popular high school basketball champions. *Hoosiers* was a warm and wonderful story, almost too good to be true. Like Milan. Like Indiana in that 1987 tournament drive, to its thousands of home-state fans.

*A Season on the Brink* was a story of its own. Feinstein, a Duke graduate and basketball devotee, conceived the idea of following an Indiana team from its first October practice through its final game —

Indiana, because Feinstein considered its coach, Bob Knight, to be "the most compelling" figure in the sport. Feinstein made the suggestion to Knight at the 1985 NCAA tournament's Final Four in Lexington, Ky., and Knight agreed to provide the access necessary. Probably, the only one who thought much about the project in the next few weeks and months was Feinstein. Knight's priorities were getting his Indiana basketball program back at the top after a bottoming-out season: 19-14, missing an NCAA tournament spot. It was the year he threw a chair on the floor during a game. It was a year that prompted Knight to change his longheld reluctance to recruit junior college players, feeling he had waited too long for high school talent to surface in the areas that had sustained him for so many years —Indiana, Ohio and Illinois, notably Indiana, which was in a rare drought of college-sized players.

In that summer of 1985, Knight also was to take his team around the world, a trip he had been counseled to give up in the wake of the long, strained 1984-85 season. He went ahead with the trip, feeling it would expedite development of the players who were coming back. It did, and it gave him a temporary center: 6-foot-7 Daryl Thomas, who had never played the position before the trip began. Knight returned to the U.S. from the five-week swing through Japan, China, Hong Kong, Yugoslavia and Finland and worked in only a little of the fishing and hunting that usually fill his summer. His mind was on integrating his holdover players with the first two products of his new attention to junior colleges, Andre Harris and Todd Jadlow, and with Rick Calloway, a high school recruit Knight felt could be outstanding.

Then Feinstein showed up in Bloomington in October, so did the new basketball season, and the year forever to be known as the Indiana-Knight-Feinstein "season on the brink" began, took place, and ended in the abruptness of first-round NCAA tournament elimination by

Phil Whitlow

underrated Cleveland State.

Long before then, predictably, Knight had tired of the project and the author, not necessarily in that order. Lengthy and intimate conversations far into the night had taken place between Knight and Feinstein rather frequently in late October, November and much of December. Those ended, and there were occasional flareups that put Feinstein's literary season on a brink of its own, but Knight never cut off the access to his team that he had promised. The chill of the Knight-Feinstein relationship through those finishing months, however, was represented in their last Bloomington moment before Feinstein headed off to write. Knight was in his lockerroom-office just off the Assembly Hall playing court, watching films and talking with some of the assistant coaches who share the room.

"What do you want?" he asked when Feinstein entered the room.

**Bob Knight — a new season, a new team, and a new problem**

'We have good talent . . .

quickness, ability to shoot . . .

mentally tough enough?'

Phil Whitlow

"I'm leaving and I just wanted to say goodbye."

"Don't let the door hit you in the ass on your way out."

Artificial niceties are not prominent in the makeup of Robert Montgomery Knight.

Theirs was one of the most unusual book arrangements ever arrived at. Knight, the subject who — through a national prominence both positive and negative — unquestionably had far, far more to do with the book's soaring success than the arduous work of its author, is not a man prone to naivete where money matters are concerned. He's very good at making a buck. Yet, he concluded the arrangement with Feinstein without a contract, without an editing voice, without a penny in compensation or profit-sharing. Each became oversights he surely later regretted.

No money involvement was the reason there was no contract, but no contract meant nothing in writing that proved conclusively a few agreements that Knight thought were his rather tiny price for providing the subject matter and the access central to the book's success.

One of those involved language. Feinstein has heard of Knight's dissatisfaction with him on that subject and defended himself by saying, "I can't say that Bob Knight said, 'Please box out.' " Nor was that ever Knight's insistence or expectation. Bob Knight employs the language of the lockerroom as saltily and unapologetically as any sailor or longshoreman at work. Naturally there would be profanity in the book. However, two words that showed up in the book — not God-damn, or son of a bitch, or any of several extensions beyond, or a barnyard phrase or two — to Knight represented a clear and simple breach of faith on an issue about which he had been explicit. They're not difficult to sort out. They're words no family newspaper in the land would use, and Knight was under the impression he was talking to a newspaperman, used to such strictures.

Obviously, Knight could have kept

both words out of the book by going the entire season without using them. He did make strides toward reducing his use of the two last year. And a high percentage of the lapses that did come popped out in private conversation when the book or the author came up.

What Knight certainly didn't anticipate was how often that would happen, that in every road stop along the entire season, he would run into local newspaper coverage with a new Feinstein interview, a new probe of the book to pinpoint local grievances, a new team and populace with documented reasons to be angry and aroused.

Not dumb, Knight realized from the beginning that any public reaction by him would help sell the book. It ran counter to every inflammable instinct of his to keep his mouth shut on the subject, but he dammed up his growing rage till the late January week when Illinois was to play at Indiana and Terry Boers of the Chicago *Sun-Times* asked Knight to verify some criticisms of Illinois coach Lou Henson attributed to him. To one, Knight responded: "When did I say that?" Boers read directly from the book. And, for the first time, more than three months after the book hit print, Knight said to hell with judgment and book sales and erupted: about Feinstein, about the book, about misrepresentations, about views attributed to him without quotations backing them up. Before and almost without fail thereafter, Knight declined to answer questions regarding the book, as well known as his displeasure became.

Nevertheless, well into Final Four week, it was common to hear, "Doesn't he realize that every time he pops off, all he does is increase sales?" He certainly did realize it, but he had supplied Boers with enough material that the same pithy quotes kept coming up in news stories — so frequently they seemed freshly re-uttered. And sales kept climbing, through more than two months with the book No. 1 on the non-fiction best-seller list.

The Hoosiers' first road trip of the year showed him a new problem created by the book. When the Hoosiers arrived at Notre Dame's Athletic and Convocation Center for their game-morning practice Dec. 2, Irish coach Digger Phelps, as close a friend as Knight has on his regular schedule, somewhat mysteriously and icily demanded that Knight go with him for a moment of private conversation.

The moment became more than an hour, more than the length of the Hoosiers' practice. Phelps was both angered and hurt by some things in the book, such as:

• Knight's asking an assistant who had scouted Notre Dame: "Could we bury them?"

• Knight's consideration, right up to tipoff time in Bloomington a year before, of using a 2-3 zone defense — knowing what a surprise it would be to Phelps and all basketball, given Knight's intransigence about altering his defensive philosophy to include anything but man-to-man coverage.

The "bury" question Phelps interpreted as an implication that Knight wanted to beat the Irish as badly as he could. Not at all, Knight said. "I'll guarantee you that the very next question I asked was, 'Could they bury us?' It's something I have always done, to get an idea of just how the guy who saw the team play thinks we compare."

The zone matter came across to Phelps as an indication Knight felt he could not only beat but also embarrass Phelps and his team, by — in effect, given Knight's well known views — taking them on with one hand tied behind Hoosier backs. Not at all, Knight said one more time. Indeed he did consider using a zone — that wasn't misreported. "I think that would have been the absolute best way to play that team you had last year," Knight said. "You had good inside players who weren't particularly good shooters, and you had David Rivers, who can kill any team if he penetrates, and he's hard as hell to stop from penetrating with man-to-man defense."

**Knight counsels Steve Alford, Dean Garrett, Joe Hillman, Tony Freeman**

An ironic followup to the conversation was that Knight came out that night with a 2-3 zone defense. The game was carried nationally by ESPN, and across the country, jaws dropped. In Iowa City, Iowa guard and Hoosier native Jeff Moe was watching the game. "When they came out in a zone, I almost did a backflip. I couldn't believe that."

Knight stayed in it for more than half the game, and it was a key to the Hoosiers' 67-62 victory in an arena where, later in the year, Top 20 clubs from North Carolina, Duke and DePaul were to fall.

After the game, the relationship patched, Phelps shook Knight's hand in congratulation of victory and said of the zone, and the morning conversation: "You didn't do that just to stick it to me, did you?" The answer, given and in truth, was no, for the very reasons Knight gave Phelps in their crisis-time chat: the zone was in the Hoosier game plan from the beginning.

The experience showed Knight the side-effect he hadn't anticipated: on other coaches and teams.

For years, he has realized — and taken some justifiable pride in the fact — that he and the Indiana program have become very special targets. He had commented on the very subject at a fans' luncheon in Bloomington the day before the Hoosier season opened:

"This team I think could beat anybody in the country just playing basketball — just come out and play, and the other team plays . . . I think this team is capable of beating anybody. But what happens is emotion. There is an emotional involvement in play against us that probably only a couple of teams in college athletes face. Notre Dame in football has exactly the same thing.

"Because of all the things over the years that have happened in Indiana basketball, our kids get the best shot, the best effort, that the other team can give.

"Our team will play some really good games this year. It always has. It always will. We'll beat some teams rather easily that probably have pretty good talent.

"That talent always seems to come to the front when they're playing us — a lot of times here, always when we go on the road. That's what this team has to learn to cope with and deal with more than anything else.

"We have had some teams that were very, very good at it. In 1976, I used to breathe a sigh of relief when we played on the road, because they, too, knew what happened when we played away — biggest crowd of the season, most charged-up atmosphere imaginable. They beat some very good teams under very difficult circumstances because they understood that.

"That's the thing more than anything else that this team has to understand. This team plays with a lot of ability. This team plays with a lot of championships, a lot of tradition that started here long before I ever thought about coming.

"We have a good blend of talent,

**A warm sideline reception for Steve Alford from fellow senior Todd Meier and Coach Bob Knight**

John Terhune

quickness, ability to shoot the ball, board, depth — a lot of things. And yet I'm not convinced that we are mentally tough enough to understand that some teams can play not particularly well but end up winning because they're a little bit better or a little bit better organized. That can't happen to us."

After the experience with Phelps, Knight felt an obligation to expand on the theme to his players. At a game-day team meeting, he asked how many had read the book and was a little surprised when not one said he had. Basically, they're an honest, upright, honorable, God-fearing lot, but it's possible a few of the Hoosiers felt fibbing might be an allowable, indeed advisable, sin, under the circumstances.

Knight explained what had just happened with Phelps, and how the book no doubt included other passages that would be used to incite teams to a special pitch. He apologized for his role in allowing the book to be done and adding to the players' pressures. It was a low-key, pleasant, humor-spiced session with the basic message: "Be ready for anything, from here on out. I've made it even tougher for you by allowing this book."

He had, which made a 30-4 year all the more remarkable, achieved as it was by a team that was as uncertain in makeup when practice began as any Knight ever has had. It turned out to be a season that soared far above and beyond the one of the book, in spite of the book, in a sense in answer to the book.

It was a most unusual way to win a national championship — in the public's eye from Day 1 to year's end, the team's holdover performers under scrutiny to see what carryovers could be detected from the season that had been described to more than 600,000 book-buyers.

Success is never, in itself, justification of method. The success of Indiana's 1986-87 Hoosiers, however, certainly was an answer to the Indianapolis question:

"The 'brink' of what?"

Something very nice.

Bob Knight — a very public championship

# 1 Smart, at start

It was a routine pre-season. Before practice even began Oct. 15, the Hoosiers lost two freshman guards to surgery — Tony Freeman (shoulder) and Jeff Oliphant (foot). The first time the Hoosiers went public, in an intra-squad scrimmage at Gary, coach Bob Knight announced at the end of it all that returning starter Daryl Thomas had been dropped from the team. Three days after that, Thomas returned to the team but two more players went down that very day with injuries — Rick Calloway (knee) and Kreigh Smith (ankle). In Marion, the two most celebrated players in Indiana high school basketball, guards Lyndon Jones and Jay Edwards, made a joint announcement that they would enroll at Indiana next year. And, in New York a book came out.

Just a routine pre-season at Indiana.

There was an element of adaptation to the start of this new season for every Hoosier player, including the most seasoned of them all: Steve Alford. Alford and the rest of the Hoosiers had packed away their gear the previous season just before the college game's rulesmakers dropped a bomb on the sport by adding the three-point shot, effective in the 1986-87 season. Around the nation, it quickly took on the tag of "the Steve Alford rule." The basketball-conscious were quite aware that, as a freshman, Alford had made the 1984 Olympic team, and eventually its starting lineup, on his outside shooting skill. As a junior, he had become the first consensus all-America player from the Big Ten in five years, primarily on his outside shooting skill. The day that news of the rule came out, Alford's reaction was "Great!" And it never changed.

He still felt good about it when pre-season workouts began. After a few days of practicing with the line in place on-court, Alford was reluctant to say he was particularly conscious of it as he worked to get shots. "I notice it," he said. "I'd be lying if I said I didn't. I enjoy it.

"I haven't approached the year much differently than I did before. I wanted to come in in as good condition as possible, and I think I'm all right there. I worked harder on the weights during the summer than I ever did before — four or five days a week, where it used to be only two or three. I seem to be staying right around 185 pounds. I came here (as a freshman) weighing 150. It's nice. It feels good. I know my strength is improved, and my endurance is better.

"I tried to work this summer on defense and seeing the floor, getting everybody involved. And I think it's important for the seniors — Daryl, Todd (Meier) and I — that our leadership qualities continue to get better.

"With our junior-college transfers, for example. I know they can really help us. The quicker I can help them get ready, the better it will be for all of us. There's a lot to learn with our motion offense and our defensive rules. But they're great kids and they're working hard. They've made tremendous strides already."

Keith Smart must have wondered who in the world Alford was talking about. While Alford was playing with a top-of-the-world feeling in October, Smart was so low he thought every day of quitting.

That wasn't the way he had thought it would go at all. Because of Knight's position as chairman of the

'I was lying on the bed thinking, I can't take it. I'm going to waste a year and sit on the bench. Oh, man, I'll never fit in here.'

Jim Rider

**For Keith Smart, getting introduced to Bloomington and IU basketball, even a walk to the fieldhouse was no easy matter**

Player Selection Committee for the U.S. Olympic basketball program, Smart had been given a spot on a U.S. select team that Dayton coach Don Donoher took to Taiwan in June. Calloway also was on that team, and Calloway and Smart formed a friendship, while Smart — the only player on the Donoher team straight from junior college basketball — also was building confidence that he could, indeed, play with major college stars. Smart reported to Bloomington straight from the select team's return.

Assistant coach Joby Wright checked Smart in at the dormitory where he would be staying. Wright told Smart some other Hoosiers would be playing some basketball late that afternoon at the fieldhouse, and left. "I'm all alone in the dorm now," Smart recalled, "and I'm thinking, 'Where in the hell is the fieldhouse?' I can't reach Joby, and I know no one on campus, so I take it on my own to try to walk and find the fieldhouse." It was about a mile away. His meandering search took him in the opposite direction, from his dormitory on the northeast side of campus to Kirkwood Avenue on the west side, then all the way back through to a point southeast of everything, at least a three-mile walk. "I ended up down on Third Street at a Marathon Oil place," Smart said. "I walked back to the dorm. Daryl had left a note on my door saying, 'We're going to play some basketball later on. Come up to my room before you leave.' I hadn't met Daryl. I just went up to his room and I said, 'Man, I've been all *over* the place trying to find the fieldhouse.'

"So we went down to play, and my legs were just too tight from walking all day. They cramped up. I was slow. I couldn't move. Everyone's in there watching me and they're saying (in a whispered recreation of what he was hearing): 'What's *wrong* with him?' But, Steve and I teamed up for some pretty good plays, fast break and all that, and he told me, 'I like that kind of basketball.'

"Even in pickup games like that, I

was impressed. I liked the way they played together. They'd say, 'Come on, Steve, use the screen,' always trying to give up themselves so someone else could score." The screens were an education in themselves. "One day in those pickup games I was on the team against Steve, and I was guarding him. They were actually running the offense, with Steve coming off the screens. Here I am a new guy, not used to screens, and I was just getting nailed. I think he's going inside, and he pops outside, and there's a screen. Boom! I'm getting frustrated, because here are all these big guys laying screens on me. And every shot goes in. I thought, 'Oh, man.' "

A few days later, Garrett checked in. Smart, from Garden City, Kan., Junior College, and Garrett, from San Francisco City College, had spent nine days together in an Olympic development program at Colorado Springs. "It was a quick relationship," Smart said. "Dean and I got to know each other real well. We weren't on the same team. In the format there, we played six games. He played real well. The team he had took it as an all-star game. They were *all* trying to score. They didn't look in the middle at all. He still averaged double figures in points and double figures in scoring. I was impressed."

So was Garrett. "Keith was *real* quick, a real good player. He was just running past guys."

Thomas was Garrett's roommate, and he already had become a Smart confidante. Smart remembers times when the three were in the Thomas-Garrett quarters together, Thomas studying for his summer classes and the two newcomers, not enrolled in anything then, musing about their future: " 'Man, this is amazing. Can you believe this, man? It's hard to believe we're here at Indiana. We've *got* to have a good year.' We even mentioned a national championship . . . 'We could *win* it, man. We're gonna be tough.'

"We'd say something like that, and Daryl would say, 'This is no *junior* college. You don't win a championship that way. It's going to be tough in the Big Ten. Let me tell you about the Big Ten.' And everything he said turned out to be true. He didn't oversell it at all.

"Then Daryl would go to class, and Dean and I would be there together, and we'd say, 'Man, we can't *wait* till the season starts.' "

Right up to the start of practice, Smart was starry-eyed in anticipation. Not that he hadn't been warned how tough things would be. "Guys had told me what to expect — it was going to be hard, and I was going to be very tired." Weeks of running and weight work precede the start of practice. "The guys said pre-season conditioning does the body some good. 'You're still gonna be totally exhausted. But if you had missed pre-season conditioning, you would die.'

"After going through it, they were exactly right.

"That first day . . . we were in and out of the gym in just two hours. But we were going from station to station real, real quick, everything to a beat, non-stop. I was dead tired the first day. Super tired. I hurt so bad."

The second day was a repeat. And the third day . . . the schedule the same for veterans and newcomers: fundamental instruction that is at the heart of Knight's basketball. "We were doing a lot of things I had never done before — ballhandling drills, zigzag drills. I was kinda confused, then on top of being confused, tired. That just made it even worse."

When the time came to play some real basketball, it didn't get a bit better for Smart.

"Every day throughout that six-week period was a low moment for me. I'd go home from practice thinking, 'I don't belong here.' I thought about that a whole lot. I thought about quitting so many times. I told Joby one day: 'The way I'm playing, I don't belong here.' Joby told Coach I said that . . . " Knight lost the best player he ever recruited to a similar down moment, Larry Bird walking away from school before practice ever began in the fall of 1974. Knight sees himself now as too rigid

when that happened, too hard-line to sense the emotional low that led Bird to leave without saying a word to anyone. He wasn't about to lose Smart so easily. "Coach pulled me over at practice and said, 'Don't you even think that again.' " Smart said. Knight made a point of trying to prop up Smart's confidence. He had his coaches and his senior leaders working at the same project. "I tried to fight it," Smart said, "but I just kept thinking, 'I don't belong here.' I'd make mistakes and I would think, 'Someone playing at Indiana wouldn't make those mistakes.' I looked at Indiana like it was something precious — there was no bad, you could never make a mistake and be able to play for Indiana.

"All the time, the other guys were saying, 'Hey, don't worry. You're going to be all right. It will come to you.' All the coaches were telling me, 'Isiah Thomas, Randy Wittman, all those guys went through it the first year. It's a big adjustment going from being a big star in your school to coming in here and having to learn everything all over again. It's hard.'

"I'd try to believe it, but I'd say, 'Now, wait. Isiah didn't go through this. There's no *way* Steve (Alford) went through something like this.'

"Coach had a coaches' clinic one Saturday. Open practice. And I'm terrible. I could hear guys saying, '*That's* the kid who's going to play?' . . . 'That Smart, I'll tell you, he won't be anything here.'

"It was killing me."

At the same time, Smart had some academic catching-up to do. Not all of his junior college credits counted, and the Big Ten operates with a rule that pins eligibility not only to cumulative grade average but also to attaining sufficient hours to stay on schedule toward a degree. Smart's problem was complicated by the fact that he attended one semester of junior college on his own, while trying to convince his Garden City coaches that he could play well enough to get a scholarship. By Big Ten regulations, that meant he had to be the academic equivalent of a

*I'd try to believe it, but I'd say, 'Now, wait. Isiah didn't go through this. There's no way Steve went through something like this.'*
— Keith Smart

**Daryl Thomas operates in big company**

John Terhune

senior by January. He had to take 18 hours of classes (three more than the usual student load) the fall semester to be eligible in January.

"Now I'm going home at night thinking, 'I've got to get this homework.' I had a great deal of reading — it seemed like in every class I had two books to read from. I'm tired and I have to read, and while I'm reading, my mind focused back on my bad play. I would call my mom — I would never talk to her about quitting, but just by me calling home, she knew there was some problem. She and my aunt would say, 'Keith doesn't sound good.' They'd ask me how I was doing; 'I'm doing fine.' How's basketball going? 'OK.' She knew there was something wrong.

"I was lying on the bed thinking, 'I can't take it. I've come here and now I'm going to waste a year and sit on the bench.' I'm thinking that I was overrated coming out of junior college. 'Oh man, I'll never fit in here.'

"It was never the coaches. I was just doubting myself, and I was thinking the other players were doubting me, too. I would make a bad pass, and I'd see just a quick look in a guy's eyes. I'd think, 'These guys think I can't play at all.' "

Through it all, Knight was telling outside groups that Smart could, indeed, play. Every year, shortly after practice begins, Knight has a question-and-answer session open to the full student body. From the first year he did it, it has been so popular with students that it has outgrown every hall they put it in, till it was moved into the 3,000-plus IU Auditorium. It's a highlight night for both Knight and the students, and at the session October 28th, a student asked about progress of the two new junior college players.

"Garrett has a lot of work to do," Knight said, "but he's a really hard-working, very good kid who I think has a chance to be a good player for us. Smart has the kind of ability that will enable him to be an outstanding basketball player. You're going to enjoy Smart. He probably gets the ball down the court faster than anybody I've had here."

Even trying to be patient, Knight ran into some moments of exasperation as Smart kept blundering. "I had probably a hundred turnovers in pre-season," Smart said. "And when I made one, I would always say, 'My fault.' I'd make a bad pass or a bad play: 'My fault.' Coach got tired of hearing that and he said, 'Don't say that any more. I don't want to *hear* it.'

"Right away, the very next thing, I made a turnover and I said, 'My fault.'

"He had to try to get me out of that frame of mind."

Because of the state-engulfing popularity that the Indiana basketball program has gained in the Knight years, the Hoosier coach frequently has taken his team to cities around the state for pre-season intrasquad exhibition games. On consecutive Thursdays, starting November 6th, Knight took the Hoosiers to Gary, Fort Wayne and New Castle. At Gary, Smart started with what was in essence a second unit — with Todd Jadlow, Todd Meier, Magnus Pelkowski, Kreigh Smith and Dave Minor against Alford, Rick Calloway, Garrett, Brian Sloan, Joe Hillman and Steve Eyl. Alford had 19 points as that team "won" the 20-minute game, 42-28. The news of the half was that the new man, Smart, responded to people in the stands with 17 points. The second half, Knight moved Smart and Smith onto the Alford unit, replacing Hillman and Sloan. Smart scored eight more points, a 25-point night. Two other things stood out: Smart led both teams with six turnovers, and the team he was on lost both halves — the erstwhile second unit responding to the trade with .645 shooting for a 54-51 victory, despite 16 more points from Alford and 19 from Garrett.

Freshman Minor, from Cincinnati, was the newcomer who impressed Knight most. From first look, Knight was impressed with both the 6-foot-5 Minor and the obvious polish he had attained at Purcell-Marian High School under coach Jim Stoll. "He really can

play," Knight said. "He played tonight about as well as you can expect a freshman to play." And the other newcomers, Coach? "Smart and Garrett both do some good things. I don't think that they play particularly well yet, but they make good plays." The 15-minute press conference was almost over when a writer asked about Thomas's unexpected absence. The questioner didn't know how unexpected it was. Thomas's parents had driven down from their Chicago home to watch the game, expecting to see their son play. Just before the team left for Gary, Knight received class reports that showed senior Thomas was in trouble in a couple of classes, one in folklore and one in physical education — in danger of failing at least one of the courses primarily because he wasn't showing up. Summarily, Thomas was dropped from the squad that flew to Gary. Casually, Knight responded to the question about Thomas by saying: "Daryl Thomas has been dropped from the squad because he does not think it's important to maintain academic standards." And he walked out, to join his team for a postgame buffet with Gary Mayor Richard Hatcher.

Knight hadn't arrived at the postgame press conference for about 45 minutes, because he had taken time in between the game and the conference to talk privately, in a hall, with Thomas's parents. He explained what he intended to do, why he was doing it, and he asked their support. He left the session more impressed than ever with the Thomas family, because of the backing both parents offered.

The one-sentence announcement about Thomas dwarfed all else from the evening. It spread swiftly and widely via newspaper wire services. The impact of Indiana basketball in the entire state was illustrated by newspaper handling of the story. The same day, Leon Burtnett announced his resignation as football coach at Purdue. In Fort Wayne, the *News-Sentinel* gave primary play to a story carrying the three-line headline: "IU's Thomas bounced from

## *Daryl Thomas has been dropped from the squad*

— Bob Knight

team." Directly below it, a two-line headline in smaller type said "Burt-nett resigns as Purdue coach."

Thomas remained off the squad through Friday and Saturday practices. He returned Sunday afternoon, probationary status clear. The situation was a warning that the newcomers, who had grown close to Thomas, didn't miss. "When Coach got on *him*, he kinda caught my eye and Dean's eye," Smart said. "We said, 'Hey, man, we're not getting in *that* kind of trouble. We don't want to be in that part of the doghouse.' "

The Sunday Thomas came back brought a different anxiety with the injuries to Calloway and Smith. The spindly Calloway clutched a knee. Smith sprained an ankle, severely. The incidents came barely 10 minutes apart and, even with Thomas back, the Hoosiers were down to an 11-man squad.

Calloway's problem was not serious. By Thursday, he was back, and he was the leading scorer (24 points) in the Fort Wayne scrimmage, where the story was the crowd. Fort Wayne is in the northeast corner of Indiana, about a three-hour drive from Bloomington. When the scrimmage date was announced, the 9,800-seat Fort Wayne Coliseum was sold out in a day. Checks for $10,000 went to two different Fort Wayne charities.

It wasn't a glorious night for Smart, who had 10 points and 10 turnovers. Asked how Smart's obvious speed affected Knight's defensive planning, the coach said: "Smart hasn't affected it at all, because he hasn't learned to use his quickness. He overruns things. He plays like a jackrabbit.

"The guy who I thought had real good concentration and awareness was Garrett. He made a lot of good plays (19 points, 11 rebounds, 3 blocked shots). Garrett is more agile and more mobile than anybody we've had, with the exception of (Ray) Tolbert and (Landon) Turner. And he probably anticipates things a little bit better than both of those guys. Garrett has an opportunity to have more effect on normal de-

fensive play than any of the kids that we've had."

In the half Knight mentioned, Smart teamed with Alford on a version of the No. 1 unit and the team had a 51-30 edge. The significance of that, Knight noted, was that "I think that might be the first time all year Joe Hillman's team has been beaten. Joe gives us more on-the-court direction and leadership than almost everybody else put together. He has been exceptional in his direction of things." The clear message was that Hillman was far in front in competition to fill the open guard spot opposite Alford. The route open to Smart was spelled out. "Hillman gives us a lot of things," Knight said, "but the ability to apply really good pressure isn't necessarily one of them. Smart is a real key there."

Two nights after the Fort Wayne outing, Bloomington saw the Hoosiers for the first time. They met the Soviet Union's National Team, which was back in the U.S. playing college teams for the first time since the Soviets boycotted the 1984 Los Angeles Olympic Games in obvious reprisal for America's 1980 boycott of the Moscow Olympics. No one was more stung by the Soviets' refusal to play at Los Angeles than was Knight, who felt his team — Michael Jordan, Sam Perkins, Patrick Ewing and all — would have beaten the Soviets by whatever margin he wanted, as much as 50 points. He had studied the Soviets closely during the two-year period leading up to the Olympics. Inwardly, he *knew* his team was better.

The Soviets knew of all that. When they arrived in New York to start their tour, Indiana was the game that new Soviet coach Armand Kraulin mentioned. "Knight is very popular in Russia," Kraulin was quoted in *USA Today.*

Kraulin arrived without his top star, Arvidas Sabonis. He brought a big team restyled to shoot from outside, because of the three-point shot that was added to international basketball in 1985. "This is not a stereotyped Soviet team," said Bill

*When the Soviets arrived in New York to start their tour, Indiana was the game that coach Armand Kraulin mentioned: 'Knight is very popular in Russia'*

— USA Today

## AP poll

| **Pre-season** | | |
|---|---|---|
| 1. North Carolina (35) | | 1215 |
| 2. Louisville (22) | | 1196 |
| 3. Indiana (2) | | 956 |
| 4. Purdue (2) | | 935 |
| 5. Nevada-Las Vegas (2) | | 901 |
| 6. Georgia Tech (1) | | 770 |
| 7. Oklahoma | | 684 |
| 8. Kansas | | 645 |
| 9. Navy | | 560 |
| 10. Iowa | | 531 |
| 11. Kentucky | | 500 |
| 12. Auburn | | 498 |
| 13. Alabama | | 451 |
| 14. Illinois | | 386 |
| 15. Syracuse | | 383 |

Wall, the executive director of America's amateur basketball program and a man who traveled with the Soviets on their tour. "Bob says the '84 Olympic team would have beaten them badly because they don't play defense, and he's right. But they do have quicker and better athletes than they have had."

Against Indiana, they zipped in three-point baskets the first two times downcourt and launched 17 in all, hitting nine. Indiana got 25 points from Calloway, 24 from Thomas, 23 from Alford and 17 from Garrett, who led both teams with 10 rebounds. The Hoosiers won, 97-95, because the 17th of those Soviet three-point tries, by 6-9 Valery Tikhonenko, was put up under defensive pressure from Hillman and Alford. It missed, and Garrett used his wide shoulders and long arms to screen everyone away as the rebound bounced out of bounds. Knight termed the game-closing sequence "an outstanding defensive play. Alford and Hillman both got into the ball and forced a really bad shot, and Garrett did a great job keeping them away from the ball."

The scoring balance proved a portent, in many ways. "They obviously keyed to play Alford," Knight said. "If he got 23, really being played hard as he was, I think it's very good for us to score as much as we did. Everybody else had to be doing some things."

One name was missing. After the Hoosiers had come onto the floor to warm up for the game, Smart pulled a groin muscle. "I'm not sure I ever had anybody knocked out in the warmup before," Knight mused. "That really screwed up what we were going to try to do, with substitutions and different combinations. We never work out on game day, but we worked out about an hour this morning. Smart was very, very good. He hasn't progressed quite as quickly as we had hoped, but that's asking a lot for a kid to just jump right in and be a player. I was really looking forward to him playing tonight, but we'll just have to wait on that."

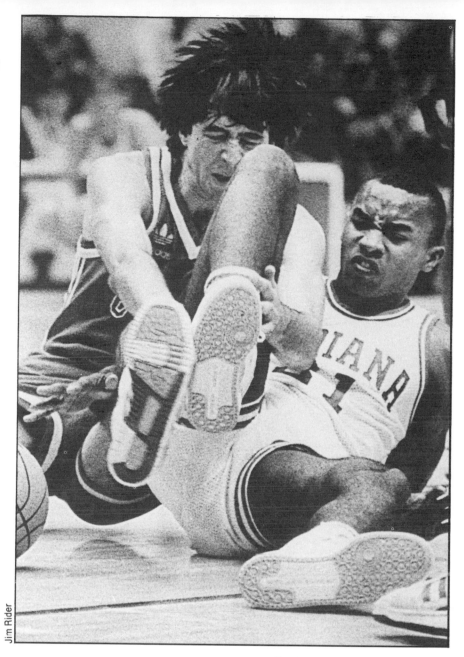

Jim Rider

**Freshman Dave Minor finds himself floored in his first Assembly Hall appearance**

Nov. 15, Assembly Hall

# Soviet Union 95

| | M | 3FG | AFG | FT | R | A | B | S | T | F | Pts |
|---|---|---|---|---|---|---|---|---|---|---|---|
| Tarakanov, f | 37 | 3- 5 | 8-13 | 2- 2 | 7 | 3 | 0 | 0 | 4 | 4 | 21 |
| Volkov, f | 31 | 0- 1 | 6-11 | 7- 9 | 6 | 2 | 0 | 2 | 0 | 5 | 19 |
| Goborov, c | 24 | | 1- 4 | 3- 4 | 3 | 1 | 2 | 1 | 2 | 3 | 5 |
| Khomichus, g | 40 | 4- 8 | 9-15 | 2- 2 | 3 | 3 | 0 | 1 | 5 | 1 | 24 |
| Marchulinis, g | 24 | 2- 2 | 2- 5 | 4- 4 | 1 | 4 | 0 | 1 | 4 | 5 | 10 |
| Tkachenko | 15 | | 3- 4 | 0- 0 | 2 | 0 | 1 | 1 | 2 | 5 | 6 |
| Tikhonenko | 16 | 0- 1 | 1- 7 | 0- 0 | 5 | 1 | 1 | 0 | 2 | 0 | 2 |
| Babenic | 12 | | 3- 4 | 2- 3 | 1 | 0 | 0 | 2 | 0 | 5 | 8 |
| Grishaev | 1 | | 0- 0 | 0- 0 | 0 | 0 | 0 | 0 | 0 | 0 | 0 |
| Team | | | | | 4 | | | | | | |
| **Totals** | | 9-17 | 33-63 | 20-24 | 32 | 14 | 4 | 8 | 19 | 28 | 95 |

# Indiana 97

| | M | 3FG | AFG | FT | R | A | B | S | T | F | Pts |
|---|---|---|---|---|---|---|---|---|---|---|---|
| Thomas, f | 35 | | 9-13 | 6- 6 | 5 | 0 | 0 | 0 | 3 | 4 | 24 |
| Calloway, f | 37 | | 7-14 | 11-13 | 8 | 1 | 0 | 0 | 1 | 3 | 25 |
| Garrett, c | 30 | | 6-14 | 5- 8 | 10 | 1 | 1 | 0 | 2 | 4 | 17 |
| Alford, g | 37 | 2 -7 | 6-13 | 9-10 | 2 | 6 | 0 | 2 | 0 | 0 | 23 |
| Hillman, g | 25 | | 0- 0 | 0- 0 | 1 | 2 | 1 | 3 | 4 | 3 | 0 |
| Pelkowski | 13 | | 2- 5 | 0- 1 | 4 | 0 | 0 | 0 | 0 | 4 | 4 |
| Minor | 18 | | 2- 4 | 0- 0 | 3 | 2 | 0 | 2 | 2 | 0 | 4 |
| Eyl | 3 | | 0- 0 | 0- 0 | 1 | 1 | 1 | 0 | 0 | 0 | 0 |
| Sloan | 2 | | 0- 0 | 0- 0 | 0 | 0 | 0 | 0 | 1 | 1 | 0 |
| Team | | | | | 2 | | | | | | |
| **Totals** | | 2- 7 | 32-63 | 31-38 | 36 | 13 | 2 | 7 | 13 | 19 | 97 |

| SCORE BY HALVES | | | 3FG | AFG | FT |
|---|---|---|---|---|---|
| Soviet Union | 46 | 49—95 | .529 | .524 | .833 |
| Indiana | 51 | 46—97 | .286 | .508 | .805 |

**Officials**—Joe Forte, Larry Limbo.
**Attendance**—17,157 (sellout).

# 2 | Early scare

If Bob Knight has a second state, it is Montana, which by governor's proclamation made him an honorary citizen a few years ago. For several weeks every summer, the citizenship is more than honorary as Knight indulges his love for hunting and fishing there. It was with the warmest feelings that Knight brought Montana State onto the schedule as the leadoff opponent on the Hoosiers' 1986-87 lineup.

A score of 90-55 doesn't seem particularly hospitable, but Indiana came out of the game with more gloom than did the Bobcats — who were to go on to win the Big Sky Conference championship. Early in the second half, the slender young basketball greyhound on whom much of Indiana's Big Ten and national hopes were based, Rick Calloway, went down in a pileup under the basket and didn't get up. It had been a festive day at Assembly Hall, where the turnout of 17,101 prompted some research that showed it was the third-biggest home-opener crowd in IU history — behind only 1975-76 and 1980-81, Knight's two NCAA championship seasons. The place was loud and red and jovial, until Daryl Thomas maneuvered for an inside basket, Calloway went up with Montana State's Steve Snodgrass and Tom Damako for a possible rebound — and everything went silent. "I remember going after the ball and getting tangled up," Calloway said. "I felt their guy (Snodgrass) fall on my leg. It hurt real bad."

Calloway's scream wasn't audible to many amid the reaction to the basket, but Snodgrass and Damako heard. Legs were entwined. Damako eased himself out of the tangle, and Snodgrass was as slow and gentle as a doctor at a crash scene in carefully working himself free. "God, that's horrible," Snodgrass said later. "I just hope that, somehow, he's back playing soon."

It didn't seem likely. The word Knight relayed after the game was: "There could be a torn cartilage in there. There could be damage to the anterior cruciate ligament, which would be very serious." Instant diagnosis isn't possible with such injuries. "The way it looked then was that I had torn something and my season was probably over," Calloway said. "I was thinking red-shirt, and all the time I had put into getting ready for the season . . . I'd have to wait another whole year to play . . .

"It was a sad moment."

He went out with the game well in hand, Indiana up 48-35. Alford (24 points) and Thomas (15) were delivering as expected, but the surprise to Montana State coach Stu Starner was the new man in the lineup, center Dean Garrett. His Assembly Hall debut included 10 points, 14 rebounds and 8 blocked shots — the most blocks for a Hoosier in a decade of record-keeping.

Starner, a former Minnesota assistant and one of Knight's summertime Montana hosts, formed some quick opinions. "Garrett makes that Hoosier team look a little different than it did last year," he said. "By 10 minutes into the game, our postmen weren't taking it to the hoop, they were taking it *away* from the hoop. That's a credit to a very active athlete inside. That intimidation factor is a big part of their defense. That wasn't in evidence last year. They are much improved. Thomas, Calloway and Garrett give them three athletes who can get to the

**In the season opener against Montana State, Rick Calloway went down in a pileup under the basket and didn't get up**

**Rick Calloway — missed early**

boards. It's hard to block an athlete out. Quickness is a tremendous ingredient. To me, that's the difference in this Hoosier team. They can really pound the boards. They really got on the Russians despite a tremendous lack of size. They made up for that with athletic ability."

Joe Hillman started for the Hoosiers and hit four of six shots, with four assists. Keith Smart came on to play 23 minutes and score 15 points in his debut. Starner included Smart in his assessment of added offensive dimensions. "Smart penetrates more, certainly has more athletic ability," Starner said. "Hillman is steady. Smart is an athlete who can draw double coverage. He'll open up some people."

His picture of optimism arrived for Indiana people with a black border around it, in uncertainty over Calloway. "We had some spurts where we played pretty well," Knight said. "I felt better about our defense than our offense for the first game. Offensively, this was as poorly as Garrett has played. He was very impatient. He positioned himself very poorly. Defensively, I thought he was really alert, anticipated very well, and he was really a force.

"Smart I thought played much better, really, than he probably should have played or I would have expected him to play. This is the kind of play we would have expected from him earlier, that he's slowly graduating toward."

The key checking time for Calloway was Sunday, a day after the injury. Swelling was expected, and that would have meant at least arthroscopic surgery. Pleasant medical surprises haven't been common for Knight, who always will feel solid national-championship teams were cut down by injuries in 1975 (all-America forward Scott May broke an arm with a month to go in the season) and 1980 (present pros Mike Woodson and Randy Wittman went out early — Woodson to back surgery that kept him out seven weeks; Wittman to a foot stress fracture that ended his season).

With Calloway, though, the most

optimistic hopes were met. Swelling was minimal. No surgery was required. The problem was a sprain: a stretched medial collateral ligament. "That was good news, very good news," Calloway said. "They told me I could go home and get right to work on rehabilitation."

It was the best possible long-range news, but short-term, there were some quick answers to find. Indiana's December schedule reached a quick highlight. Right after Montana State on the schedule came Rivalry Week: at Notre Dame on Tuesday, at home against Kentucky on Saturday.

Notre Dame had its own problems. All-America candidate David Rivers almost died in a late-August auto wreck that sliced his abdomen open. The immediate problem was massive loss of blood; once survival was assured, his barrier to a return to basketball was healing time for damaged stomach muscle and tissue. He made exceptional progress and still was unable to return to any basketball at all until a month before the season. He didn't start the Irish opener, a disappointing 80-63 home-court loss to the Western Kentucky team that went from that pre-season NIT opener to the finals before opening a 20-point lead on Nevada-Las Vegas and losing to a barrage of three-point shots. Phelps was grim after that game.

Still, Notre Dame, in its Athletic and Convocation Center, is difficult to beat in big games, as No. 1 North Carolina and high-ranked Duke and DePaul teams found later in the scason. Phelps won one major national coach of the year award for how far he brought his Irish from that dismaying start, and he got Knight's vote. "Dick Phelps is one of the really good people in college basketball," he said. "He probably gets players ready to play hard and together as well as anybody in coaching. He goes about things in exactly the right way."

Knight went about things in the Notre Dame game in exactly the opposite way from what Phelps expected. When the Irish controlled the opening tip and moved into their half-court offense, they ran a couple of preliminary cuts before a surprised shout of recognition went up: "Zone . . . ?" On ESPN, Dick Vitale recognized it as history. It wasn't, quite. Knight experimented with a zone in his second IU season. Against Ohio University on Dec. 16, 1972, the Hoosiers played one for the last four minutes of the first half and the opening seconds of the second. "But they got an easy basket right away in the second half," Knight said at the time. So he shelved that idea, for 14 years and 422 games.

The idea never really went away. He had considered making the step a year before. At times in the preseason scrimmages, at least one of the teams played a zone. In November talks to Bloomington groups, he openly said he planned to play some zone. At a Bloomington Varsity Club luncheon, he was amused by the tone of a questioner, so he repeated the man's phrasing: "Why are we 'fooling around' with a zone defense? I hope it amounts to a little bit more than fooling around.

"Basketball as I've watched it over the last seven or eight years has had many players who were very difficult to play against as individuals. There is a difference in the mental approach to playing against a zone or a man to man. The zone has a tendency to slow things down and get kids to stand around. I think probably the worst thing that people do today is attack the zone defense. If we don't play a little bit of it, then essentially what we're doing is saying, 'All right, you don't have to face what you do the worst of all against.' We're going to play it a little bit, change the tempo of the game a little bit." He was, he conceded, indulging himself a little bit in satisfying a personal curiosity. "I'm sure in my first or second year here my curiosity would not have gone to the point where I would be willing to fiddle around with what we're doing, but I've been around here long enough I figure I can do what the hell I want."

If any opponent stood out as one

For Rick Calloway (20), a stretched ligament was 'very good news. They told me I could go home and get right to work on rehabilitation.'

who was "very difficult to play against" man to man, it was Rivers. Just as Knight had said in his morning talk with Phelps, he felt a two-man front provided by the zone offered a much better chance of denying Rivers the penetration that he exploits as well as anyone in college basketball. The move helped the Hoosiers jump out to a 17-6 lead, 36-24 at halftime. Phelps had time to adjust during the break. "We figured in the first half they had nine layups," he said. He went to a 1-3-1 zone of his own and — at 43-40 with 12:20 to go — convinced Knight it no longer was a proper time to experiment. "They just got too much inside on us," Knight said. "I don't think we did a good job around the basket. But I thought we played it very well in the first half. Against a kid like Rivers, you've got to have two people to play him on top — change back and forth, give him two people to get past. It takes something away from him."

The Irish never quite caught up.

## Milestone

Indiana's first three-point basket under the present rule was not by Steve Alford. Alford tried the first one by a Hoosier a minute and a half into the opener against Montana State. He missed that and another try before Keith Smart hit the Hoosiers' first with 10:40 to go in the first half, putting the Hoosiers ahead 23-12 – Smart's number and Alford's number. Alford's first three-point basket came on his third try with 4:10 left in the half.

John Terhune

**Steve Alford stretches to get a pass around Chris Conway of Montana State**

Nov. 29, Assembly Hall

# Montana State 55

| | M | 3FG | AFG | FT | R | A | B | S | T | F | Pts |
|---|---|---|---|---|---|---|---|---|---|---|---|
| K.Ferch, f | 30 | 0- 2 | 1-14 | 1- 2 | 3 | 0 | 0 | 1 | 1 | 2 | 3 |
| Domako, f | 38 | | 8-23 | 2- 2 | 17 | 2 | 0 | 1 | 3 | 3 | 18 |
| Fellows, c | 18 | | 0- 5 | 0- 1 | 5 | 0 | 0 | 2 | 4 | 0 | |
| Willis, g | 19 | | 2- 6 | 1- 2 | 1 | 1 | 0 | 1 | 2 | 3 | 5 |
| S.Ferch, g | 24 | 0- 3 | 2-11 | 2- 2 | 2 | 1 | 0 | 2 | 3 | 5 | 6 |
| Conway | 35 | | 4-10 | 0- 0 | 7 | 6 | 0 | 0 | 4 | 4 | 8 |
| Jacobs | 14 | | 2- 5 | 1- 2 | 0 | 0 | 0 | 0 | 2 | 4 | 5 |
| Snodgrass | 14 | | 4- 9 | 2- 3 | 5 | 0 | 0 | 0 | 0 | 0 | 10 |
| Andrews | 4 | | 0- 0 | 0- 2 | 2 | 0 | 0 | 0 | 0 | 0 | 0 |
| Ligons | 2 | 0- 1 | 0- 1 | 0- 0 | 1 | 0 | 0 | 0 | 1 | 1 | 0 |
| Pierce | 2 | | 0- 0 | 0- 0 | 1 | 0 | 0 | 0 | 0 | 0 | 0 |
| Team | | | | | 8 | | | | | | |
| Totals | | 0- 6 | 23-84 | 9-16 | 52 | 10 | 0 | 5 | 18 | 26 | 55 |

# Indiana 90

| | M | 3FG | AFG | FT | R | A | B | S | T | F | Pts |
|---|---|---|---|---|---|---|---|---|---|---|---|
| Thomas, f | 20 | | 6- 9 | 3- 3 | 5 | 1 | 0 | 2 | 1 | 1 | 15 |
| Calloway, f | 19 | | 3- 5 | 1- 2 | 5 | 0 | 1 | 1 | 1 | 2 | 7 |
| Garrett, c | 33 | | 4-13 | 2- 2 | 14 | 1 | 8 | 2 | 0 | 2 | 10 |
| Alford, g | 33 | 3- 5 | 8-18 | 5- 6 | 5 | 1 | 0 | 1 | 6 | 2 | 24 |
| Hillman, g | 24 | | 4- 6 | 0- 0 | 3 | 4 | 0 | 1 | 1 | 2 | 8 |
| Smart | 23 | 1- 3 | 6-12 | 2- 3 | 3 | 3 | 0 | 0 | 2 | 2 | 15 |
| Eyl | 11 | | 1- 2 | 2- 2 | 2 | 1 | 0 | 1 | 0 | 0 | 4 |
| Minor | 15 | | 0- 1 | 1- 3 | 0 | 1 | 0 | 0 | 1 | 3 | 1 |
| Pelkowski | 12 | | 1- 3 | 0- 0 | 5 | 0 | 0 | 0 | 2 | 2 | 2 |
| Meier | 2 | | 0- 0 | 0- 0 | 0 | 0 | 0 | 0 | 0 | 0 | 0 |
| Sloan | 8 | | 1- 3 | 2- 5 | 1 | 1 | 0 | 1 | 1 | 0 | 4 |
| Team | | | | | 5 | | | | | | |
| Totals | | 4- 8 | 34-72 | 18-26 | 48 | 13 | 9 | 9 | 13 | 16 | 90 |

| SCORE BY HALVES | | | 3FG | AFG | FT |
|---|---|---|---|---|---|
| Montana St. (0-1) | 31 | 24—55 | .000 | .274 | .563 |
| Indiana (1-0) | 42 | 48—90 | .500 | .472 | .692 |

**Officials**—Gary Muncy, Mike Stockner, Ted Valentine.
**Attendance**—17,101 (sellout).

The score was 55-52 with 5:30 left when they lost one of their stars, forward Donald Royal, to an injury. It was 55-54 when Smart was fouled, setting him up to stare straight into the wildly waving Irish student section.

Smart had been Knight's choice to fill Calloway's lineup spot, the preference quickness over the size that a forward's replacement of forward Calloway would have provided. Smart seemed loose enough in handling the promotion. The IU Foundation airplane that carried the Hoosiers to South Bend landed at Michiana Airport in heavy rain. The schedule, as usual, called for a bus to be there and pick up players and gear at the airplane. No bus was there. Ten minutes passed. Twenty minutes. Twenty-five minutes, in a quiet, growingly tense atmosphere. From the back of the plane, a voice shattered the quiet.

"Coach Knight?"

"Yeah, Keith," Knight responded.

"Coach . . . this is just like Garden City."

The outburst of laughter throughout the plane recognized the running joke Knight had maintained with Smart through the days when he was trying to ease Smart through his obviously difficult transition. Big Ten budgets are a bit more generous than a junior college's. Where Garden City bused to games, Indiana flew to intrasquad scrimmages. Where Garden City ate at a McDonald's, Indiana ate steaks at excellent restaurants. Whenever he caught Smart in the slightest reaction of surprise to his new level of traveling, Knight would joke: "Just like Garden City, eh, Keith?"

Smart faced that Irish student section that is a major-college legend as a hazard, and he sank both free throws. "Just like Garden City," he said later.

The Irish didn't back off, though. Indiana's lead was 61-60 when Alford — limited to 4 points on his only previous Notre Dame visit, a low point in his difficult sophomore season — faked his way to an opening and sank a 15-foot shot for

John Terhune

a 63-60 lead with 1:10 to go. When Rivers missed and Steve Eyl rebounded, the Hoosiers seemed safe — for just an instant. Eyl gave the ball to Smart, whose careless pass was grabbed by the only Hoosier in the Notre Dame lineup, Scott Hicks of Indianapolis Cathedral, and converted into a fast basket at 0:40.

Indiana protected its one-point lead by keeping the ball in Alford's hands. "It's got to be a foul situation — deny Alford (the ball) and foul anyone," Phelps said. "Match up, find somebody and foul right away, but don't foul Alford." Finally, with the clock down to 0:11 and Alford dominating the ball, Hicks grabbed him. Alford sank both, making him 10-for-10 in a 26-point performance, and when sophomore Sean Connor's three-point try was on-line but missed, 6-foot-7 reserve Kreigh

**Notre Dame star David Rivers runs into an unexpected zone problem from Daryl Thomas, Steve Alford, and IU**

Dec. 2, South Bend

# Indiana 67

|  | M | 3FG | AFG | FT | R | A | B | S | T | F | Pts |
|---|---|---|---|---|---|---|---|---|---|---|---|
| Thomas, f | 40 |  | 4-11 | 3- 4 | 8 | 0 | 0 | 1 | 2 | 2 | 11 |
| Smart, f | 36 | 0- 1 | 7-12 | 3- 3 | 7 | 0 | 0 | 1 | 4 | 4 | 17 |
| Garrett, c | 13 |  | 2- 6 | 0- 0 | 4 | 1 | 0 | 0 | 0 | 5 | 4 |
| Alford, g | 40 | 2- 6 | 7-14 | 10-10 | 0 | 1 | 1 | 0 | 0 | 2 | 26 |
| Hillman, g | 26 |  | 1- 2 | 0- 1 | 1 | 1 | 0 | 0 | 3 | 4 | 2 |
| Meier | 18 |  | 0- 0 | 3- 4 | 5 | 0 | 0 | 0 | 2 | 2 | 3 |
| Minor | 4 |  | 0- 0 | 0- 0 | 2 | 0 | 0 | 0 | 0 | 2 | 0 |
| Eyl | 9 |  | 1- 1 | 0- 2 | 0 | 0 | 0 | 0 | 0 | 0 | 2 |
| Smith | 14 |  | 0- 1 | 2- 3 | 2 | 1 | 0 | 0 | 1 | 1 | 2 |
| Team |  |  |  |  | 4 |  |  |  |  |  |  |
| Totals |  | 2- 7 | 22-47 | 21-27 | 31 | 6 | 1 | 2 | 12 | 22 | 67 |

# Notre Dame 62

|  | M | 3FG | AFG | FT | R | A | B | S | T | F | Pts |
|---|---|---|---|---|---|---|---|---|---|---|---|
| Royal, f | 34 |  | 5- 8 | 4- 6 | 8 | 1 | 0 | 1 | 1 | 4 | 14 |
| Stevenson, f | 21 |  | 1- 4 | 3- 4 | 2 | 2 | 0 | 0 | 1 | 1 | 5 |
| Voce, c | 8 |  | 0- 2 | 0- 0 | 0 | 0 | 0 | 0 | 1 | 2 | 0 |
| Rivers, g | 40 | 0- 1 | 4- 7 | 1- 3 | 6 | 9 | 0 | 1 | 5 | 2 | 9 |
| Hicks, g | 36 |  | 8-12 | 2- 5 | 4 | 1 | 0 | 1 | 3 | 5 | 18 |
| Connor | 23 | 0- 1 | 3- 8 | 0- 2 | 3 | 2 | 0 | 0 | 1 | 4 | 6 |
| Paddock | 31 |  | 5- 8 | 0- 2 | 7 | 2 | 1 | 0 | 0 | 2 | 10 |
| J.Jackson | 3 |  | 0- 2 | 0- 0 | 0 | 0 | 0 | 0 | 1 | 4 | 0 |
| T.Jackson | 1 |  | 0- 0 | 0- 0 | 0 | 0 | 0 | 0 | 0 | 0 | 0 |
| Frederick | 3 |  | 0- 1 | 0- 0 | 0 | 0 | 0 | 0 | 0 | 1 | 0 |
| Team |  |  |  |  | 4 |  |  |  |  |  |  |
| Totals |  | 0- 2 | 26-52 | 10-22 | 34 | 17 | 1 | 3 | 13 | 25 | 62 |

| SCORE BY HALVES |  |  | 3FG | AFG | FT |
|---|---|---|---|---|---|
| Indiana (2-0) | 36 31—67 |  | .286 | .468 | .778 |
| Notre Dame (0-2) | 24 38—62 |  | .000 | .500 | .455 |

**Officials**—Roger Parramore, John Carr, Steve Welmer.
**Attendance**—11,415 (sellout).

Todd Meier, Steve Alford, Daryl Thomas drop in on ND's Scott Paddock

John Terhune

Smith grabbed the rebound to assure victory.

"As good as Alford is, he wins the game for them, there's no doubt about that," Phelps said.

Smart's log in his first start read 17 points, seven rebounds. Good Calloway numbers. And four turnovers. Garrett's followup to his impressive start wasn't quite so sparkling. He played only 13 minutes and fouled out, contributing four points and four rebounds.

The week allowed no time for celebrating. Kentucky was on the horizon, and that is a rivalry that starts for Hoosiers and Kentuckians somewhere right after the cradle. "Long before I came to Kentucky, when I thought about college basketball I thought about all the great games Kentucky and Indiana have had through the years," second-year Wildcat coach Eddie Sutton said he told Knight at a game-eve chat. Sutton was working to continue the series. Knight had indicated at Lexington the year before he was less than excited about continuing it.

Kentucky was on its way to what was, for the Wildcats, a subpar season — 18-11, a spot in the NCAA tournament but a fast exit courtesy of Ohio State (91-77). The 'Cats were frisky in early December in Bloomington, though, and they opened a 30-24 lead. At that point, an errant pass by Alford sent Kentucky freshman Derrick Miller driving for a layup. He missed, but 6-11 Rob Lock came along behind and tried a dunk-rebound that also missed. Smith salvaged the play for Indiana with a rebound, and he stopped a seven-point Kentucky run by hitting two free throws.

The game swung just that quickly. It was 30-28 when Alford used a Smith screen to fire a jump shot just as Kentucky guard Ed Davender, trying to fight his way to Alford, crashed into Smith. Officials counted Alford's basket and gave Smith a one-and-one, which he converted into an odd but lead-switching four-point play. Indiana, playing reserves Smith, Steve Eyl and Dave Minor with Alford and Garrett, ran its point streak to 10 with another Alford basket to go to halftime up 34-30, and Kentucky never quite caught up — or quit trying. Freshman Rex Chapman had his first big day as a Wildcat, matching the 26 points Alford had for Indiana. The Hoosiers seemed to have a little breathing room at 60-56, with the basketball, but a turnover and a Chapman three-pointer made it 60-59. Chapman's last basket, a remarkable double-pump baseline jump shot over Eyl, cut an Indiana edge to 65-64 with 1:35 to go. Indiana ran the 45-second shot clock down before Joe Hillman put up a try. He missed, but Garrett rebounded. He missed, but Thomas rebounded. Thomas missed once, recovered the ball and he was fouled.

It was a pressure time to be going to the line: 42 seconds to play, one-and-one, leading by one. "My freshman and sophomore years I was a horrendous free-throw shooter," Thomas said. "Coach Knight would take me aside and tell me to relax and develop a smooth stroke I was comfortable with." He was so smooth in stroking two home that even Knight felt more comfortable, especially after a traveling call against Chapman and a one-and-one conversion by Hillman (at 0:19) finally shook Indiana loose.

Garrett came back from his Notre Dame problems with a 13-point, 12-rebound game. Smart slipped: five points, one rebound, four turnovers.

Alford was happy that he was able to shake off a cold start (2-for-7) and sizzle in the final minutes (hitting his last four shots and then four straight free throws). "Coach has been harping on us for three years about mental toughness," he said. "We've had to play these last two games without Ricky. This is a real good chance for us to show some mental toughness."

Thomas, with a senior's disinclination to overreact, said, "We have a lot of work to do and a lot to look forward to. If we keep working and get clicking, maybe we can be as good a team as everybody seems to be saying we are."

Larry Crewell

**Kentucky's Irving Thomas does not agree with the foul that put him out of Indiana's 71-66 rivalry victory**

Dec. 6, Assembly Hall

# Kentucky 66

| | M | 3FG | AFG | FT | R | A | B | S | T | F | Pts |
|---|---|---|---|---|---|---|---|---|---|---|---|
| Madison, f | 36 | | 2- 6 | 0- 0 | 5 | 1 | 0 | 0 | 1 | 2 | 4 |
| Blackmon, f | 33 | | 2- 3 | 0- 1 | 4 | 2 | 0 | 1 | 0 | 5 | 4 |
| Thomas, c | 28 | | 5- 7 | 0- 4 | 10 | 1 | 1 | 1 | 3 | 5 | 10 |
| Davender, g | 29 | | 2- 9 | 2- 2 | 3 | 4 | 0 | 1 | 0 | 5 | 6 |
| Chapman, g | 36 | 3- 5 | 10-18 | 3- 6 | 3 | 0 | 1 | 1 | 2 | 2 | 26 |
| Andrews | 10 | | 1- 3 | 0- 0 | 0 | 0 | 0 | 0 | 0 | 1 | 2 |
| Lock | 14 | | 2- 4 | 0- 0 | 5 | 0 | 0 | 0 | 1 | 2 | 4 |
| Miller | 14 | 2- 2 | 4- 6 | 0- 2 | 2 | 0 | 0 | 1 | 0 | 0 | 10 |
| Team | | | | | 1 | | | | | | |
| **Totals** | | 5- 7 | 28-56 | 5-15 | 33 | 8 | 2 | 5 | 7 | 22 | 66 |

# Indiana 71

| | M | 3FG | AFG | FT | R | A | B | S | T | F | Pts |
|---|---|---|---|---|---|---|---|---|---|---|---|
| Thomas, f | 20 | | 4- 7 | 4- 4 | 7 | 1 | 0 | 0 | 1 | 4 | 12 |
| Smart, f | 23 | 1- 1 | 2- 6 | 0- 0 | 1 | 1 | 0 | 2 | 4 | 1 | 5 |
| Garrett, c | 39 | | 6-11 | 1- 4 | 12 | 1 | 2 | 0 | 1 | 3 | 13 |
| Alford, g | 39 | 2- 2 | 10-19 | 4- 5 | 2 | 6 | 0 | 2 | 3 | 2 | 26 |
| Hillman, g | 27 | | 1- 2 | 3- 4 | 0 | 4 | 0 | 0 | 2 | 4 | 5 |
| Eyl | 23 | | 0- 0 | 2- 2 | 2 | 1 | 0 | 0 | 1 | 1 | 2 |
| Smith | 18 | 1- 1 | | 4- 4 | 2 | 1 | 0 | 0 | 1 | 2 | 6 |
| Minor | 10 | | 1- 2 | 0- 0 | 2 | 1 | 0 | 0 | 2 | 0 | 2 |
| Meier | 1 | | 0- 0 | 0- 0 | 0 | 0 | 0 | 1 | 0 | 0 | 0 |
| Team | | | | | 1 | | | | | | |
| **Totals** | | 3- 3 | 25-48 | 18-23 | 29 | 16 | 2 | 5 | 15 | 17 | 71 |

| SCORE BY HALVES | | | 3FG | AFG | FT |
|---|---|---|---|---|---|
| Kentucky (2-1) | 30 36 | 66 | .714 | .500 | .333 |
| Indiana (3-0) | 34 37 | 71 | 1.000 | .521 | .783 |

**Officials**—Tom Rucker, Eric Harmon, Paul Galvan.
**Attendance**—17,232 (sellout).

# 3 A lesson learned

**M**ike Kenn, a former Michigan tackle now starring for the Atlanta Falcons, said as a National Football League veteran, "The only time you think about the (college) draft is when your team's No. 1 pick is at your position." It didn't work that way for Daryl Thomas when Indiana recruited Dean Garrett as the likely starter at the position Thomas played in 1985-86, center. From the first day Garrett reported to campus, his biggest fan and supporter was Thomas.

It wasn't altogether a manifestation of selflessness and team play. Garrett's arrival meant Indiana could move a 6-foot-10, 225-pound "legitimate" center into the position that Thomas (6-7) had played for the first time in his life during his junior season as a Hoosier. His was the most uncommon of all position shifts. Most major-college players have to adjust to a new role after their high school days. Many 6-4 guards were the biggest man on their high school team so they played center or forward, where they could be around the basket. Virtually all forwards, 6-6 or up, were high school centers. Thomas was a guard as he was growing up in the same Westchester, Ill., St. Joseph's program that sent Isiah Thomas (no relation to Daryl) to Indiana. When he attained his height, Daryl became a forward, because of his own ability to play out on the court and because the team also had 6-6 Tony Reeder, who played center and was recruited by Marquette.

When Indiana's returning players from the 1984-85 season went on a round-the-world trip with Knight and assistant coaches Royce Waltman, Joby Wright and Kohn Smith in the summer of 1985, Thomas — who had played sparingly at forward in his first two seasons — became the center. By the end of the five-week, 18-game trip, Knight was convinced Thomas could do the job better than anyone else on the roster. He had the assignment throughout the 21-8 season, and he did well: a 14.5 scoring average, third-team all-Big Ten status, season highs of 31 points against Iowa State and 30 against Illinois. Still, a front line that had Thomas as its biggest man had its limitations, as Michigan's huge front line showed in overwhelming the Hoosiers for an 80-52 victory in a season-ending game for the Big Ten championship.

Thomas at forward, with a 6-10 center? That was a different matter. As much as the idea appealed to Knight, whose every move is aimed toward being able to beat the best opponents, not the majority, it surely meant more to Thomas. And his year of experience at center was a bonus in a couple of ways: It improved his own inside skills, and it made him an invaluable confidante for newcomer Garrett, who roomed with him.

"He helped me a lot," Garrett said. "He told me who I was going against, when I didn't know them at all. The first time around the Big Ten, just his presence, being there, knowing that if I'm not going, Daryl could — all of that really helped me."

Personality played a role, too. "Everything's not always serious with Daryl," Garrett said. "He has a great sense of humor. He's always joking. I can relate to that."

Garrett didn't have the emotional lows that fellow junior college transfer Keith Smart had during the pre-season, perhaps because of Thomas' presence. "It wasn't that bad for me," Garrett said. "The guys made me feel comfortable when I first got here. Everything just kinda went well. Daryl had a lot to do with that — and Ricky (Calloway) and Keith.

"I was excited to start practice and the season and see how I played against different guys. My major priority was to try to play well. I wasn't thinking about an NCAA championship. I was just trying to play."

A tenet of Knight coaching is leveling off the peaks and valleys that are common in athletics. Invariably, a team that plays exceptionally well in an obviously peaked performance is ripe for plucking in its next game. It works that way in individual cases, too. The experience and the demeanor of a Steve Alford combine to flatten those out, for the most part. Garrett is an emotional, excitable young man who entered his first major-college season with minimal experience. And it showed.

His opener won him grand reviews. Three nights later, he was ineffective at Notre Dame. A pattern of ups and downs was started, and however much Knight, or Thomas, or anyone else tried to anticipate and head off the lows, they happened.

For an Indiana basketball team, it's difficult to find a much more predictable valley-after-peak situation than playing any team immediately after beating annual rivals Notre Dame and Kentucky. For the '86-87 Hoosiers, the team in that position was Vanderbilt, new on the Indiana schedule.

Vanderbilt has a grand basketball tradition. It has one of the best coaches in the sport, C.M. Newton, who was on Knight's 1984 Olympic staff. The professional respect between the two coaches couldn't be higher. At New Orleans, when preparing for the national-championship game, Knight said one more time what he has said for 11 years: the best team one of his clubs ever has played was Newton's Alabama team that led the 1976

Hoosiers in the last two minutes of play before losing, 74-69, in a regional tournament game at Baton Rouge, La.

"I know he has said that," Newton said, "and it is a real compliment. That was a hell of a team, the only one I've coached in 32 years that was good enough to win the national championship." When the two worked together, along with George Raveling (now at Southern California) and Don Donoher (Dayton), in the summer leading up to the 1984 Olympics, the result was what Newton called "the best amateur basketball team that was ever put together. They absolutely were relentless. Bob was able to take that team and convince them to play hard every possession. That's what upset him in the West German game (an 11-point victory). That was the only one we played in the whole shooting match where they violated that principle."

That was the principle Knight counted on to carry the Hoosiers from the crest of Notre Dame and Kentucky week through the Vanderbilt trip. It didn't. Vanderbilt, with outstanding guard play from sophomores Barry Goheen and Barry Booker and effective inside work by 7-foot Will Perdue, came from nine points behind in the second half to win, 79-75. Alford had 28 points and Smart 13, but Goheen had a career-high 26 points as he and Booker combined for 30 last-half points. "We were supposed to get the ball into Will," he said, "but if we had a shot, we were supposed to take it."

Knight called the victory "a great game for them — I'm really pleased for C.M. and his kids." When he got to his own team, he was considerably less pleased. "I really got on them," Knight said weeks later about his old-style screaming session. "Losing the game didn't really bother me that much, because of how I feel about C.M. I didn't think we played very well, though, and I just wanted to see how they would react. I got on them pretty hard then and the next couple of nights in practice.

*Daryl helped me a lot. The first time around the Big Ten, just his presence, being there — all of that really helped me.*

— Dean Garrett

"And it didn't work. We almost lost to North Carolina-Wilmington. If we *had* lost, it wouldn't have been anybody else's fault but mine."

Against Vanderbilt, he had been particularly upset with the second-half defensive play of guards Alford and Smart, the worst he had seen at Indiana, he told them. He wasn't much more pleased with Joe Hillman, who made a big play by drawing a charge from Goheen with the score 76-73 and just over a minute to play, then gave the ball back with a poor shot. Hillman drove to the basket, seeking a possible three-point play, but he got up in the air and had to force up an off-balance left-handed shot that Perdue, well-positioned, smothered and retrieved.

Coming up three days after Vanderbilt was the 13th Indiana Classic. Traditionally, that has been get-well time for the Hoosiers. Indiana never has lost in the four-team tournament, and the average winning margin has been 25 points. Good teams, average teams, mediocre teams have been swallowed up by Indiana teams that have played at a consistent Classic level that has mildly baffled even Knight. The 13th tournament seemed to be the weakest field ever.

Jim Rider

**Magnus Pelkowski is a barrier for Wilmington's Kevan Miles**

Dec. 9, Nashville

# Indiana 75

| | M | 3FG | AFG | FT | R | A | B | S | T | F | Pts |
|---|---|---|---|---|---|---|---|---|---|---|---|
| Thomas, f | 39 | | 7-14 | 7-13 | 10 | 1 | 1 | 3 | 1 | 0 | 21 |
| Smart, f | 28 | 1- 1 | 5-10 | 2- 2 | 1 | 6 | 0 | 0 | 2 | 5 | 13 |
| Garrett, c | 26 | | 4-13 | 1- 3 | 11 | 0 | 3 | 0 | 2 | 3 | 9 |
| Alford, g | 40 | 4- 5 | 9-17 | 6- 6 | 2 | 5 | 0 | 0 | 2 | 1 | 28 |
| Hillman, g | 23 | | 0- 2 | 2- 2 | 4 | 3 | 0 | 1 | 1 | 2 | 2 |
| Smith | 13 | | 0- 0 | 0- 0 | 1 | 0 | 0 | 1 | 3 | 0 | 0 |
| Minor | 9 | | 0- 2 | 0- 0 | 2 | 0 | 0 | 0 | 1 | 0 | 0 |
| Eyl | 8 | | 0- 0 | 0- 0 | 0 | 0 | 0 | 0 | 0 | 0 | 0 |
| Sloan | 5 | | 1- 2 | 0- 0 | 2 | 0 | 0 | 0 | 0 | 0 | 2 |
| Pelkowski | 4 | | 0- 0 | 0- 0 | 0 | 0 | 0 | 0 | 0 | 2 | 0 |
| Meier | 5 | | 0- 0 | 0- 0 | 1 | 1 | 0 | 0 | 0 | 3 | 0 |
| Team | | | | | 1 | | | | | | |
| **Totals** | | 5- 6 | 26-60 | 18-26 | 35 | 16 | 4 | 4 | 10 | 19 | 75 |

# Vanderbilt 79

| | M | 3FG | AFG | FT | R | A | B | S | T | F | Pts |
|---|---|---|---|---|---|---|---|---|---|---|---|
| Reece, f | 25 | | 5- 8 | 2- 2 | 7 | 3 | 0 | 0 | 2 | 5 | 12 |
| Clem, f | 31 | 0- 2 | 1- 4 | 1- 2 | 4 | 2 | 0 | 0 | 0 | 4 | 3 |
| Perdue, c | 27 | | 7-12 | 1- 2 | 9 | 5 | 2 | 0 | 3 | 2 | 15 |
| Booker, g | 35 | 2- 5 | 5-11 | 1- 2 | 4 | 2 | 0 | 0 | 3 | 2 | 13 |
| Goheen, f | 36 | 1- 1 | 7-10 | 11-12 | 6 | 1 | 0 | 0 | 4 | 1 | 26 |
| Kornet | 13 | | 2- 5 | 1- 2 | 2 | 0 | 0 | 0 | 0 | 5 | 5 |
| Neff | 10 | | 0- 2 | 0- 0 | 1 | 0 | 0 | 0 | 1 | 1 | 0 |
| Draud | 10 | 1- 1 | 1- 2 | 0- 0 | 2 | 2 | 0 | 0 | 1 | 0 | 3 |
| Adams | 9 | 0- 2 | 0- 3 | 0- 0 | 0 | 1 | 0 | 0 | 0 | 0 | 0 |
| Reid | 4 | | 1- 1 | 0- 0 | 1 | 0 | 0 | 0 | 0 | 1 | 2 |
| Team | | | | | 0 | | | | | | |
| **Totals** | | 4-11 | 29-58 | 17-22 | 36 | 16 | 2 | 0 | 14 | 21 | 79 |

| SCORE BY HALVES | | | 3FG | AFG | FT |
|---|---|---|---|---|---|
| Indiana (3-1) | 38 37—75 | | .833 | .433 | .692 |
| Vanderbilt (5-1) | 32 47—79 | | .364 | .500 | .773 |

**Officials**—Joe Silvester, Jim Burr, Tim Higgins.
**Attendance**—15,626 (sellout).

John Terhune

Center Brian Rowsom of North Carolina-Wilmington rewrote the scoring records and was named MVP of the Indiana Classic, but IU captains Todd Meier, Daryl Thomas and Steve Alford got the team trophy.

John Terhune

A couple of last-minute cancellations left Indiana facing a field of North Carolina-Wilmington and East Carolina from the Southern Conference and independent Southern Illinois.

The name of Brian Rowsom hadn't even penetrated the Midwest, when he and his North Carolina-Wilmington teammates arrived. It was about to.

Knight carried out his displeasure with the guards by making his first lineup change since the enforced one after Calloway's injury. Smart and Hillman were benched in favor of Brian Sloan and freshman Dave Minor, and Garrett — outscored 15-9 by Perdue — was sat down to give 6-10 Magnus Pelkowski, a native of Bogota, Colombia, a start. In five minutes, the Hoosiers were down 12-5 and Knight had made his first change: freshman Tony Freeman for Minor.

Freeman — smallest Knight recruit ever at 5-foot-7 — reported to campus in the fall with a shoulder injury. In pick-up play before practice even began, he dislocated it and had to have surgery. He returned to the playing floor the day before the Wilmington game, logging less than an hour's practice time with his new teammates before Knight gave him the call. "You're going to love Tony

Freeman," Knight had promised Indiana fans in pre-season, before any had seen him. Quite quickly, they did. Freeman ignited a Hoosier spurt that put them ahead, 20-19, before he sat down, eight minutes after entering.

He returned with four minutes left in the half, Indiana leading 34-21 — the lead attained primarily because of ferocious rebounding and de-

Dec. 12, Assembly Hall

## N.C.-Wilmington 72

| | M | 3FG | AFG | FT | R | A | B | S | T | F | Pts |
|---|---|---|---|---|---|---|---|---|---|---|---|
| Bender, f | 23 | | 0- 6 | 3- 4 | 4 | 2 | 0 | 1 | 1 | 4 | 3 |
| Miles, f | 22 | | 2- 5 | 4- 4 | 7 | 0 | 0 | 1 | 2 | 5 | 8 |
| Rowsom, c | 40 | | 15-32 | 5- 7 | 18 | 1 | 0 | 3 | 1 | 4 | 35 |
| Porter, g | 34 | 1- 1 | 6- 8 | 1- 1 | 4 | 3 | 0 | 2 | 7 | 3 | 14 |
| Anderson, g | 22 | | 1- 5 | 0- 0 | 2 | 2 | 1 | 3 | 2 | 1 | 2 |
| Gary | 20 | | 1- 4 | 2- 2 | 0 | 2 | 0 | 1 | 1 | 1 | 4 |
| Pittman | 15 | | 0- 3 | 0- 0 | 1 | 0 | 0 | 0 | 2 | 3 | 0 |
| Wagner | 7 | | 1- 3 | 0- 0 | 1 | 0 | 0 | 0 | 1 | 2 | 2 |
| Griffin | 5 | | 1- 2 | 0- 0 | 1 | 0 | 0 | 0 | 0 | 3 | 2 |
| Cherry | 12 | | 1- 3 | 0- 0 | 2 | 0 | 0 | 0 | 0 | 3 | 2 |
| Team | | | | | 5 | | | | | | |
| Totals | | 1- 1 | 28-71 | 15-18 | 45 | 10 | 1 | 11 | 17 | 29 | 72 |

## Indiana 73

| | M | 3FG | AFG | FT | R | A | B | S | T | F | Pts |
|---|---|---|---|---|---|---|---|---|---|---|---|
| Thomas, f | 36 | | 5-14 | 7- 9 | 5 | 1 | 1 | 2 | 3 | 3 | 17 |
| Sloan, f | 6 | | 0- 0 | 0- 0 | 1 | 0 | 0 | 0 | 0 | 1 | 0 |
| Pelkowski, c | 9 | | 0- 0 | 0- 0 | 1 | 0 | 0 | 0 | 1 | 1 | 0 |
| Alford, g | 40 | 4-10 | 8-21 | 0- 1 | 2 | 1 | 0 | 0 | 3 | 1 | 20 |
| Minor, g | 4 | | 0- 1 | 0- 0 | 0 | 1 | 0 | 0 | 3 | 0 | 0 |
| Freeman | 22 | 0- 1 | 1- 4 | 5- 7 | 3 | 3 | 0 | 2 | 5 | 1 | 7 |
| Smart | 22 | 0- 1 | 2- 5 | 4- 6 | 1 | 3 | 0 | 2 | 2 | 4 | 8 |
| Garrett | 33 | | 6- 8 | 5- 9 | 16 | 0 | 7 | 2 | 2 | 3 | 17 |
| Eyl | 20 | | 0- 0 | 4- 5 | 4 | 0 | 0 | 1 | 0 | 2 | 4 |
| Hillman | 8 | | 0- 1 | 0- 0 | 2 | 0 | 0 | 0 | 0 | 0 | 0 |
| Team | | | | | 6 | | | | | | |
| Totals | | 4-12 | 22-54 | 25-37 | 39 | 11 | 8 | 9 | 19 | 16 | 73 |

| SCORE BY HALVES | | | 3FG | AFG | FT |
|---|---|---|---|---|---|
| N.C.-Wilmington (2-2) | 29 | 43—72 | 1.000 | .394 | .833 |
| Indiana (4-1) | 43 | 30—73 | .333 | .407 | .676 |

**Officials**—Tom Rucker, Eric Harmon, Sam Lickliter.
**Attendance**—13,725.

fensive play by Garrett, once he got a summons from the bench a little more than six minutes into the game. The lead reached 43-25 before leveling off with two Wilmington baskets in the final seconds of the first half. As a reward for his surprise performance, Knight started Freeman in the second half, and the Hoosiers seemed to be breezing at 56-43. Very suddenly, things changed. Rowsom, a 6-9 senior center, scored three straight baskets to highlight a 12-2 run that pulled Wilmington within 56-51. Knight pulled Freeman after two straight turnovers but went back to him with 3:27 to go and the Indiana lead a shaky 69-66. With 1:10 to go, Kevan Miles scored to pull Wilmington within 73-72.

The time left guaranteed that Indiana would have to put up one more shot — the general presumption, by Alford. With more than 15 seconds left on the shot clock, Freeman saw an opening to the basket, bolted in — and missed, his attempt to slip a layup through last-second pressure bouncing off the underside of the goal. Wilmington recovered, took timeout with 38 seconds left,

Jim Rider

**Dean Garrett's seven Classic blocks won his job back**

and went to work at isolating Rowsom for a possible game-winning shot. It was logical. By then, Rowsom already had a tournament-record 35 points.

With about 12 seconds to go, the Seahawks got the ball to him, posted along the right baseline. He turned for the jump shot that had been killing the Hoosiers, but Garrett slammed his shot aside — out of bounds, at 0:10. Wilmington kept possession and, with Indiana packed around Rowsom, got the ball to forward Greg Bender for an open shot about 14 feet out on the left baseline. Bender missed. So did a gang tip by the Seahawks, and Steve Eyl assured an escape for the Hoosiers by pulling the rebound in.

Knight second-guessed himself for playing Freeman 22 minutes in just his second day back on the court. Starting him the second half "was almost a mistake I knew I was making at the time," Knight said. "Tony was a little bit tired, so we weren't running up and down the floor like we were in the first half. He had some turnovers, and we never got back in it."

Rowsom came back the next night with another tournament record, 36 points, in the consolation round to become the first non-In-

### Dec. 13, Assembly Hall
# East Carolina 68

| | M | 3FG | AFG | FT | R | A | B | S | T | F | Pts |
|---|---|---|---|---|---|---|---|---|---|---|---|
| Henry, f | 36 | | 7-11 | 4- 5 | 6 | 1 | 0 | 3 | 4 | 2 | 18 |
| Edwards, f | 34 | | 4-11 | 2- 2 | 3 | 2 | 0 | 3 | 3 | 3 | 10 |
| Bass, c | 31 | | 6- 9 | 4- 6 | 5 | 1 | 1 | 0 | 1 | 2 | 16 |
| Brown, g | 20 | | 2- 9 | 0- 0 | 2 | 0 | 0 | 0 | 8 | 1 | 4 |
| Sledge, g | 30 | 3- 6 | 4- 8 | 0- 0 | 2 | 2 | 0 | 3 | 2 | 1 | 11 |
| Kelly | 20 | | 1- 1 | 0- 0 | 4 | 0 | 1 | 2 | 2 | 2 | 2 |
| Lose | 11 | 0- 1 | 0- 1 | 0- 0 | 2 | 0 | 0 | 1 | 2 | 2 | 0 |
| Battle | 1 | | 0- 0 | 0- 0 | 0 | 0 | 0 | 0 | 0 | 0 | 0 |
| King | 7 | | 1 2 | 0- 2 | 4 | 0 | 0 | 0 | 2 | 0 | 2 |
| Grady | 5 | 0- 2 | 0- 4 | 3- 4 | 2 | 0 | 0 | 0 | 0 | 0 | 3 |
| Jones | 5 | | 1- 1 | 0- 0 | 1 | 0 | 0 | 0 | 0 | 0 | 2 |
| Team | | | | | 6 | | | | | | |
| **Totals** | | **3- 9** | **26-57** | **13-19** | **33** | **10** | **1** | **8** | **25** | **14** | **68** |

# Indiana 96

| | M | 3FG | AFG | FT | R | A | B | S | T | F | Pts |
|---|---|---|---|---|---|---|---|---|---|---|---|
| Thomas, f | 24 | | 10-13 | 2- 3 | 4 | 2 | 0 | 2 | 4 | 2 | 22 |
| Eyl, f | 24 | | 3- 4 | 0- 0 | 4 | 5 | 0 | 1 | 2 | 0 | 6 |
| Garrett, c | 23 | | 5- 9 | 1- 2 | 6 | 1 | 2 | 0 | 2 | 2 | 11 |
| Alford, g | 28 | 1- 3 | 6-13 | 1- 1 | 6 | 3 | 0 | 4 | 0 | 1 | 14 |
| Smart, g | 23 | | 3- 6 | 1- 1 | 3 | 4 | 0 | 0 | 2 | 2 | 7 |
| Freeman | 13 | | 2- 3 | 0- 0 | 1 | 3 | 0 | 2 | 2 | 3 | 4 |
| Sloan | 10 | | 1- 4 | 0- 1 | 1 | 0 | 1 | 0 | 0 | 2 | 2 |
| Meier | 4 | | 1- 1 | 2- 2 | 2 | 0 | 0 | 0 | 0 | 3 | 4 |
| Minor | 13 | | 1- 5 | 0- 0 | 1 | 1 | 0 | 0 | 1 | 1 | 2 |
| Hillman | 10 | | 2- 3 | 3- 3 | 1 | 5 | 0 | 0 | 0 | 0 | 7 |
| Pelkowski | 14 | | 4- 7 | 1- 2 | 4 | 0 | 0 | 0 | 0 | 4 | 9 |
| Smith | 14 | 2- 2 | 3- 5 | 0- 0 | 0 | 0 | 0 | 1 | 1 | 1 | 8 |
| Team | | | | | 3 | | | | | | |
| **Totals** | | **3- 5** | **41-73** | **11-15** | **36** | **24** | **3** | **10** | **14** | **21** | **96** |

| SCORE BY HALVES | | 3FG | AFG | FT |
|---|---|---|---|---|
| East Carolina (5-2) | 22 46—68 | .333 | .456 | .684 |
| Indiana (5-1) | 49 47—96 | .600 | .562 | .733 |

**Officials** —Tom Rucker, Eric Harmon, Sam Lickliter.
**Attendance**—14,139.

**Pervis Ellison, meet Keith Smart, Steve Alford, Dean Garrett**

John Terhune

## Morehead State 62

| | M | 3FG | AFG | FT | R | A | B | S | F | Pts |
|---|---|---|---|---|---|---|---|---|---|---|
| Davis, f | 24 | | 4- 9 | 1- 4 | 5 | 2 | 0 | 2 | 1 | 9 |
| Griffin, f | 26 | 1- 2 | 3- 4 | 0- 0 | 1 | 2 | 0 | 4 | 1 | 7 |
| McCann, c | 34 | | 8-16 | 9-15 | 11 | 0 | 1 | 5 | 5 | 25 |
| Curry, g | 27 | | 1- 5 | 0- 0 | 1 | 2 | 0 | 0 | 3 | 4 | 2 |
| Rivers, g | 26 | 0- 1 | 2- 4 | 1- 1 | 6 | 1 | 0 | 0 | 3 | 3 | 5 |
| Mason | 23 | | 2- 7 | 1- 2 | 3 | 2 | 1 | 1 | 2 | 2 | 5 |
| Turner | 14 | 1- 1 | 2- 6 | 0- 0 | 1 | 1 | 0 | 1 | 2 | 1 | 5 |
| Clements | 7 | | 1- 1 | 0- 0 | 0 | 0 | 0 | 0 | 0 | 2 |
| Feldhaus | 12 | | 0- 0 | 0- 0 | 0 | 0 | 1 | 1 | 0 | 0 |
| Simpson | 2 | | 1- 1 | 0- 0 | 1 | 0 | 0 | 0 | 0 | 2 |
| Chaney | 1 | | 0- 0 | 0- 0 | 1 | 0 | 0 | 0 | 1 | 0 |
| Smith | 1 | | 0- 0 | 0- 0 | 0 | 0 | 0 | 0 | 0 | 0 |
| Hale | 1 | | 0- 0 | 0- 0 | 0 | 0 | 0 | 0 | 0 | 0 |
| Brooks | 1 | | 0- 0 | 0- 0 | 0 | 0 | 0 | 0 | 1 | 0 |
| Lott | 1 | | 0- 1 | 0- 0 | 0 | 0 | 0 | 0 | 0 | 0 |
| Team | | | | | 5 | | | | | |
| Totals | | 2- 4 | 24-54 | 12-22 | 35 | 10 | 2 | 6 | 21 | 18 | 62 |

## Indiana 84

| | M | 3FG | AFG | FT | R | A | B | S | T | F | Pts |
|---|---|---|---|---|---|---|---|---|---|---|---|
| Thomas, f | 31 | | 8-13 | 0- 0 | 5 | 2 | 1 | 3 | 2 | 1 | 16 |
| Calloway, f | 24 | | 4- 7 | 1- 1 | 4 | 5 | 1 | 2 | 1 | 2 | 9 |
| Garrett, c | 28 | | 7-11 | 4- 4 | 9 | 2 | 0 | 0 | 1 | 3 | 18 |
| Alford, g | 28 | 4- 8 | 6-12 | 2- 3 | 1 | 4 | 0 | 2 | 1 | 0 | 18 |
| Smart, g | 18 | | 3- 8 | 0- 0 | 1 | 3 | 0 | 0 | 2 | 2 | 6 |
| Pelkowski | 16 | 1- 1 | 5- 9 | 0- 0 | 1 | 0 | 0 | 0 | 3 | 3 | 11 |
| Eyl | 6 | | 0- 1 | 0- 0 | 1 | 1 | 0 | 1 | 1 | 1 | 0 |
| Hillman | 7 | | 1- 3 | 0- 0 | 1 | 2 | 0 | 0 | 0 | 0 | 2 |
| Freeman | 5 | | 0- 0 | 0- 0 | 1 | 1 | 0 | 2 | 0 | 0 |
| Sloan | 11 | | 0- 0 | 0- 0 | 2 | 0 | 0 | 3 | 0 |
| Smith | 13 | | 1- 1 | 0- 0 | 0 | 0 | 0 | 1 | 0 | 2 |
| Minor | 9 | | 0- 1 | 0- 0 | 2 | 0 | 0 | 2 | 0 | 0 |
| Meier | 4 | | 1- 2 | 0- 1 | 2 | 1 | 1 | 0 | 0 | 2 |
| Team | | | | | 4 | | | | | | |
| Totals | | 5- 9 | 36-68 | 7- 9 | 32 | 23 | 3 | 8 | 16 | 15 | 84 |

| SCORE BY HALVES | | | 3FG | AFG | FT |
|---|---|---|---|---|---|
| Morehead State (3-4) | 25 | 37—62 | .500 | .444 | .545 |
| Indiana (7-1) | 42 | 42—84 | .556 | .529 | .778 |

**Officials**—Gary Muncy, Ted Valentine, Mike Stockner.
**Attendance**—15,397 (sellout).

diana player to win MVP honors in the tournament and put his name in many a pro scout's file. North Carolina-Wilmington's conference partner, East Carolina, had reached the finals breezing, an 89-71 winner over Southern Illinois. The victory provided a chance drawling, courageous East Carolina coach Charlie Harrison had dreamed of. Harrison, a polio victim as a boy, was a college coach because Knight had given him a chance to assist the IU staff, then recommended him for an assistant's job under Tates Locke, whom Knight had assisted at Army when his own coaching career was beginning. "I've told my kids what a class act this place is," Harrison said when he brought the Pirates into Bloomington. "I keep thinking myself what a great opportunity I was given here." He got no opportunity at all in the championship game. The Hoosiers used a 12-point string to open a 24-11 lead on the way to 49-22 by halftime and a more classically Indiana Classic final score: 96-68. "They played extremely well," Harrison said.

Knight praised the defensive play of Steve Eyl, given his first start as an antidote to 6-5 East Carolina forward Marchell Henry, who had matched Rowsom's 35 the previous night. Henry had just 2 points the first half. "I thought Eyl played Henry very well," Knight said. "He just took him out of the game." Knight couldn't forget the lesson he had learned in the scare against North Carolina-Wilmington. "That was my fault, not the players'," he said. "I just didn't do a very good job of preparing them to play. I was too hard on them after the Vanderbilt game. I don't think I can do that with these kids."

The Hoosiers spent a week focusing on semester exams, but the biggest test came when Calloway rejoined them in midweek. By Friday, he was cleared to play, some. He started Saturday against Morehead State and contributed nine points, four rebounds and five assists to an 84-62 Hoosier victory. "I didn't want to fool around," Knight said. "I just wanted to get him started and let him play as much as he could. He didn't have to play his way back into the lineup. He did that last year." Morehead State coach Wayne Martin said Calloway "makes Indiana an immeasurably better basketball team than the one anybody else has played since Montana State."

The Morehead State game marked the first time the Hoosiers had started the lineup that had seemed inevitable all along — Thomas, Calloway, Garrett, Alford and Smart. It became the first long-term lineup Knight had found since 1981, his last NCAA championship team, when the lineup that blew the national tournament field away stayed intact through the last three games of the regular season and the five in the tournament. In the 1983-84 season, Knight tried 18 different combinations; in the chaotic 1984-85 season, 21; in 1985-86, just 11. During the 1986-87 season, seven combinations started games, but the Thomas, Calloway, Garrett, Alford, Smart group opened 24 of the last

John Terhune

**Daryl Thomas gets up and over Pervis Ellison, once, in what Thomas called 'a lousy game' for him — and a pivotal game. After it, he stopped 'running to the middle and clogging things up for Dean (Garrett).'**

Dec. 23, Assembly Hall

# Louisville 58

| | M | 3FG | AFG | FT | R | A | B | S | T | F | Pts |
|---|---|---|---|---|---|---|---|---|---|---|---|
| Crook, f | 37 | | 12-23 | 0- 0 | 10 | 0 | 0 | 0 | 2 | 3 | 24 |
| Payne, f | 30 | | 2- 7 | 0- 0 | 3 | 0 | 0 | 0 | 3 | 3 | 4 |
| Ellison, c | 40 | | 3-14 | 2- 3 | 12 | 4 | 4 | 3 | 3 | 1 | 8 |
| Hawley, g | 20 | 0- 1 | 1- 2 | 0- 0 | 1 | 2 | 0 | 0 | 2 | 4 | 2 |
| Kimbro, g | 34 | 0- 1 | 4- 8 | 0- 2 | 2 | 0 | 2 | 0 | 2 | 4 | 8 |
| Abram | 12 | | 2- 3 | 2- 2 | 4 | 1 | 0 | 1 | 1 | 3 | 6 |
| McSwain | 13 | | 1- 4 | 1- 2 | 4 | 2 | 1 | 0 | 2 | 1 | 3 |
| Walls | 2 | | 0- 0 | 0- 0 | 0 | 0 | 0 | 0 | 0 | 1 | 0 |
| Williams | 12 | | 1- 1 | 1- 2 | 0 | 0 | 0 | 0 | 3 | 1 | 3 |
| Tcam | | | | | 4 | | | | | | |
| **Totals** | | 0- 2 | 26-62 | 6-11 | 40 | 9 | 7 | 4 | 18 | 21 | 58 |

# Indiana 67

| | M | 3FG | AFG | FT | R | A | B | S | T | F | Pts |
|---|---|---|---|---|---|---|---|---|---|---|---|
| Thomas, f | 25 | | 2- 7 | 1- 2 | 5 | 0 | 0 | 1 | 2 | 2 | 5 |
| Calloway, f | 32 | | 8-14 | 3- 6 | 2 | 1 | 0 | 2 | 2 | 3 | 19 |
| Garrett, c | 40 | | 6-10 | 0- 0 | 11 | 1 | 2 | 3 | 1 | 0 | 12 |
| Alford, g | 40 | 3- 7 | 4-17 | 6- 7 | 3 | 2 | 0 | 2 | 1 | 2 | 17 |
| Smart, g | 29 | | 4- 7 | 5- 6 | 2 | 5 | 0 | 2 | 2 | 3 | 13 |
| Eyl | 22 | | 0- 1 | 1- 2 | 5 | 0 | 0 | 0 | 4 | 3 | 1 |
| Smith | 8 | | 0- 0 | 0- 0 | 1 | 1 | 0 | 0 | 0 | 1 | 0 |
| Meier | 4 | | 0- 1 | 0- 0 | 1 | 0 | 0 | 0 | 0 | 1 | 0 |
| Team | | | | | 5 | | | | | | |
| **Totals** | | 3- 7 | 24-57 | 16-23 | 35 | 10 | 2 | 10 | 12 | 15 | 67 |

| SCORE BY HALVES | | | | 3FG | AFG | FT |
|---|---|---|---|---|---|---|
| Louisville (4-5) | | 34 | 24—58 | .000 | .419 | .545 |
| Indiana (7-1) | | 28 | 39—67 | .429 | .421 | .696 |

**Officials**—Ted Hillary, Jim Burr, Dan Rutledge.
**Attendance**—17,253 (sellout).

Phil Whitlow

**Pete Carril, 3-0 against Bob Knight teams at Army and Indiana, won Knight's praise when the string ended with Indiana's 83-54 victory over Carril's Princeton team in the Hoosier Classic. Carril could only wince as Steve Alford stung his team for 8-for-11 shooting from three-point range.**

27 games.

Knight had hoped to get Calloway's testing and uncertainty out of the way before the third big game of December: the visit of reigning national champion Louisville to Assembly Hall.

Denny Crum didn't have the combination that had clicked for his second NCAA title the previous March at Dallas. Louisville came in 4-4 and unranked. Garrett hardly noticed. What he did know was that the Cardinals still had the player who received the 1986 tournament's Outstanding Player Award as a freshman, 6-9 center Pervis Ellison.

"I was *really* pumped up," Garrett said. "I had been thinking about Pervis Ellison since the summertime. Guys back home, when they knew we were playing Louisville, were telling me, 'He's gonna eat you alive.' Just guys I'd see on the street. They saw how Pervis Ellison played in the tournament. It was, like, 'He's gonna tear you up. You haven't played against guys like that.' It might have been all in joking, but it just built up till that time. That was

the game I was probably most pumped up for all season. I thought it was a chance to prove myself and make a name."

Both Garrett and Ellison were virtual spectators while the other starter back from Crum's championship team, forward Herbert Crook, shot the Hoosiers into trouble early. Louisville opened a 30-21 lead and Crook had 18 of the points. Crook still was bedeviling the Hoosiers in the second half, his rebound basket lifting him to 24 points and opening a 49-42 Louisville lead with nine minutes to go.

What the Cardinals had graduated was guards. Four straight times, they turned the ball over. Alford followed one with a three-point shot, Garrett one with a dunk. Garrett;s rebound basket tied the game, 49-49, and a free throw by Smart broke the tie. Calloway followed with a three-point play to complete an 11-point run that put the Hoosiers ahead, 53-49, and Louisville was on a slide that carried it out of the game, a 67-58 loser.

Garrett had 12 points and 11 rebounds; Ellison, 8 points and 12 rebounds. "It was a game I'll never forget," Garrett said. "My mom was there; my family came — my sister, my cousin, my uncle."

It was a game Knight couldn't forget when Garrett followed it with two points and three rebounds in just a 10-minute role in Indiana's 83-54 victory over Princeton on opening night of the fifth Hoosier Classic at Indianapolis. Alford provided all the offense Indiana needed that night by going 8-for-11 from three-point range and scoring 26 points. "I've seen a lot of things like that by him in practice," Smart said, "but that's the first *game*. He said in his eyes, 'Bring it back to me.' I just kept bringing it back. I may set a tournament record for assists."

Smart and teammates brought the ball back for 21 more Alford points as Indiana stayed unbeaten in both of its December tournaments by beating Illinois State and former Knight assistant Bob Donewald, 82-58. Alford was the tourna-

### Dec. 26, Indianapolis
## Princeton 54

| | M | 3FG | AFG | FT | R | A | B | S | T | F | Pts |
|---|---|---|---|---|---|---|---|---|---|---|---|
| Thompson, f | 30 | | 4- 5 | 1- 2 | 0 | 2 | 0 | 0 | 3 | 3 | 9 |
| Scrabis, f | 32 | 0- 2 | 4-10 | 1- 1 | 5 | 2 | 0 | 3 | 3 | 1 | 9 |
| Williams, c | 30 | | 8-11 | 4- 5 | 3 | 0 | 2 | 0 | 1 | 3 | 20 |
| Scott, g | 36 | 0- 3 | 0- 5 | 0- 0 | 2 | 4 | 0 | 2 | 3 | 4 | 0 |
| Orlandini, g | 29 | 1- 1 | 3- 3 | 1- 1 | 1 | 0 | 0 | 1 | 3 | 1 | 8 |
| Harnum | 7 | 0- 1 | 0- 1 | 0- 0 | 0 | 1 | 0 | 0 | 1 | 1 | 0 |
| Betz | 5 | 0- 1 | 0- 1 | 0- 0 | 0 | 1 | 0 | 1 | 1 | 0 | 0 |
| Vestegaard | 6 | | 1- 3 | 0- 0 | 1 | 0 | 0 | 1 | 0 | 0 | 2 |
| Neff | 8 | 0- 2 | 1- 3 | 0- 0 | 2 | 0 | 0 | 0 | 0 | 0 | 2 |
| Katz | 5 | 0- 1 | 0- 2 | 0- 0 | 0 | 0 | 0 | 0 | 0 | 0 | 0 |
| Miley | 3 | | 1- 3 | 0- 0 | 1 | 0 | 0 | 0 | 0 | 0 | 2 |
| Kennedy | 4 | | 0- 0 | 0- 0 | 0 | 0 | 0 | 0 | 1 | 0 | 0 |
| Nash | 3 | | 0- 3 | 0- 0 | 1 | 0 | 0 | 0 | 0 | 0 | 0 |
| Nikolai | 1 | | 0- 0 | 2- 2 | 0 | 0 | 0 | 0 | 0 | 0 | 2 |
| Lapin | 1 | | 0- 0 | 0- 0 | 1 | 0 | 0 | 0 | 0 | 0 | 0 |
| Team | | | | | 6 | | | | | | |
| **Totals** | | **1-11** | **22-50** | **9-11** | **23** | **10** | **2** | **8** | **16** | **13** | **54** |

## Indiana 83

| | M | 3FG | AFG | FT | R | A | B | S | T | F | Pts |
|---|---|---|---|---|---|---|---|---|---|---|---|
| Thomas, f | 30 | | 8-13 | 1- 1 | 2 | 0 | 0 | 1 | 1 | 2 | 17 |
| Calloway, f | 29 | | 5-11 | 3- 4 | 4 | 1 | 0 | 0 | 2 | 2 | 13 |
| Garrett, c | 10 | | 1- 1 | 0- 0 | 3 | 0 | 0 | 0 | 0 | 2 | 2 |
| Alford, g | 32 | 8-11 | 9-13 | 0- 0 | 3 | 3 | 0 | 1 | 0 | 1 | 26 |
| Smart, g | 21 | 0- 1 | 1- 4 | 0- 0 | 3 | 5 | 0 | 0 | 3 | 2 | 2 |
| Eyl | 19 | | 2- 2 | 1- 2 | 6 | 0 | 1 | 1 | 2 | 1 | 5 |
| Hillman | 15 | 0- 1 | 0- 1 | 2- 2 | 2 | 4 | 1 | 0 | 2 | 1 | 2 |
| Smith | 16 | 2- 2 | 3- 4 | 0- 0 | 3 | 2 | 0 | 0 | 0 | 0 | 8 |
| Sloan | 8 | 0- 1 | 2- 4 | 0- 0 | 1 | 0 | 2 | 1 | 1 | 1 | 4 |
| Pelkowski | 8 | | 2- 5 | 0- 0 | 3 | 0 | 0 | 0 | 0 | 2 | 4 |
| Minor | 6 | | 0- 1 | 0- 0 | 1 | 1 | 0 | 0 | 0 | 0 | 0 |
| Meier | 6 | | 0- 2 | 0- 0 | 2 | 1 | 0 | 0 | 1 | 1 | 0 |
| Team | | | | | 1 | | | | | | |
| **Totals** | | **10-16** | **33-61** | **7- 9** | **34** | **17** | **4** | **4** | **12** | **15** | **83** |

| SCORE BY HALVES | | | 3FG | AFG | FT |
|---|---|---|---|---|---|
| Princeton (4-4) | 25 | 29—54 | .091 | .440 | .818 |
| Indiana (8-1) | 38 | 45—83 | .625 | .541 | .778 |

**Officials**—Tom Rucker, Rich Weiler, Gary Muncy.
**Attendance**—15,926.

ment's MVP, and Knight seconded the vote. "I really thought over the 80 minutes Alford played about as well as I've ever seen him play."

Garrett was looking for a new start. He wasn't much more effective against Illinois State (six points, eight rebounds) than against Princeton. Knight laid it to a failure to come down from the Louisville clouds. "I might still have been thinking about that," Garrett admitted after the season. "My head might have got a little big. I played real bad in the Hoosier Classic. It was a good lesson for me."

His tutor sat down and did some thinking, too. Happy as he was to have a genuine big man around so he could play forward, Thomas felt he was hampering his play at his new position by reverting to last year's habits. "I had just a lousy game against Louisville — I didn't play my game at all. I kept running to the paint. That's where I had my success last year, so I kept running to the middle, and I was clogging things up for Dean. Louisville was giving me the outside shot and I never took it. It wasn't that I didn't want to take it — I didn't know when to take it. After the Louisville game, I took some shots. Eventually I felt confident enough to go out on the floor and handle the ball."

Steve Eyl's work off the bench made it easy for MVP Steve Alford and assistant coach Ron Felling to smile at Hoosier Classic awards time

**Dec. 27, Indianapolis**

## Illinois State 58

| | M | 3FG | AFG | FT | R | A | B | S | T | F | Pts |
|---|---|---|---|---|---|---|---|---|---|---|---|
| Sanders, f | 38 | | 6-13 | 1-2 | 9 | 1 | 1 | 1 | 4 | 2 | 13 |
| Peterson, f | 16 | | 3-5 | 0-1 | 4 | 0 | 0 | 0 | 4 | 4 | 6 |
| Holifield, c | 32 | | 4-5 | 4-6 | 5 | 0 | 2 | 1 | 3 | 2 | 12 |
| Harris, g | 34 | 2-3 | 4-10 | 0-0 | 4 | 2 | 0 | 1 | 3 | 3 | 10 |
| Starks, g | 37 | | 4-9 | 0-2 | 3 | 4 | 1 | 2 | 4 | 4 | 8 |
| Jackson | 25 | | 2-7 | 1-2 | 1 | 2 | 1 | 0 | 0 | 4 | 5 |
| Coleman | 9 | | 1-3 | 0-1 | 2 | 0 | 0 | 0 | 1 | 2 | 2 |
| Taphorn | 3 | | 0-2 | 0-0 | 2 | 0 | 0 | 0 | 1 | 0 | 0 |
| Skarich | 2 | | 1-1 | 0-0 | 0 | 0 | 0 | 0 | 0 | 0 | 2 |
| Blair | 2 | | 0-0 | 0-0 | 0 | 0 | 0 | 0 | 0 | 0 | 0 |
| Roberts | 2 | | 0-1 | 0-0 | 0 | 0 | 0 | 0 | 0 | 0 | 0 |
| Team | | | | | 6 | | | | | | |
| **Totals** | | 2-3 | 25-56 | 6-14 | 36 | 9 | 5 | 5 | 20 | 21 | 58 |

## Indiana 82

| | M | 3FG | AFG | FT | R | A | B | S | T | F | Pts |
|---|---|---|---|---|---|---|---|---|---|---|---|
| Thomas, f | 26 | | 6-15 | 1-1 | 6 | 0 | 1 | 4 | 1 | 4 | 13 |
| Calloway, f | 33 | | 8-13 | 3-3 | 5 | 2 | 1 | 0 | 2 | 3 | 19 |
| Garrett, c | 22 | | 2-6 | 2-2 | 8 | 0 | 3 | 2 | 0 | 3 | 6 |
| Alford, g | 36 | 1-3 | 6-16 | 8-8 | 5 | 7 | 0 | 0 | 3 | 1 | 21 |
| Smart, g | 28 | | 5-11 | 0-1 | 5 | 4 | 1 | 0 | 2 | 2 | 10 |
| Eyl | 14 | | 1-4 | 0-1 | 5 | 1 | 1 | 0 | 0 | 1 | 2 |
| Hillman | 12 | | 0-0 | 0-0 | 1 | 0 | 0 | 0 | 2 | 1 | 0 |
| Smith | 9 | 1-1 | 1-1 | 0-0 | 0 | 2 | 0 | 0 | 0 | 0 | 3 |
| Meier | 4 | | 1-1 | 0-0 | 1 | 0 | 0 | 0 | 0 | 0 | 2 |
| Pelkowski | 7 | | 1-1 | 2-2 | 1 | 0 | 0 | 0 | 0 | 1 | 4 |
| Minor | 5 | | 0-0 | 0-0 | 0 | 0 | 0 | 0 | 0 | 0 | 0 |
| Sloan | 4 | | 1-1 | 0-0 | 0 | 0 | 0 | 0 | 0 | 2 | 2 |
| Team | | | | | 3 | | | | | | |
| **Totals** | | 2-4 | 32-69 | 16-18 | 40 | 16 | 7 | 6 | 10 | 18 | 82 |

| SCORE BY HALVES | | | 3FG | AFG | FT |
|---|---|---|---|---|---|
| Illinois State (5-4) | 19 | 39—58 | .667 | .446 | .429 |
| Indiana (9-1) | 41 | 41—82 | .500 | .464 | .889 |

**Officials**—Tom Rucker, Rich Weiler, Gary Muncy.
**Attendance**—16,585 (sellout).

Phil Whitlow

# 4 On the road

*For Steve Alford, Daryl Thomas and Todd Meier, it was a special Big Ten season, their last-chance season*

It was not at all difficult for Steve Alford to flip a mental switch from the demands of December to the pressures of January. As a senior, Alford knew exactly what the change of the calendar meant: the start of Big Ten play. For Alford and fellow seniors Daryl Thomas and Todd Meier, it was a special Big Ten season, their last-chance season.

Certainly coach Bob Knight had mentioned to them that they were in position to be the first players ever to be with him at Indiana for four years and not win a Big Ten championship, but it was not something he had to repeat and repeat. At Indiana, basketball tradition is as omnipresent as the championship banners that hang as reminders of what others in Indiana basketball uniforms have done, constant and silent goals for those who practice under them. Only one Big Ten championship was represented among the eight 15½-by-7 foot red and white nylon-like banners that hung in Assembly Hall in 1986-87. It marked the latest of Indiana's 15 Big Ten titles, the one in 1983 when all-Big Ten forward Ted Kitchel went out with back surgery with the race tied and three games left, at home against contenders Purdue, Illinois and Ohio State. Kitchel's roommate and close friend, Randy Wittman, capped an all-America season by leading the way in a three-game sweep that won the championship outright. Knight was so touched by the way the Assembly Hall crowd responded to the homestretch crisis that he promised to put up a banner in honor of the fans.

Absence of banners for all the others doesn't represent a lack of appreciation on Knight's part for what a Big Ten basketball championship represents. There's a growing tendency within the league to say the title doesn't mean much any more, with the top five or six teams getting NCAA tournament bids. Knight makes it clear every year to his team that the principal aim of the season is leading the Big Ten.

Alford grew up in first Martinsville, Ind., 20 miles from Bloomington, then New Castle, about a 100-mile drive, with a reverence for Indiana basketball and the Big Ten. He knew all about league pressures. New Castle plays in as good a high school replica of the Big Ten as there is in the entire country. Indiana's North Central Conference — Marion, Muncie Central, Anderson, Kokomo, Lafayette Jefferson, Logansport, Richmond and New Castle — has dominated the state high school tournament. The last three years in a row, NCC teams have had *both* spots in the state championship game. The gyms are huge; Alford's senior year, he played before an average of 8,500 in his home arena, and the average around the conference was about 6,000. Counting tournament and all-star play, Alford may have played before something around 500,000 people in high school. At Indiana, he added almost another million in home games, nearly as much on the road. As a 1984 Olympian, he played before sellouts across the country on a preparation tour, then sellouts at the Games. The most spectacular production of all drew 67,596 — biggest basketball crowd in American history — for an appearance of the Olympic team at the Hoosier Dome. Then, this year, Alford played at New Orleans before the two bas-

ketball crowds that rank next to the Olympians' Hoosier Dome appearance on the all-time U.S. list — 64,959. Thus, he's the only player to play before America's all-time top three basketball crowds, and he must be the first player ever to approach 3 million in attendance for his games before reaching the NBA.

The numbers were hollow for him without a championship. He set as his greatest goal winning a state title for his Dad and coach at New Castle, Sam Alford. He gave it a 94-point effort on his last day of high school, 57 points in a morning game and 37 at night, and still couldn't even get his team to the Final Four. Now, he was heading into his last Big Ten season, and he was determined not to settle for that negative Knight Era first without an all-out try to avoid it.

"The change I wanted to make was in my leadership role," he said. "I've been through a lot.

"Daryl, Todd and I knew the problems our team in the past had had in the area of mental toughness. Coach had always harped about that. That was one thing we wanted to correct right at the beginning. We had so many new guys — two from junior college, two freshmen and six guys coming off red-shirt years. The red-shirts had practiced, but as far as competing in game situations, we had 10 guys who were completely new. We wanted to make sure right from the beginning when we got together in September everybody knew what kind of season we could have but how much work had to go into it."

When January came, it wasn't difficult for Alford to restress the step up that the newcomers could expect in Big Ten play, because he's a devout believer. Around the league, he was a favorite target of bleacher signs and crowd taunts. "That never really bothered me," he said. "I guess as a fan from another school, there has to be someone you get on. I guess I was the perfect person."

That was, indeed, one of the nettling things about Alford on the road: he came across as too, too perfect, right down to his hair —

parted near the middle, and never ruffled. "There were a lot of things said about my hair. Those were always amusing. People talked about my using hair spray or some kind of gooey shampoo. I just take a shower and comb my hair. I keep it short and I've got my mother's thick hair. I don't know if the other guys don't know how to comb their hair or what. I got that more than anything anywhere I went, and it always amused me."

On the floor, he didn't sense the same sort of antagonism. "You run into occasional ribbings," he said. "For the most part, I think they really respected my view on things. The majority of the players, especially in the Big Ten, just played basketball. You find that outside of the league maybe more than you do inside the league. Inside the league, you know each other and really you're pretty good friends. You respect the Big Ten schools and you appreciate the conference that we're in."

That was one of the messages he had for the newcomers, especially starters Keith Smart and Dean Garrett. Alford, Thomas and Meier sold their message with such gusto that Garrett felt they went almost too far. "Everybody was trying to pump me up so much," he said. "They were telling me a little bit too much, more than really happened. They were telling me how it was so aggressive, which it is, but it isn't as bad as they made me think it was going to be."

Indiana had the most challenging start of all Big Ten teams: three straight games on the road — at Ohio State, Michigan State and Michigan, none of the three expected to be a championship contender, all figured to be in the battle to pick off an NCAA tournament spot.

Ohio State was a sentimental journey for ex-Buckeye Knight when his own college coach, Fred Taylor, was coaching there. The careers of Knight at Indiana and Taylor at Ohio State overlapped for five seasons. Appropriately, Taylor's last game as a coach was at Bloomington against the best team coached by Knight,

*There were a lot of things said about my hair. Those were always amusing. I don't know if the other guys don't know how to comb their hair or what.*

— Steve Alford

who was a member of Taylor's three best Ohio State teams.

The sentiment went out for Knight when Taylor left. Eldon Miller had the Buckeye job for 10 years, then resigned last year and was replaced by fiery Gary Williams, from Boston College. As he left to take his team to Columbus the evening of January 3rd, Knight — mellowed a bit by the 49-3 victory his buddy Bill Parcells' New York Giants had over San Francisco that afternoon to win a spot in the Super Bowl — wasn't really thinking of anything but getting off to a successful league start against a team he knew would be frisky and a player he considered the league's best: 6-5 forward Dennis Hopson.

Bus drivers who pick up visiting teams at airports around the league tend to have a longevity of their own. Knight, in his 16th year of touring the league, knows many of them by first names — Leo at Iowa, Jake at Minneapolis. A new man made the pickup at Don Scott Airport in Columbus, about 15 minutes from St. John Arena where the Hoosiers were headed for a short practice. Normally, the Hoosiers don't work out in a road arena the night before a game. They practice at home, fly in, check in at their hotel and have dinner and, if the game is played at night, get up around 10 o'clock the next morning to put in about an hour at a "shoot-around" in the road arena — as much to get exercise and fill in a long day as to familiarize with the shooting conditions.

The Ohio State opener had been picked up by CBS for national airing on Sunday afternoon, so Knight wanted at least a brief shooting session there the night before. Scheduling problems cropped up; a wrestling tournament booked into the arena at first seemed likely to crowd the Hoosiers out. Athletic director Rick Bay worked out a window in the schedule to get Indiana in, but the Hoosiers got away from Assembly Hall a little late and they were pressing their scheduled time when they landed in Columbus.

It didn't matter. The new bus driver got lost. He took a right turn, heading away from the campus, when he needed a left. Columbus has changed some since Knight's playing days, but the bus hadn't gone far when Knight raised a question: "Where *are* we?" The answer was "Lost," though that wasn't the one given. "We're not lost," the driver said. "But it will take us a little longer. I knew I should have gone the way I knew." The bus

Larry Crewell

*We didn't think Smart could shoot, to be honest. We wanted him to shoot. Obviously, we were wrong.*

— Gary Williams

rambled over country roads for miles, and minutes, with no highway or Columbus in sight. The Hoosiers' practice time came, then ticked away, minute by minute. The city limits sign for Hilliard flashed by in the night. Fifteen minutes and several turns later, another Hilliard sign was passed. The driver was elderly, which helped him. Patience is not a Knight long suit, but kindliness toward older people — if they're not overweight and officiating a basketball game — is. While all else in the bus awaited a blowup, Knight put his hat on and took it off a few times but otherwise wasn't even restive. The driver confessed his dilemma, after about an hour, and stopped to get directions. They were complex. Finally, Interstate 70 loomed. "Let's just take this and forget the other directions you got," Knight said. "Why, yes," the driver said. An hour and 15 minutes after starting the jaunt, the Hoosiers arrived, Knight halfway expecting to find a dark arena.

Instead, the building was available. CBS announcers Billy Packer and Gary Bender were around, as was Taylor. Knight had a jovial time with all, found out where Hilliard was (in eastern Franklin County, miles from Scott Field *and* Columbus), put his team through the workout, set dinner plans with a group that included Packer, Bender and Taylor, then put his team back on the bus with only one light quip: "Suppose we could go direct to the hotel this time?"

It was an awesome show of restraint, the Big Ten season's first really big upset.

The next day didn't follow expectations, either. Hopson, averaging almost 30 points a game, burned the Hoosiers with a pass to center John Anderson for a basket in the game's opening seconds. With less than three minutes gone and Ohio State up 6-2, Hopson left the game. He returned in six minutes, with Indiana leading 18-13, and contributed a couple of baskets, then left again with 8:22 to go in the half and Indiana's lead 23-17. He never re-

turned, and he didn't even come back the second half to sit on the bench — ill, from something eaten the night before, it was explained later.

Hopson represented the heart of the planned Buckeye offense, but he wasn't vitally involved in the key defensive planning. Williams set up to stop Alford, who had two 32-point games against the Buckeyes the year before. Williams opened in a zone defense, and not Alford but Smart riddled it for three straight field goals, then two three-pointers, then another field goal for a 20-13 lead. After a timeout, Ohio State came out in a box-and-one defense, a 2-2 zone with the extra man sticking with Alford. "Even without the box, they were going to Steve and leaving me open," Smart said. "It was like they were saying, 'Keep a man on Alford and help out on him. Leave Smart out there.' "

That, essentially, was what the Buckeyes were doing. "We didn't think Smart could shoot, to be honest," Williams said. "We *wanted* him to shoot.

"Obviously, we were wrong."

By halftime, Smart had 20 points (his previous IU high for a game was 17). When he opened the second half with another three-point basket to put Indiana up 50-33, with Hopson nowhere in sight, the game appeared over.

It wasn't. "At halftime, Coach Williams told us to start getting after it and quit embarrassing ourselves," guard Jay Burson said. Burson and backcourt partner Curtis Wilson took on the Smart-Alford combination and sparked a charge. With 4:20 to go, Burson drove inside the Indiana defense and dropped off a pass to Keith Wesson for a layup that gave the Buckeyes a stunning 75-74 lead.

Rick Calloway, son of Cincinnati, had made big plays that helped Indiana sweep his home-state team in two games his freshman year. This time, with the Buckeye lead fresh, Calloway drew a foul, sank both halves of a one-and-one, and Indiana was ahead again. When

## Sagarin
**Jeff Sagarin computer rankings**
**Pre-Big Ten season**

| | | | |
|---|---|---|---|
| 1. North Carolina | 9-1 | 97.27 |
| 2. Clemson | 9-0 | 95.98 |
| 3. Purdue | 7-1 | 95.74 |
| 4. Iowa | 10-0 | 94.46 |
| 5. Duke | 7-1 | 94.40 |
| 6. Nevada-LV | 11-0 | 93.91 |
| 7. DePaul | 9-0 | 92.62 |
| 8. Alabama | 7-2 | 92.01 |
| 9. Illinois | 8-2 | 91.84 |
| 10. Temple | 11-1 | 91.12 |
| • • • | | |
| 13. Syracuse | 10- 0 | 89.74 |
| 15. Indiana | 9- 1 | 89.36 |

Indiana got the ball back on a turnover, Calloway set up in the low post, took a pass from Alford, and swished a turn-around jump shot for a 78-75 lead.

Alford took over from there: in 82 seconds, 10 straight Indiana points, including two three-point backbreakers. The spurt broke the Hoosiers away to a deceiving 92-80 winning margin.

Smart, who scored 31 points, was on the sidelines during the crucial moments, his exit much more spectacular than Hopson's. With Indiana leading 74-70, Alford shot from the left baseline. Garrett (6-10), Wesson (6-9) and the other big men on-court dutifully maneuvered to spots on the far side of the rim and went up for the ball. Far above them, a hand grabbed the basketball and spiked it toward the goal. The rebound try missed, and its author, the 6-foot-1 Smart, sailed on into the crowd. He emerged (1) injured, a sore ankle that led to his removal for Joe Hillman, and (2) charged with a foul.

But the play was one for history. "It was *not* a foul," Knight said after looking at films. But it was some jump.

As he slapped the rebound back toward the goal, Smart said, "I remember I was looking at Steve over the rim." For a 6-1 player to get his eyes far enough above the rim to see anything beyond it would require roughly a 51- to 53-inch vertical jump — 47 inches to put top of head at rim level, four to six more to get eyes over it. Buckeye Tony White (6-7) was a believer. "I could feel — I *swear* — Smart's knees on my shoulders," White said. "Can he get up or what?"

Alford, who finished with 22 points (Calloway had 20 and Daryl Thomas 14 — Wilson a career-high 30 for Ohio State), knew Smart would be high about his performance, too, which was good —considering his gloomy start to the season — but dangerous, in Alford's view, Garrett's problems after his big performance against Louisville's Per-

**At home, the signs tended to be friendlier than the ones Steve Alford frequently read on the road**

John Terhune

**After a 31-point Big Ten debut, Keith Smart was warned by Steve Alford that future opponents 'more than anybody' will know of the big performance. 'They don't want to see your name in the headlines anymore. They want to see theirs.'**

Jan. 4, Columbus

## Indiana 92

| | M | 3FG | AFG | FT | R | A | B | S | T | F | Pts |
|---|---|---|---|---|---|---|---|---|---|---|---|
| Thomas, f | 39 | | 6- 9 | 2- 5 | 8 | 4 | 1 | 0 | 4 | 4 | 14 |
| Calloway, f | 39 | | 9-12 | 2- 3 | 4 | 5 | 1 | 0 | 8 | 4 | 20 |
| Garrett, c | 18 | | 1- 3 | 1- 2 | 5 | 0 | 1 | 0 | 2 | 4 | 3 |
| Alford, g | 40 | 3- 5 | 7-13 | 5- 6 | 5 | 9 | 0 | 0 | 3 | 4 | 22 |
| Smart, g | 32 | 5- 5 | 13-18 | 0- 0 | 2 | 4 | 0 | 0 | 2 | 4 | 31 |
| Eyl | 22 | | 1- 1 | 0- 0 | 6 | 0 | 1 | 1 | 1 | 2 | 2 |
| Smith | 1 | | 0- 0 | 0- 0 | 0 | 1 | 0 | 0 | 0 | 0 | 0 |
| Hillman | 8 | | 0- 0 | 0- 0 | 1 | 0 | 0 | 0 | 0 | 1 | 0 |
| Meier | 1 | | 0- 0 | 0- 0 | 0 | 0 | 0 | 0 | 0 | 0 | 0 |
| Team | | | | | 2 | | | | | | |
| Totals | | 8-10 | 37-56 | 10-16 | 32 | 24 | 4 | 1 | 20 | 23 | 92 |

## Ohio State 80

| | M | 3FG | AFG | FT | R | A | B | S | T | F | P |
|---|---|---|---|---|---|---|---|---|---|---|---|
| Hopson, f | 10 | | 2- 6 | 0- 0 | 2 | 1 | 1 | 0 | 1 | 0 | 4 |
| Francis, f | 29 | | 3- 9 | 2- 3 | 7 | 0 | 0 | 0 | 1 | 4 | 8 |
| J.Anderson, c | 22 | | 2- 3 | 0- 0 | 2 | 1 | 0 | 1 | 1 | 4 | 4 |
| Wilson, g | 39 | 2- 2 | 12-23 | 4- 7 | 1 | 7 | 0 | 6 | 3 | 3 | 30 |
| Burson, g | 39 | 1- 3 | 6-12 | 4- 4 | 1 | 4 | 0 | 2 | 1 | 4 | 17 |
| White | 22 | | 4- 5 | 1- 3 | 2 | 1 | 0 | 0 | 1 | 3 | 9 |
| Wesson | 26 | | 2- 5 | 2- 4 | 5 | 0 | 0 | 0 | 3 | 4 | 6 |
| Dumas | 11 | | 1- 2 | 0- 0 | 2 | 0 | 0 | 0 | 0 | 1 | 2 |
| S.Anderson | 2 | | 0- 0 | 0- 0 | 0 | 0 | 0 | 0 | 0 | 0 | 0 |
| Team | | | | | 2 | | | | | | |
| Totals | | 3- 5 | 32-65 | 13-21 | 24 | 14 | 1 | 9 | 11 | 20 | 80 |

| SCORE BY HALVES | | | 3FG | AFG | FT |
|---|---|---|---|---|---|
| Indiana (10-1, 1-0) | 47 | 45—92 | .800 | .661 | .625 |
| Ohio State (9-4, 0-1) | 33 | 47—80 | .600 | .492 | .619 |

**Officials**—Joe Silvester, Jim Burr, Tim Higgins.
**Attendance**—13,541 (sellout).

vis Ellison in mind.

"The thing I told Keith, and I tried to tell Dean the same thing because both of them struggled with it a little bit, is, 'If you have a good game, it's not your mom and dad who's going to see it in the paper — if you're playing at Michigan next, it's Joubert and Grant and those guys who see that. They more than anybody will see that you got 31 points or 16 rebounds. Believe me, they're really going to come at you. They don't want to see your name in the headlines any more. They want to see theirs: 'Grant Stops Smart.' Or 'Joubert Stops Smart.' "

Antoine Joubert and Gary Grant of Michigan were not next up. First, the Hoosiers had a trip to Michigan State to start the two-stop Michigan swing that only two teams had swept in the four years the Big Ten had played under a "travel-partner" concept. Sixteen others had gone 0-2.

In East Lansing, Michigan State coach Jud Heathcote was doing just what Alford predicted: taking note of Smart's big game. "It made me mad," Heathcote said. "Our original scouting report on Smart said 'limited range.' That changes your strategy in terms of throwing all your outside concentration on Alford. Alford wasn't even really in the game the first half and still they get up by 17. That's scary."

Scary for Knight was having to pull Daryl Thomas with three fouls before Michigan State even scored a point. No. 3 came with 17:07 to go in the half, and Todd Meier replaced him. Smart had the dropoff Alford feared, but the whole club went with him. The Hoosiers hit just four of their first 16 shots, then turned the ball over four straight times as Michigan State opened a 20-10 lead. It was 27-15 with 4:55 to go in the half when Hillman replaced Smart, whose only offensive contribution up to then was a dunk.

By then, Knight had pulled every starter but Calloway and Alford, and those two combined for 10 of the points in a 12-6 closing rush that cut Michigan State's halftime lead to 33-27. Less than 2½ minutes into the second half, Hillman's basket gave Indiana a 36-35 lead, but Michigan State steadied to go up 43-40 and push Knight to a timeout with 13:22 to go.

The Hoosiers came out of the break in a 3-2 zone, the first time they had tried that one. Its effect was to neutralize the outside scoring of Vernon Carr and Darryl Johnson, holdover starters from the team Scott Skiles led to the NCAA regional last year. Simultaneously, Indiana's offense heated up. The Hoosiers scored 20 of the next 21 times they had the ball, and Michigan State disappeared, the final score 79-60.

Knight didn't have much time to celebrate. One of the first questions asked him in the postgame press conference was his reaction to a news report he hadn't heard: the decision by the NCAA, in convention at the time, to cut basketball scholarships from 15 to 13 effective in August 1988. It was a totally unexpected move that came with no warning, and Knight was angered.

"That's one of the dumbest things . . . I'd rather not even get started," he said. "I'm so sick and tired of the things the NCAA comes up with. I used to be a really big supporter of the NCAA, and I've drifted so far away from it. You cannot operate a basketball program today with 13 scholarships. Anybody who would propose that or vote for that is an absolute idiot. That's just absolutely ridiculous."

In the game, Alford scored 33 points — his high for the year and second-best total ever. "Alford is awfully tough," Heathcote said. "Last year, we had (6-8) Larry Polec on him. We tried the same thing with (6-6) Ed Wright in a box-and-one, and it worked very well for a while. But our players get tired and Alford just keeps working and working." That's the idea, Alford said. "It's kind of a hard defense to play. If I'm going to be in constant movement, somebody else is going to be in constant movement."

Calloway scored 17 points and Thomas, coming back to play 11 second-half minutes, scored 11.

"This Indiana team has more athletic ability," Heathcote said. "If they improve like Bobby's teams do, they could be great by the end of the season." Smart played 28 minutes and scored four points. Garrett, for the fourth game in a row, failed to reach double figures, scoring eight points. Their Big Ten baptism had begun.

The Hoosiers came home for three days, then flew to Michigan for a new item on the Big Ten schedule: Monday night basketball, late-night. League coaches, excluding the one from Bloomington, were so concerned with the league's national exposure after a year of no Big Ten telecasts on ESPN that they asked the conference to get on the cable network any way it could. Monday nights already had been taken by the Big East, but ESPN agreed to put a Big Ten game on second, which meant 9 p.m. or 9:30 starts in the league's Eastern time zone cities. At about 9:12 in Ann Arbor, Indiana and Michigan began to play.

Actually, Indiana began a little later than that. Garrett struggled again at the start, and with nine minutes gone and Michigan leading

*This Indiana team has more athletic ability. If they improve like Bobby's teams do, they could be great by the end of the season.*

— Jud Heathcote

**Jan. 8, East Lansing**

# Indiana 79

| | M | 3FG | AFG | FT | R | A | B | S | T | F | Pts |
|---|---|---|---|---|---|---|---|---|---|---|---|
| Thomas, f | 14 | | 3- 7 | 5- 6 | 3 | 0 | 0 | 0 | 0 | 4 | 11 |
| Calloway, f | 38 | | 7-13 | 3- 5 | 4 | 3 | 0 | 0 | 3 | 17 |
| Garrett, c | 24 | | 3- 8 | 2- 2 | 8 | 2 | 3 | 0 | 2 | 3 | 8 |
| Alford, g | 38 | 3- 5 | 11-19 | 8- 8 | 2 | 3 | 0 | 1 | 1 | 0 | 33 |
| Smart, g | 28 | 0- 1 | 2- 5 | 0- 0 | 6 | 2 | 0 | 2 | 0 | 2 | 4 |
| Meier | 7 | | 0- 0 | 0- 0 | 2 | 1 | 0 | 0 | 3 | 2 | 0 |
| Pelkowski | 1 | | 0- 0 | 0- 0 | 0 | 0 | 0 | 0 | 0 | 1 | 0 |
| Eyl | 18 | | 0- 0 | 0- 0 | 4 | 1 | 0 | 0 | 0 | 2 | 0 |
| Sloan | 10 | | 1- 2 | 0- 0 | 0 | 0 | 1 | 0 | 1 | 0 | 2 |
| Hillman | 19 | | 1- 2 | 2- 2 | 2 | 3 | 0 | 1 | 0 | 0 | 4 |
| Minor | 2 | | 0- 1 | 0- 0 | 0 | 0 | 0 | 0 | 0 | 0 | 0 |
| Freeman | 1 | | 0- 0 | 0- 0 | 0 | 0 | 0 | 0 | 1 | 0 | 0 |
| Team | | | | | 1 | | | | | | |
| **Totals** | | 3- 6 | 28-57 | 20-23 | 32 | 15 | 4 | 4 | 8 | 17 | 79 |

# Michigan State 60

| | M | 3FG | AFG | FT | R | A | B | S | T | F | Pts |
|---|---|---|---|---|---|---|---|---|---|---|---|
| Carr, f | 35 | 1- 3 | 3- 8 | 4- 4 | 6 | 5 | 0 | 2 | 3 | 4 | 11 |
| Valentine, f | 26 | | 7-12 | 3- 5 | 8 | 0 | 0 | 0 | 2 | 4 | 17 |
| Fordham, c | 36 | | 3- 3 | 0- 0 | 6 | 1 | 0 | 0 | 2 | 3 | 6 |
| Johnson, g | 39 | 1- 3 | 5-19 | 2- 2 | 5 | 6 | 0 | 1 | 2 | 4 | 13 |
| Wright, g | 28 | | 3- 6 | 0- 0 | 1 | 1 | 0 | 1 | 5 | 4 | 6 |
| Wolfe | 12 | | 0- 3 | 2- 2 | 4 | 0 | 0 | 0 | 0 | 2 | 2 |
| Papadakos | 9 | | 1- 3 | 3- 3 | 2 | 0 | 0 | 0 | 0 | 1 | 5 |
| Manns | 9 | 0- 2 | 0- 2 | 0- 0 | 0 | 0 | 0 | 0 | 0 | 1 | 0 |
| Redfield | 4 | | 0- 1 | 0- 0 | 0 | 0 | 0 | 0 | 1 | 0 | 0 |
| Worthington | 1 | | 0- 0 | 0- 0 | 0 | 0 | 1 | 1 | 0 | 0 | 0 |
| Izzo | 1 | | 0- 0 | 0- 0 | 0 | 0 | 0 | 0 | 0 | 0 | 0 |
| Team | | | | | 2 | | | | | | |
| **Totals** | | 2- 8 | 22-57 | 14-16 | 34 | 13 | 0 | 5 | 16 | 23 | 60 |

| SCORE BY HALVES | | | 3FG | AFG | FT |
|---|---|---|---|---|---|
| Indiana (11-1, 2-0) | 27 | 52—79 | .500 | .491 | .870 |
| Michigan St. (5-8, 0-3) | 33 | 27—60 | .250 | .386 | .875 |

**Officials**—Jim Bain, Ron Winter, Malcolm Hemphill. **Attendance**—10,004 (sellout).

*A lot of guys would have stopped and taken the jump shot. Steve got it all the way down.*

— Bob Knight

20-10, Steve Eyl replaced him. The Hoosiers got scoring from everybody except Eyl in pulling within 26-23, and along the way they picked up a third foul on Wolverine guard Gary Grant — in Alford's eyes, the best Big Ten defender he ever faced.

With Grant on him, Alford had committed three turnovers in the first nine minutes, two of them leading directly to layups as a sell-out crowd howled. Grant had barely sat down, replaced by freshman Jack Kramer, before Alford made the Wolverines pay with his most productive play of the year — Indiana's first five-pointer, ever.

With the Michigan lead 26-23, Alford fired a three-point shot, and Kramer came crashing into him after the shot. The ball went in to tie the game, and Alford sank both halves of a one-and-one to complete the five-point bonanza and swing the lead to the rallying Hoosiers, 28-26. Indiana kept dashing to zoom ahead, 51-34, at the half, Michigan coach Bill Frieder anxiously but determinedly keeping Grant on the bench to avoid a possible fourth foul.

Frieder's second-guessers were ready to argue the wisdom of caution when Daryl Thomas opened the second half with a rebound basket that put the Hoosiers ahead, 53-34. Meanwhile, Knight kept Garrett seated. With 8:10 to go, Thomas scored and Indiana led 73-58, just a two-point shrinkage from the halftime score. Michigan revived with seven points in a row, and the Wolverines kept coming. With 1:05 to go, Grant hit a jump shot for an 83-81 Michigan lead. Eyl, a .368 free-throw shooter the year before, sank both halves of a one-and-one to tie the game again with 45 seconds left, and Michigan set up to play for a last shot.

With about 12 seconds to go, Grant was maneuvering to set up a final sequence when Smart reached in and slapped the ball loose. The ball rolled into the corner, where Grant grabbed it. "Now it's a broken play and he's got to respond," Michigan coach Bill Frieder said. Grant went up for a shot, earlier than planned, and Eyl was called for hitting his arm. With 0:08 left in a tie game, Grant had two free throws. He hit the first for an 84-83 lead, then missed the second.

Thomas fielded the rebound and passed to Alford, who dashed up the left side of the floor as time ran down. Grant dashed alongside of Alford but didn't chance a steal attempt. "I didn't want to foul him," Grant said, "because if I did, he'd make both." Alford cut past a man at midcourt, drove to the center of the court, cut to the basket and pulled up just before the final line of pressure converged to put up a driving 10-foot shot. "A lot of guys would have stopped and taken the jump shot," Knight said. "Steve got it all the way down." His shot used a lot of rim, bounced a time or two, and fell through. The Wolverines threw the pass-in away, and Indiana had an 85-84 victory — a sweep of the three-game road start.

Alford had shown himself to be a master of buzzer-beating shots at halftime of games, but he couldn't remember another time at any level when he scored the game-winning basket. "At the buzzer, I think that's the first one," he said. It was just another exercise in leadership, because it started a grand pattern for the Hoosiers.

### Jan. 12, Ann Arbor

# Indiana 85

| | M | 3FG | AFG | FT | R | A | B | S | T | F | Pts |
|---|---|---|---|---|---|---|---|---|---|---|---|
| Thomas, f | 40 | | 10-13 | 2-4 | 8 | 1 | 0 | 0 | 8 | 3 | 22 |
| Calloway, f | 33 | | 4-9 | 5-6 | 2 | 2 | 0 | 2 | 1 | 4 | 13 |
| Garrett, c | 10 | | 1-3 | 0-0 | 6 | 0 | 0 | 0 | 1 | 0 | 2 |
| Alford, g | 39 | 3-3 | 9-16 | 2-2 | 5 | 4 | 0 | 1 | 4 | 1 | 23 |
| Smart, g | 37 | 0-1 | 6-11 | 3-3 | 1 | 2 | 1 | 2 | 3 | 4 | 15 |
| Eyl | 30 | | 3-5 | 3-3 | 8 | 3 | 0 | 1 | 2 | 5 | 9 |
| Hillman | 10 | | 0-0 | 1-2 | 0 | 0 | 0 | 0 | 1 | 3 | 1 |
| Minor | 1 | | 0-0 | 0-0 | 0 | 0 | 0 | 0 | 0 | 0 | 0 |
| Team | | | | | 0 | | | | | | |
| Totals | | 3-4 | 33-57 | 16-20 | 30 | 12 | 1 | 6 | 20 | 20 | 85 |

# Michigan 84

| | M | 3FG | AFG | FT | R | A | B | S | T | F | Pts |
|---|---|---|---|---|---|---|---|---|---|---|---|
| Rice, f | 35 | | 4-8 | 3-3 | 7 | 3 | 0 | 1 | 3 | 2 | 11 |
| Joubert, f | 40 | 0-2 | 9-18 | 2-4 | 4 | 6 | 0 | 1 | 2 | 3 | 20 |
| Hughes, c | 34 | | 5-11 | 1-1 | 7 | 3 | 0 | 1 | 2 | 5 | 11 |
| Grant, g | 32 | | 5-12 | 8-12 | 3 | 2 | 0 | 4 | 4 | 4 | 18 |
| Thompson, g | 30 | 4-5 | 8-11 | 0-0 | 4 | 4 | 0 | 2 | 1 | 3 | 20 |
| Griffin | 8 | | 1-2 | 0-0 | 1 | 1 | 0 | 0 | 2 | 2 | 2 |
| Oosterbaan | 1 | | 0-0 | 0-0 | 0 | 0 | 0 | 0 | 1 | 0 | 0 |
| Kramer | 8 | | 0-0 | 0-0 | 0 | 1 | 0 | 0 | 1 | 2 | 0 |
| Vaught | 12 | | 1-1 | 0-0 | 2 | 1 | 2 | 0 | 0 | 2 | 2 |
| Team | | | | | 3 | | | | | | |
| Totals | | 4-7 | 33-63 | 14-20 | 31 | 21 | 2 | 9 | 16 | 23 | 84 |

| SCORE BY HALVES | | | 3FG | AFG | FT |
|---|---|---|---|---|---|
| Indiana (12-1, 3-0) | 51 | 34—85 | .750 | .578 | .800 |
| Michigan (9-6, 1-3) | 34 | 50—84 | .571 | .523 | .700 |

**Officials**—Tom Rucker, Eric Harmon, Sam Lickliter.
**Attendance**—13,434 (sellout).

# Pizzo had 'Hoosiers' in mind

On the night of March 30, when Hollywood gave out its Oscars, Angelo Pizzo wanted very much to be there. As the writer and co-producer of the movie *Hoosiers*, which had two Oscar nominations, Pizzo was understandably, deservedly proud. "To have the first film that one does be nominated . . ." he said. He wanted to be there, "but it just *killed* me that I wasn't in New Orleans."

So, he and director David Anspaugh, an Indiana University alumnus as is Pizzo, skipped the Oscars and served as hosts to a TV party at Anspaugh's house. "We had three or four televisions," he said, both the NCAA championship game and the Oscars telecast coming in. "I didn't pay *any* attention to the Academy Awards. Once the game started — forget it. You go back to your roots in times of stress."

Pizzo's roots are in Bloomington, his hometown. Now 38, he was an IU basketball fan long before Bob Knight arrived, which made Pizzo all the more sensitive to and appreciative of the changes — both subtle and radical — that Knight made in the game as it was played first at Indiana, then in the Big Ten, then in America and the world. Gene Hackman plays the coach in *Hoosiers*, the story of Milan's 1954 state champions, fictionalized. Hackman consciously avoided styling the role after Knight. Pizzo said Hackman told him, "He's such a strong character; I'd rather make my own character choices." Long before, Pizzo had begun writing the movie not with a Knight in mind at all — rather, someone like the 26-year-old coach who actually won with Milan, Marvin Wood. For the story he had in mind, "it didn't work. One of the reasons, I figured out, was that there was nothing at stake for this coach.

If he didn't win, so what? He had the rest of his life in front of him. So I had to rethink who this coach was and create a situation for him that gave him this . . . last chance. 'Let's have a coach come into town who is in his 40s, who has failed somewhere in his past, and he gets a second chance, and create a story about second chances.'

"I am fascinated with Knight. He has more charisma than almost anybody I know. He is as fascinating in his personality strengths as in his flaws. I have, ultimately, tremendous respect for the man because I think he represents a standard of excellence that just doesn't exist any more in college basketball. I wanted to use as much of his basketball philosophy as possible." Hackman thus plays the *Hoosiers* coach coolly, not, as Pizzo said, "like a walking time bomb," but the lines that Pizzo gave him talk of four passes before a shot, of no zone defense, of no outside interference: staples that Knight brought with him in changing IU basketball. "Actually, there was much more," Pizzo said. "Much was cut out because we didn't want to overwhelm the public."

Analogies to *Hoosiers* were everywhere when Indiana won the NCAA championship on a last-seconds shot. Only Pizzo knew the true symmetry of the Hoosiers' championship in relationship to *Hoosiers*. "I saw the games in Philadelphia (when Indiana won Knight's second NCAA title) in '81," he said. "I got so pumped up, it was such a great experience, I went back home and thought, 'Maybe this is a perfect time to do this script that I've been thinking about for a long time.' I thought it was such a perfect circle that it would come around to this."

Writer Angelo Pizzo, a Bloomington native and rabid Indiana basketball fan, said in writing the script for *Hoosiers*, IU basketball coach Bob Knight was a true role model. "I started thinking about coaches — all the coaches I have had in my life, and the coaches who interested me," Pizzo said. "Certainly, Coach Knight is one of the most fascinating."

# 5 The scoutmaster

Daryl Thomas wants very much to play professional basketball, but he's sufficiently wise and realistic to know the chance might not come. Whether it does or doesn't, he has a goal in life that is not based on basketball.

"I would like to go back home and work with kids," he said. Home is Chicago, inner-city Chicago. "I've lived there all my life. I know what's going on there. I know what it takes to get out. I've seen a lot of people do it, not just in sports — students, who have made it from the inner city. I think I can share a lot with them on that." He won't ignore his basketball background — certainly not the national championship ring he will always wear proudly. "It'll make them listen," Thomas said. "That's the first problem."

He was to graduate from Indiana as a forensics major "on time," in the spring of his fourth academic year. He already has his job internship logged. Sort of one, anyway. And he has two-way experience in what he was covering with his laughing reference to his ring and the effect it might have on a wide-eyed young audience some day: "It'll make them listen. That's the first problem."

Thomas, as Keith Smart said in reliving his tough early days, was a Big Brother, a scoutmaster-in-residence, for both Smart and Dean Garrett in their transition from the relatively free-and-easy life of junior college to the intensity of basketball at Indiana.

His greatest contribution to grounding them in Indiana basketball life wasn't at all intentional. It was his own pre-season academic conflict with coach Bob Knight that,

for a long three days, had Thomas off the Hoosier ball club. There is the chance that Knight used the situation to make a dramatic and unforgettable point to all watching — say, Smart and Garrett, for example. "If he *didn't*," Thomas said, "it worked that way. He definitely got a message across."

Daryl Thomas and Bob Knight. It's the most controversial relationship portrayed in *A Season on the Brink*. Drawn is a portrait of a tyrannical coach and a cowed player, a man with a scathing verbal whip and a whipping boy, a relationship with no respect at all at one end and no self-respect left at the other. It's not the relationship Thomas describes in discussing his own trip to the brink: his November suspension for skipping folklore classes and getting himself in danger of flunking the course — and flunking out of Professor Knight's demanding basketball school.

That Thursday afternoon when Indiana's basketball team was making its first public appearance as a team with a flying visit to Gary for an intrasquad game, Thomas knew the midterm report from his folklore class had arrived and Knight would not be pleased. "I was telling Dean when we were going to The Hall to go to Gary, 'Coach Knight got a bad letter on me. I might not even be making the trip to Gary with you.' I was saying that joking. Then I got there and didn't make the trip. I was shocked myself."

And then again, he wasn't really surprised at all. "I didn't know exactly what to expect. If I had caught him on a good day, he might have let things go. But then again, seeing that I've had problems in the past in doing what I was supposed to

**Daryl Thomas — aiming high**

*Seeing it was me, a senior, Coach Knight had to put his foot down, as a father should*

— Daryl Thomas

## Milestone

Steve Alford used Indiana's favorite out-of-bounds play to get open for the three-point shot that gave him his 2,000th collegiate point. Alford's basket from the left corner came with 17:25 to go in Indiana's 103-65 victory over Wisconsin at Assembly Hall January 15th. At the time, the basket made the score 51-26. Alford had 1,999 when he shot. Alford was the third player from Indiana to reach 2,000 and the 11th from the Big Ten. Dennis Hopson of Ohio State became the Big Ten's 12th later in the year. By coincidence, the shot that made Alford Indiana's career recordholder also was a three-point basket from the left corner, against Wisconsin - in the team's rematch at Madison February 16th. It came with 14:43 left in the first half and put Indiana ahead, 7-3, in a game that went three overtimes before Indiana won, 86-85.

do — academically, in class — I don't think that would have been the case with me. If it had been any other player, like a younger player, I'm sure Coach Knight would have sat them down, talked to them, given them another chance, and wouldn't have made a bigger deal of it. Seeing it was me, being a senior, Coach Knight had to put his foot down, as a father should.

"So I wasn't *sure* what was going to happen, and when he went to the extreme he did, I was shocked."

Any senior on an Indiana basketball team is experienced in what is jokingly, and privately, known as Bob Knight Theater: Actions, sometimes explosive, designed to get what laws of physics guarantee, reactions — *i.e.,* markedly better basketball. Thomas had no feelings of theatrics in his situation. He felt there was a very real possibility his Indiana basketball career could be over.

"I thought of that, after the first two days when I didn't practice," he said. "That happened on a Thursday. That Friday I didn't practice. That Saturday I didn't practice. I kept coming into The Hall (player shorthand for Assembly Hall, where Indiana plays and practices). The team had practice; I'd be there. I waited. I waited for the guys afterward. I tried to talk to the coach. He was upset about the situation and didn't want to talk to me.

"On Sunday, I didn't go. I told Keith and Dean, 'I'm going to stay back here (at Ashton Dormitory) today. I'm going to keep the phone on the hook' — I'd been leaving it off the hook because it was just ringing constantly, reporters calling with questions. I told them, 'If *anything* happens, have somebody call.'

"I sat there. I was waiting, I was answering the phone all afternoon. Then the phone rang and it was Joby (Wright, an assistant coach). He said, 'Somebody got hurt and we need you to practice.' I said, 'OK! I'll be right there.' I don't think it took me 10 minutes to get there and get taped."

By that time, a second somebody

had gone down — Rick Calloway and Kreigh Smith, only a few minutes apart. "I think Fate was on my side," Thomas laughed.

He, of course, wasn't all the way back, as he knew he wouldn't be. At Indiana, the six or seven players expected to do most of the playing in the next game wear red shirts in practice, and the rest of the squad is in white — the training squad assigned to simulate the opponent and get the starters ready. "I was a white-shirt for three days," Thomas said. "We practiced and practiced. Coach made comments, and I was, like, non-existent. He never commented on me. I just practiced. Then he called me into his office and asked me if all the craziness had stopped, if I understood that if I did anything wrong from then on out, I'm out of there. I said, 'Well, yeah.' He said, 'Concentrate on basketball. I don't want to have to do that again.' From that point on, things were back to normal."

*A Season on the Brink* readers might smile at Thomas' reference to normalcy for him and Knight. Long after his senior season had ended, Thomas insisted he hadn't read the book. "We lived it, we don't have to read it," he quipped to non-believers at New Orleans. "I want to get far away from it," he said later. But he knew what was in it, how he was portrayed. "Oh, yeah," he said. "A lot of my friends at home purchased the book, and they would say, 'How could you sit there and take all that abuse — all that language and yelling and screaming?' I said, 'Well, it got me a national championship.' "

There was more to the Thomas end of the relationship than that, of course. There are days when Knight criticism comes, in torrents, and a fourth-year player has to have learned how not only to live with that but also to extract the message. "OK," he said. "I know in my mind when I've done something wrong. When I *know* I'm wrong, I just take it and I try to improve. But there are times when I know I'm trying hard and I know it wasn't my fault — maybe Coach didn't see the whole thing develop and the way it ended up looked like it was my fault. It doesn't get discouraging when it happens once, but there are some days when it seems like a situation like that just happens to you all day long. You try to work harder; the harder you try to push yourself, you stop thinking about playing, and you start making mistakes.

"You try to calm yourself down, listen to what Coach is saying, and then just start over again. That's what I do in practice when things are going bad for me. When we have a free-throw break, I stop, I think about what I'm doing wrong, and I just try to start all over again. I say, 'OK, Coach is saying that I'm getting backcut too much. So I'll be leery of the backcut.' And yet I still want to do the things I've been doing. I want to keep looking for my shot, I want to look to screen, I want to rebound, I want to play defense, but next play, whatever happens, I'm *not* going to get back-cut. If they're gonna get me, they've got to get me with something else, but I'm *not* gonna get backcut."

Normal life for Daryl Thomas in 1986-87 included bringing his two young associates along through their own rough times. Garrett's hadn't come early, as Smart's had. Three games into the Big Ten season, the big man brought onto the club to make it more competitive in the toughest games had bottomed out. Since hitting a career peak with his strong performance head-to-head with Ellison in Indiana's victory over Louisville, Garrett not only had gone into the next-game valley Knight had hoped not to see but also had stayed there. In the five games immediately after Louisville, his point totals were two, six, three, eight, two.

"He *really* had himself geared toward the Louisville game," Thomas said. "He played a really good game. I told him, 'OK, you played a good game. What Coach is going to be looking for now is whether you can carry that over into the next game.' "

When five games had passed without improvement, Garrett wasn't positive he would even be in

Jan. 15, Assembly Hall

Phil Whitlow

# Wisconsin 65

| | M | 3FG | AFG | FT | R | A | B | S | T | F | Pts |
|---|---|---|---|---|---|---|---|---|---|---|---|
| Ripley, f | 17 | 1- 4 | 1- 4 | 0- 0 | 2 | 0 | 0 | 1 | 1 | 0 | 3 |
| Jones, f | 25 | | 2- 6 | 1- 2 | 0 | 0 | 0 | 0 | 3 | 3 | 5 |
| Weber, c | 32 | | 3- 9 | 2- 2 | 6 | 3 | 1 | 1 | 3 | 3 | 8 |
| Smith, g | 28 | 2- 5 | 6-11 | 2- 2 | 2 | 0 | 0 | 1 | 6 | 2 | 16 |
| Heineman, g | 32 | 0- 3 | 2- 9 | 2- 2 | 12 | 6 | 0 | 0 | 2 | 2 | 6 |
| Portmann | 19 | | 1- 4 | 0- 0 | 2 | 1 | 0 | 0 | 0 | 2 | 2 |
| Tapp | 9 | 0- 2 | 1- 3 | 0- 0 | 0 | 0 | 0 | 0 | 1 | 0 | 2 |
| Jackson | 22 | 3- 9 | 7-15 | 5- 5 | 1 | 0 | 0 | 0 | 2 | 4 | 22 |
| Fleming | 3 | | 0- 0 | 1- 2 | 0 | 0 | 0 | 0 | 1 | 0 | 1 |
| Schubring | 5 | | 0- 0 | 0- 1 | 0 | 0 | 0 | 0 | 0 | 1 | 0 |
| Molaski | 5 | | 0- 0 | 0- 1 | 0 | 0 | 0 | 0 | 1 | 0 | 0 |
| Robertson | 3 | | 0- 1 | 0- 0 | 1 | 0 | 0 | 0 | 0 | 1 | 0 |
| Team | | | | | 5 | | | | | | |
| **Totals** | | 6-23 | 23-62 | 13-17 | 31 | 10 | 1 | 4 | 19 | 20 | 65 |

# Indiana 103

| | M | 3FG | AFG | FT | R | A | B | S | T | F | Pts |
|---|---|---|---|---|---|---|---|---|---|---|---|
| Thomas, f | 19 | | 4- 6 | 8- 8 | 7 | 0 | 0 | 2 | 0 | 4 | 16 |
| Calloway, f | 26 | | 2- 4 | 5- 5 | 2 | 4 | 0 | 1 | 3 | 2 | 9 |
| Garrett, c | 26 | | 4-10 | 2- 2 | 8 | 0 | 6 | 0 | 1 | 3 | 10 |
| Alford, g | 26 | 7- 8 | 7- 9 | 0- 1 | 0 | 5 | 0 | 2 | 2 | 0 | 21 |
| Smart, g | 20 | 2- 4 | 3- 6 | 0- 0 | 1 | 2 | 0 | 0 | 3 | 2 | 8 |
| Eyl | 13 | | 2- 3 | 2- 2 | 4 | 0 | 0 | 1 | 1 | 0 | 6 |
| Hillman | 13 | | 3- 5 | 0- 0 | 2 | 3 | 0 | 0 | 0 | 1 | 6 |
| Meier | 10 | | 1- 2 | 3- 4 | 1 | 1 | 0 | 1 | 2 | 1 | 5 |
| Freeman | 21 | 1- 2 | 3- 6 | 4- 6 | 2 | 0 | 0 | 2 | 2 | 2 | 11 |
| Pelkowski | 15 | 1- 1 | 4- 6 | 0- 0 | 4 | 1 | 2 | 0 | 0 | 3 | 9 |
| Sloan | 11 | | 1- 1 | 0- 1 | 2 | 0 | 0 | 0 | 1 | 1 | 2 |
| Team | | | | | 6 | | | | | | |
| **Totals** | | 11-15 | 34-58 | 24-29 | 39 | 16 | 8 | 9 | 15 | 19 | 103 |

| SCORE BY HALVES | | | 3FG | AFG | FT |
|---|---|---|---|---|---|
| Wisconsin (10-8, 0-5) | 26 | 39— 65 | .261 | .371 | ./65 |
| Indiana (13 1, 4-0) | 48 | 55—103 | .733 | .586 | .827 |

**Officials**—Ed Maracich, Verl Sell, Randy Drury.
**Attendance**—17,035 (sellout).

**Daryl Thomas, working inside against Northwestern's Shon Morris, helped get roommate Dean Garrett going again**

John Terhune

**Dean Garrett's play against Northwestern and Wisconsin was, to Daryl Thomas, 'the turning point — he was really consistent from then on'**

Jan. 17, Assembly Hall

# Northwestern 43

| | M | 3FG | AFG | FT | R | A | B | S | T | F | Pts |
|---|---|---|---|---|---|---|---|---|---|---|---|
| Morris, f | 37 | | 4-12 | 1- 1 | 8 | 1 | 0 | 2 | 4 | 3 | 9 |
| Buford, f | 26 | | 1- 7 | 0- 0 | 2 | 2 | 0 | 0 | 3 | 1 | 2 |
| Ross, c | 17 | | 0- 4 | 0- 0 | 2 | 0 | 0 | 5 | 5 | 0 | |
| Fullen, g | 29 | 0- 1 | 4-11 | 2- 2 | 2 | 0 | 0 | 0 | 6 | 0 | 10 |
| Watts, g | 29 | | 2- 4 | 0- 0 | 1 | 2 | 0 | 1 | 2 | 1 | 4 |
| Grose | 17 | | 2- 4 | 2- 2 | 3 | 0 | 0 | 0 | 3 | 1 | 6 |
| Cucuz | 23 | | 3- 6 | 0- 0 | 4 | 0 | 0 | 0 | 3 | 1 | 6 |
| Polite | 5 | | 1- 1 | 2- 2 | 0 | 0 | 0 | 0 | 1 | 2 | 4 |
| Wyss | 12 | 0- 1 | 1- 3 | 0- 0 | 2 | 3 | 0 | 2 | 0 | 1 | 2 |
| Petrovic | 5 | | 0- 1 | 0- Q | 0 | 0 | 0 | 0 | 0 | 0 | 0 |
| Team | | | | | 3 | | | | | | |
| **Totals** | | 0- 2 | 18-53 | 7- 7 | 27 | 8 | 0 | 5 | 27 | 15 | 43 |

# Indiana 95

| | M | 3FG | AFG | FT | R | A | B | S | T | F | Pts |
|---|---|---|---|---|---|---|---|---|---|---|---|
| Thomas, f | 20 | | 9-13 | 0- 0 | 1 | 2 | 0 | 3 | 0 | 2 | 18 |
| Calloway, f | 21 | | 6- 8 | 0- 0 | 3 | 2 | 0 | 3 | 2 | 0 | 12 |
| Garrett, c | 23 | | 7- 9 | 2- 4 | 8 | 0 | 3 | 1 | 0 | 0 | 16 |
| Alford, g | 26 | 3- 6 | 4- 9 | 0- 0 | 3 | 6 | 0 | 2 | 1 | 0 | 11 |
| Smart, g | 13 | | 3- 5 | 0- 0 | 1 | 2 | 0 | 4 | 2 | 2 | 6 |
| Freeman | 21 | | 2- 3 | 1- 2 | 4 | 13 | 0 | 1 | 1 | 1 | 5 |
| Hillman | 15 | 0- 1 | 4- 7 | 0- 0 | 2 | 1 | 0 | 1 | 2 | 3 | 8 |
| Pelkowski | 20 | 0- 1 | 4- 8 | 0- 0 | 5 | 0 | 1 | 2 | 1 | 0 | 8 |
| Sloan | 17 | | 2- 5 | 1- 2 | 5 | 2 | 0 | 2 | 1 | 2 | 5 |
| Minor | 10 | | 1- 1 | 2- 2 | 2 | 1 | 0 | 0 | 1 | 1 | 4 |
| Eyl | 5 | | 0- 0 | 0- 0 | 0 | 0 | 0 | 0 | 1 | 0 | 0 |
| Meier | 9 | | 1- 1 | 0- 2 | 2 | 0 | 0 | 0 | 0 | 0 | 2 |
| Team | | | | | 1 | | | | | | |
| **Totals** | | 3- 8 | 43-69 | 6-12 | 37 | 29 | 4 | 19 | 12 | 11 | 95 |

| SCORE BY HALVES | | | 3FG | AFG | FT |
|---|---|---|---|---|---|
| Northwestern (5-11, 0-6) | 19 | 24—43 | .000 | .340 | 1.000 |
| Indiana (14-1, 5-0) | 40 | 55—95 | .375 | .623 | .500 |

**Officials**—Rich Weiler, Ted Hillary, Phil Robinson.
**Attendance**—17,125 (sellout).

the next game. "He was getting really low, really down on his confidence and shooting," Thomas said. "His judgment in shooting was not as good as it should have been. To take a lot of pressure off him, Coach told him, 'Don't even look to shoot. Get yours off the board and then we'll just go from there.' He had to start all over, so to speak. Where Coach would tolerate the mistakes he made earlier, Coach wouldn't tolerate them any more. Dean had to learn the system."

The Knight system says play every game the same way: not against an opponent but against your own potential. It has become almost a coaching cliche, but it started right there in "The Hall" where it remains an insistence, definitely not a cliche.

The message had gone through to Dean Garrett. Wisconsin came in with an excellent center in J.J. Weber, though Garrett's California friends had never heard of him. Wisconsin came in 0-4 in the Big Ten, tied for last in the league. For a player whose tendency had been to get up for the name teams and ease off against those who didn't inspire him, the potential was there for another Garrett dropoff. But not after the five games he had just gone through. "I was determined to try to play well against Wisconsin," Garrett said.

In the first minute of play, Thomas, Smart and Garrett scored to put Indiana ahead 6-0. In the next two minutes, Steve Alford hit two three-point shots, Garrett and Thomas shut off the interior and swept the Wisconsin backboard, and the Hoosiers' lead was 12-0, their best start of the year. Wisconsin answered with nine straight points, but in a 75-second stretch, Smart hit one three-point shot and Alford two to restart the Hoosiers toward a 48-26 halftime lead and an eventual 103-65 romp. The Hoosiers got 21 points by Alford, including No. 2,000 of his career, 16 by Thomas, and some by each of the eleven players used in the game. Tony Freeman, who hadn't scored since his splashy debut in the Indiana Classic and hadn't even played in five of the seven games after that, scored 11 points. Against all that, Garrett's numbers were not especially notice-able: 10 points, 8 rebounds, 6 blocked shots. Knight noticed. "I was really pleased with Garrett's play," Knight said as almost his opening remarks in his postgame press con-ference. "I don't even know how many points he got — 10? That's great. To do what he did on the boards and to do the things he did defensively and to come up with 10 points — that's a hell of a ball game for him." To Thomas, "That was the turning point as far as getting him-self ready. He was really consistent from then on."

Northwestern followed the Bad-gers into Assembly Hall, and first-year coach Bill Foster said he told his 0-5 team: "It's a new day, a new game. Indiana's not going to play as well as it did against Wisconsin." Wrong, he said to himself as he watched a 95-43 hammering take place. "They probably did." The score at one time was 37-8.

Knight fanned the flames of the Garrett revival by letting him play a little more than he might have other-wise, though still just 23 minutes. He scored 16 points, with 8 re-bounds and 3 blocks.

The most spectacular Hoosier was the 5-foot-7 Freeman, who scored just five points but had 13 assists — which stood up as the most by anyone in a Big Ten game in 1987. Freeman got an early call to replace Smart, who had two fouls and a turnover in a bumpy offensive start for the Hoosiers. After four minutes and four seconds, leading 6-2, Knight went to Freeman, who hit Thomas for a basket 26 seconds later and zipped a pass to Garrett for another 29 seconds after that. The show got rather flashy. A blind pass to Rick Calloway cutting through the middle gave Indiana a 23-6 led, and another whistling feed produced a Garrett dunk, a 25-6 lead and a seven-minute total of seven assists for Freeman — all to inside players, a phase of the attack that, to Knight's great exasperation, had

Phil Whitlow

**Tony Freeman gave IU's offense a midseason boost**

Phil Whitlow

**First-year Iowa Coach Tom Davis saw his team stay undefeated and No. 1 in the land with a 101-88 victory over Indiana, the first time a Bob Knight team ever allowed 100 collegiate points**

been missing up to then.

The opening pass to Thomas was appropriate. Thomas and Freeman go back a long while. Thomas was a senior and Freeman a sparkplug freshman under coach Gene Pingatore on a Westchester St. Joseph's team that was ranked No. 1 among Class AA teams in Illinois in 1982-83. Thomas remembered well what happened the first time he broke open with Freeman on the court that high school year together. A pass he never saw coming bashed him square in the nose. "Daryl and I only had a chance to play together one year in high school," Freeman said, "but the passes are still the same. He's gotten used to me now."

At 5-0 in Big Ten play for the first time since the glory years of '75 and '76, the Hoosiers were overshadowed. Iowa was 17-0 overall and — for the first time in Hawkeye history — No. 1 in the polls, Indiana (14-1) No. 3. The voting already was in by the time Iowa completed the Big Ten weekend by winning at Purdue, 70-67. For the Hawkeyes, it had been some weekend. Iowa began it by spotting Illinois a 19-point lead at Champaign and then roaring from behind to win in overtime. The Illinois-Purdue road swing was the league's toughest in 1987. No one else won even one game on it.

And the Hawkeyes kept rolling, defending No. 1 with a 101-88 victory over Indiana.

It was a clamorous night, a sensational game. Iowa blitzed Indiana with a 15-5 start, led 33-20 about seven minutes before halftime, then lost the whole lead before going up at halftime 46-44 on a shot by sophomore star Roy Marble with seven seconds left. Indiana moved ahead briefly in the second half, fell behind by as much as 83-68, then came clawing back once more. The score was 93-88 when Alford ran behind a screen on the left side of the court and swished an apparent three-point shot with 1:25 to go. No basket, official Sid Rodeheffer gestured. Rocking back to launch the shot, Alford's foot had touched the sideline, Rodeheffer said. Reprieved

from 93-91 pressures, Iowa ended the game with a flourish that, on a tipin by Ed Horton with two seconds left, made the Hawkeyes the first collegiate team ever to reach 100 against Knight.

It was quite a performance. New Iowa coach Tom Davis used his bench liberally, as he had all year, and he bunched six scorers from 13 to 17 — sixth-man Jeff Moe, a former Indianapolis Brebeuf star unrecruited by Indiana or Purdue and eager ever since to make both regret it, one of two Hawkeyes who had 17. Knight was impressed, giving Iowa's ranking a quick ratification, almost. "I've not seen everybody play, but I don't think there can be many teams better than Iowa," he said. "I have a pretty good idea how good you have to be to be No. 1, and I think Iowa is *very* good."

To his team, he went even farther. Iowa, he told the Hoosiers, probably would not lose. Thomas remembers, "He told us, 'If we win every game and beat Iowa (in a rematch at Assembly Hall), we have a chance to tie for the Big Ten championship.' " That was no small if; it required an eight-game winning streak. Thomas also remembers the second half of Knight's message: "As good as Iowa is, and I think they very well may be the best team in the country, you could have beaten them if you had done just a few things better. You were outrebounded 46 to 19. *Forty-six to nineteen.* And if Steve's shot had counted, you could have won the game. You let a game get away that you could have won, yes, and you have to make up your minds that kind of rebounding discrepancy will never happen again, but what you also can take away from that game is that if you play the way you can, there isn't anybody in the country you can't beat."

That was the game in which Indiana stepped onto the national-championship track, Thomas feels. "Although we lost that game, I really felt we had potential to be pretty good. We lost that game on the boards. That was my responsibility

Jan. 22, Iowa City

# Indiana 88

| | M | 3FG | AFG | FT | R | A | B | S | T | F | Pts |
|---|---|---|---|---|---|---|---|---|---|---|---|
| Thomas, f | 37 | | 7- 9 | 8- 8 | 5 | 2 | 2 | 0 | 0 | 2 | 22 |
| Calloway, f | 19 | | 4- 9 | 1- 2 | 1 | 0 | 0 | 0 | 1 | 3 | 9 |
| Garrett, c | 36 | | 9-11 | 0- 1 | 5 | 0 | 4 | 0 | 0 | 1 | 18 |
| Alford, g | 39 | 5- 8 | 6-11 | 4- 4 | 0 | 3 | 0 | 0 | 2 | 2 | 21 |
| Smart, g | 18 | 0- 1 | 4- 7 | 2- 2 | 1 | 2 | 0 | 0 | 2 | 4 | 10 |
| Eyl | 4 | | 0- 0 | 0- 0 | 0 | 0 | 0 | 0 | 0 | 1 | 0 |
| Hillman | 7 | | 0- 0 | 0- 0 | 3 | 0 | 1 | 0 | 1 | 0 | 0 |
| Meier | 3 | | 0- 0 | 0- 1 | 0 | 1 | 0 | 0 | 1 | 0 | 0 |
| Sloan | 18 | | 1- 2 | 2- 2 | 2 | 2 | 0 | 0 | 1 | 3 | 4 |
| Freeman | 19 | | 1- 5 | 2- 2 | 0 | 7 | 0 | 1 | 0 | 3 | 4 |
| Team | | | | | 4 | | | | 6 | | |
| **Totals** | | 5- 9 | 32-54 | 19-21 | 19 | 19 | 6 | 2 | 13 | 20 | 88 |

# Iowa 101

| | M | 3FG | AFG | FT | R | A | B | S | T | F | Pts |
|---|---|---|---|---|---|---|---|---|---|---|---|
| Marble, f | 30 | | 6- 8 | 4- 5 | 7 | 2 | 0 | 0 | 1 | 2 | 16 |
| Lohaus, f | 24 | 0- 2 | 6- 9 | 1- 2 | 3 | 3 | 0 | 0 | 0 | 5 | 13 |
| Horton, c | 29 | | 5-12 | 4- 5 | 11 | 3 | 0 | 0 | 3 | 3 | 14 |
| Armstrong, g | 30 | 1- 1 | 7-11 | 1- 1 | 3 | 5 | 0 | 3 | 2 | 2 | 16 |
| Gamble, g | 29 | 0- 2 | 7-11 | 3- 5 | 7 | 2 | 0 | 2 | 1 | 2 | 17 |
| Moe | 23 | 3- 7 | 6-16 | 2- 2 | 5 | 1 | 0 | 1 | 2 | 1 | 17 |
| Wright | 4 | | 0- 0 | 0- 0 | 0 | 0 | 0 | 0 | 0 | 3 | 0 |
| Lorenzen | 15 | | 1- 3 | 1- 2 | 3 | 2 | 0 | 0 | 1 | 2 | 3 |
| Jones | 10 | | 1- 3 | 1- 2 | 1 | 0 | 0 | 0 | 0 | 2 | 3 |
| Hill | 6 | | 1- 2 | 0- 0 | 4 | 1 | 1 | 0 | 0 | 0 | 2 |
| Team | | | | | 2 | | | | 1 | | |
| **Totals** | | 4-12 | 40-75 | 17-24 | 46 | 19 | 1 | 6 | 11 | 22 | 101 |

| SCORE BY HALVES | | 3FG | AFG | FT |
|---|---|---|---|---|
| Indiana (14-2, 5-1) | 44 44— 88 | .556 | .593 | .905 |
| Iowa (18-0, 6-0) | 46 55—101 | .333 | .533 | .708 |

**Officials**—Bob Showalter, Ed Hightower, Sid Rodeheffer
**Attendance**—15,570 (sellout).

and Dean's responsibility, so (after a postgame flight to Minnesota for a game two nights later) we were talking about it, and we said, 'If we had rebounded with them, we could have won by 12 or 14 points.' We talked a great deal about the season, and how things were going to go, and how we were going to match up, and how if things went wrong, how we were going to correct each other's mistakes.

"I really *felt* we had a good team. But the key was we had to win every game and then play Iowa again."

Meanwhile, Dean Garrett had hit nine of eleven shots and scored 18 points. "They beat us up pretty bad," Garrett said, "but that's the game I remember most of the whole Big Ten season. That was my best game up to that time against the best team we had played against." Thomas was starting to be convinced that Garrett was on his way to becoming a genuine Big Ten center — and that Knight's different approach was a key. "Our team seemed to respond well when the mood was good," Thomas said. "Not to say that we had a soft team, but I don't think yelling at Dean or Keith would have improved them any more than sitting back and explaining."

**Daryl Thomas — even in defeat, uplifted at Iowa**

Phil Whitlow

# 6 | A rosy time

*I am interested in Knight because I am interested in teaching. I think he's the best teacher I've ever seen.*

— Prof. Robert Byrnes

The average college basketball season doesn't get into petunias and daffodils, but average and Indiana are words rarely coupled in basketball. Things just happen . . .

On Jan. 20, two days before the Indiana-Iowa game, the Indiana University Faculty Council voted 18-16 in support of a statement of student rights designed, it was said, to protect the university's athletes from abuse by their coaches. Indiana athletes "have been hit, pushed, shoved, and . . . they have been molested," sociology professor Whitney Pope said in pushing for adoption of the statement. There was little mystery about the specific target. Basketball coach Bob Knight subjects athletes to "humiliation of the worst kind," economics professor Elmus Wicker said.

It was a thorny proposal. To some on the council, a no vote seemed to put them in the position of saying student-athletes don't have rights or abuse is OK. At Indiana, the Faculty Council does not have a long, impressive record of having influenced university policies or procedures. To its frustration, far more often than not it has been ignored by the school's administration. With the Knight matter, however, the council made Page 1 of the local newspapers and sports pages all around the country. Clearly, the matter was an embarrassment to Knight, but he declined immediate comment. It didn't die. Knight supporters on the faculty pointed out that (1) the man's longtime stands on academic fidelity in a sport continually stained by abuses should have the faculty supporting him, not attacking him, and (2) the "hit, pushed, shoved,

### Jan. 24, Minneapolis

## Indiana 77

| | M | 3FG | AFG | FT | R | A | B | S | T | F | Pts |
|---|---|---|---|---|---|---|---|---|---|---|---|
| Thomas, f | 16 | | 1- 6 | 1- 2 | 3 | 0 | 0 | 0 | 1 | 4 | 3 |
| Calloway, f | 35 | | 8- 8 | 1- 2 | 6 | 2 | 0 | 1 | 2 | 5 | 17 |
| Garrett, c | 24 | | 7-12 | 0- 1 | 9 | 0 | 1 | 2 | 3 | 4 | 14 |
| Alford, g | 36 | 4- 8 | 7-16 | 6- 6 | 2 | 1 | 0 | 2 | 2 | 0 | 24 |
| Hillman, g | 21 | | 0- 3 | 0- 0 | 1 | 2 | 0 | 1 | 3 | 2 | 0 |
| Eyl | 22 | | 2- 2 | 0- 0 | 5 | 0 | 0 | 0 | 0 | 1 | 4 |
| Smart | 21 | | 3- 3 | 3- 3 | 2 | 2 | 0 | 1 | 3 | 3 | 9 |
| Meier | 13 | | 0- 1 | 0- 1 | 2 | 0 | 0 | 0 | 1 | 3 | 0 |
| Minor | 3 | | 1- 1 | 0- 0 | 1 | 0 | 0 | 0 | 0 | 0 | 2 |
| Sloan | 3 | | 0- 1 | 0- 0 | 0 | 0 | 0 | 0 | 0 | 0 | 0 |
| Pelkowski | 2 | | 2- 2 | 0- 1 | 0 | 0 | 0 | 0 | 0 | 0 | 4 |
| Freeman | 2 | | 0- 0 | 0- 0 | 0 | 0 | 0 | 0 | 0 | 1 | 0 |
| Smith | 2 | | 0- 0 | 0- 0 | 0 | 0 | 0 | 0 | 0 | 0 | 0 |
| Team | | | | | 3 | | | | | | |
| Totals | | 4- 8 | 31-55 | 11-16 | 34 | 7 | 1 | 7 | 15 | 23 | 77 |

## Minnesota 53

| | M | 3FG | AFG | FT | R | A | B | S | T | F | Pts |
|---|---|---|---|---|---|---|---|---|---|---|---|
| Burton, f | 29 | | 1- 7 | 3- 5 | 8 | 2 | 2 | 0 | 2 | 3 | 5 |
| Hanson, f | 27 | 1- 2 | 3- 9 | 5- 5 | 6 | 2 | 0 | 2 | 0 | 3 | 12 |
| Coffey, c | 32 | | 5- 8 | 2- 3 | 7 | 0 | 0 | 1 | 2 | 1 | 12 |
| Zurcher, g | 15 | 0- 2 | 0- 4 | 2- 2 | 1 | 0 | 0 | 0 | 3 | 2 | 2 |
| Woods, g | 31 | 0- 3 | 2- 9 | 4- 4 | 2 | 0 | 0 | 1 | 1 | 2 | 8 |
| Gaffney | 31 | | 3- 6 | 2- 3 | 3 | 3 | 0 | 1 | 3 | 1 | 8 |
| Smith | 10 | | 0- 1 | 1- 4 | 3 | 0 | 0 | 1 | 2 | 1 | 1 |
| Shikenjanski | 14 | | 1- 1 | 0- 2 | 1 | 0 | 0 | 0 | 0 | 3 | 2 |
| Williams | 6 | | 0- 1 | 0- 0 | 0 | 0 | 0 | 1 | 2 | 0 | 0 |
| Lewis | 3 | | 0- 1 | 0- 0 | 0 | 0 | 0 | 0 | 0 | 0 | 0 |
| Retzlaff | 2 | 1- 1 | 1- 1 | 0- 0 | 0 | 0 | 0 | 0 | 0 | 0 | 3 |
| Team | | | | | 3 | | | | | | |
| Totals | | 2- 8 | 16-48 | 19-28 | 34 | 7 | 2 | 6 | 14 | 17 | 53 |

| SCORE BY HALVES | | | 3FG | AFG | FT |
|---|---|---|---|---|---|
| Indiana (14-2, 6-1) | 34 | 43—77 | .500 | .564 | .688 |
| Minnesota (9-8, 2-5) | 17 | 36—53 | .250 | .333 | .679 |

**Technical foul**—Minnesota.
**Officials**—Jim Bain, Ron Winter, Malcolm Hemphill.
**Attendance**—14,453.

## Big Ten

### After Indiana-Iowa Jan. 22

| | | |
|---|---|---|
| 1. Iowa | 6- 0 | |
| 2. Purdue | 6- 1 | |
| 3. Indiana | 5- 1 | |
| 4. Illinois | 5- 2 | |
| 5. Michigan | 3- 3 | |
| Ohio State | 3- 3 | |
| 7. Minnesota | 2- 4 | |
| Michigan State | 2- 4 | |
| 9. Wisconsin | 0- 7 | |
| Northwestern | 0- 7 | |

molested" charges essentially boil down to Knight's screaming at players on the sidelines during games.

Robert Byrnes's faculty title is Distinguished Professor of History. Early in Knight's Indiana career, Byrnes began going to Hoosier practices (they're not open, but a half-dozen or so professors have *carte blanche*), and he formed a close friendship with Knight. Byrnes is a quiet, soft-spoken man, recognized as one of the university's most prominent scholars and teachers. He shuns profanity and works at taming Knight's. He is not a man hesitant to put forth sharply stated views, and — though not a member of the Faculty Council — he wasn't at all reticent when asked his view.

"Very few teachers at Indiana or

anywhere else have thought very clearly about the goals of education," Byrnes said. "I am interested in Knight because I am interested in teaching. I think he's the best teacher I've ever seen. That's why I go to practices. He's an extremely able, dedicated teacher. Faculty, we really don't work very hard at teaching. If we did, this would be the greatest university in the world.

"The most important student right is the right to get a good education, and a lot of kids here are being cheated."

The matter did not come up after the Indiana-Iowa game. After Indiana's game at Minnesota, four days after the Faculty Council action, the question came up late in Knight's postgame press conference, and he declined comment. The reporter rephrased the question, and Knight again declined comment. When he asked a third time, Knight snapped an angry answer at the writer ("Jeeezus Christ!") and walked away. He returned in seconds and had a few more angry words, walked off, then returned and invited the writer — Rick Morrissey of the Fort Wayne *Journal-Gazette* — into the dressing room to talk the matter out. No apologies came, but they did talk. The no-comment became the lead item on the game in one Twin Cities newspaper, another "Knight incident."

On Knight's Monday night radio show with the IU network's play-by-play broadcaster, Don Fischer, the subject of the Faculty Council vote came up. Fischer mentioned the barrage of mail he had received from Indiana fans outraged by the faculty's action. "It's really unfair, I think, to use this as an indictment of the entire faculty," Knight said. "I've gotten all kinds of letters and calls, with the same things that you are talking about, Don. In fact, a lot of the names that have been used for the Bloomington faculty are known only to a guy with a vocabulary like I have. But it's really, really unfair. We have a great faculty."

Knight's sense of humor wouldn't let him drop the subject with

Dean Garrett gets a shot away over Lowell Hamilton

Jim Rider

peaches and cream. With tongue deeply in cheek, he said the Faculty Council's next soul-searching issue was over whether to plant petunias or daffodils in a plot behind the Old Library, and he said he was concerned whether it would solve that issue in time to tell him what lineup to use in the next game. He liked the pseudo-issue he had raised, and brought it up again on his Sunday television show, in straight-faced fashion supplying on-screen the address for IU fans who wished to give the council suggestions on the petunias-or-daffodils issue. Personally, he said, he would prefer bright red roses. Next TV show, a vaseful of bright red roses brightened the set and at times during the telecast Knight stopped, as in the counsel of the late Walter Hagen, to smell the roses. Meanwhile, the mail came in. One report said a one-day count reached 996 cards or letters. A few weeks after the issue was raised, Knight's contract was formally extended through 1997, and at year's end, the Brown Derby — a prestigious award annually given by Sigma Delta Chi, the national journalism(!) honorary — went to Knight, representing his selection in a student vote as the most popular professor on campus.

Through it all, basketball went on

### Jan. 28, Assembly Hall

# Illinois 66

| | M | 3FG | AFG | FT | R | A | B | S | T | F | Pts |
|---|---|---|---|---|---|---|---|---|---|---|---|
| Norman, f | 36 | 0- 1 | 5-18 | 6- 9 | 1 | 1 | 1 | 3 | | 16 |
| Altenberger, f | 38 | 1- 6 | 3-12 | 1- 2 | 3 | 1 | 1 | 0 | 1 | 3 | 8 |
| Kujawa, c | 13 | | 0- 1 | 0- 0 | 3 | 1 | 0 | 0 | 3 | 0 |
| Blackwell, g | 20 | 0- 1 | 5-10 | 2- 2 | 5 | 1 | 0 | 4 | 3 | 12 |
| Bardo, g | 26 | | 2- 4 | 0- 0 | 3 | 0 | 0 | 1 | 0 | 3 | 4 |
| Hamilton | 33 | | 8-13 | 0- 0 | 8 | 2 | 0 | 0 | 3 | 2 | 16 |
| Gill | 5 | | 0- 0 | 0- 0 | 0 | 0 | 0 | 0 | 0 | 1 | 0 |
| Wysinger | 29 | 0- 2 | 5-10 | 0- 0 | 5 | 1 | 0 | 3 | 2 | 3 | 10 |
| Team | | | | | 3 |
| **Totals** | | 1-10 | 28-68 | 9-10 | 39 | 7 | 2 | 5 | 11 | 21 | 66 |

# Indiana 69

| | M | 3FG | AFG | FT | R | A | B | S | T | F | Pts |
|---|---|---|---|---|---|---|---|---|---|---|---|
| Thomas, f | 34 | | 3- 8 | 3- 6 | 6 | 1 | 0 | 0 | 2 | 3 | 9 |
| Calloway, f | 29 | | 6-13 | 1- 2 | 2 | 1 | 0 | 2 | 3 | 4 | 13 |
| Garrett, c | 36 | | 8-13 | 4- 5 | 9 | 0 | 6 | 0 | 0 | 2 | 20 |
| Alford, g | 39 | 0- 3 | 3-11 | 4- 4 | 3 | 2 | 0 | 2 | 1 | 3 | 10 |
| Smart, g | 28 | | 4- 5 | 1- 2 | 3 | 1 | 0 | 1 | 3 | 2 | 9 |
| Eyl | 22 | | 1- 1 | 6- 8 | 6 | 3 | 0 | 0 | 3 | 0 | 8 |
| Freeman | 6 | | 0- 0 | 0- 0 | 1 | 0 | 1 | 0 | 0 | 0 |
| Hillman | 2 | 0- 1 | 0- 1 | 0- 0 | 0 | 2 | 0 | 1 | 0 | 0 |
| Meier | 4 | | 0- 0 | 0- 0 | 0 | 0 | 0 | 0 | 1 | 0 |
| Team | | | | | 5 |
| **Totals** | | 0- 4 | 25-52 | 19-27 | 34 | 11 | 6 | 7 | 12 | 15 | 69 |

| SCORE BY HALVES | | | 3FG | AFG | FT |
|---|---|---|---|---|---|
| Illinois (14-5, 5-3) | 32 | 34—66 | .100 | .412 | .900 |
| Indiana (16-2, 7-1) | 34 | 35—69 | .000 | .481 | .704 |

**Officials**—Ed Hightower, Bob Showalter, Ted Hillary.
**Attendance**—17,249 (sellout).

and a Big Ten race was pursued.

Immediately after the Thursday night loss at Iowa, the Hoosiers flew to Minneapolis for a Saturday night game. It was there, after the pregame meal on the afternoon of the game, that Knight delivered his half-critical, half-uplifting analysis of the Iowa game and its ramifications. The players went back to their rooms, and the late-afternoon quiet was shattered about an hour later when a surprising score came in: Ohio State 80, Iowa 76, *at Iowa.*

"I remember I was laying down before the game," Dean Garrett said. "Todd Meier came by and told us Iowa lost, and everybody just jumped up. There was a lot of electricity in the bus going to the game, to play against Minnesota. It really changed things." To Knight, what it meant was that winning those next eight games would put the Hoosiers in a position to take the Big Ten lead by beating Iowa, not just tie. It didn't alter the necessity of winning everything between the Iowa games at all.

The Hoosiers started in that direction with a rather easy 77-53 victory in the Gophers' ancient basketball home, Williams Arena. Indiana led 34-12 after 15 minutes, Steve Alford scoring 15 of his 24 points in the fast start. He didn't have a good shooting night (7-for-16), but Gopher forward Tim Hanson was impressed. "They set three to four picks every time down the court for Alford. And once he's open, ring up three." Rick Calloway was 8-for-8 from the field to tie an IU record. He scored 17 points, 13 in the last half after both Garrett and Daryl Thomas had been lifted with four fouls and Minnesota had cut the lead to 11 points. "His first step is so explosive," Hanson said. "It's one of the best first steps I've ever run into." The Calloway second-half scoring was a simple matter of positioning, Knight felt. "He had more room. I kept screaming at them the first half to get the offense higher, but we kept throwing the ball to Garrett in the low post."

The late-night Minnesota game kept Knight from seriously consid-

A loose basketball attracts attention fast when Indiana (with Steve Eyl and Dean Garrett) and Purdue (Doug Lee and diving Melvin McCants) play

John Terhune

ering an invitation from his friend, New York Giants coach Bill Parcells, to be his guest at the Super Bowl in Pasadena. Knight couldn't have been pulling harder for Parcells, but "I couldn't be back in Bloomington until Monday night, and there's no way I can do that," Knight said. "Not this week."

"This week" was Illinois on Wednesday, Purdue on Saturday — two collisions with contenders, must games for Indiana because they were at home, the start of a rare four-game home stand that also would bring in Michigan State and Michigan. It was time to peak.

All four Big Ten contenders — Iowa, Indiana, Illinois and Purdue — had been Top 10 teams virtually all season long. Illinois dropped to 12th

the week of its Indiana visit, after losing the big lead against Iowa and then losing at Purdue in an overtime game that the Illini had in their hands till their defense let Doug Lee get loose for a three-point shot at the buzzer to create the overtime. The Illini were getting a luckless feeling, and Indiana was not a good place for them to go in that mood. A year before, Indiana had won over Illinois, 71-69 and 61-60.

Both teams started tight. After six minutes, Indiana had more turnovers (five) than points (Illinois, not finding many openings, either, led 6-4). As had become common, the reserves brought on late in the first half to forestall foul problems finished the half well — Steve Eyl scoring seven points in the last 3:10

John Terhune

**Former Indiana high school "Mr. Basketball" selections Troy Lewis of Purdue and Steve Alford tangle on a day when each scored well — Lewis 23, Alford 31**

Jan. 31, Assembly Hall

## Purdue 77

| | M | 3FG | AFG | FT | R | A | B | S | F | Pts |
|---|---|---|---|---|---|---|---|---|---|---|
| Mitchell, f | 26 | | 6-11 | 3- 5 | 6 | 1 | 0 | 1 | 3 | 15 |
| Lee, f | 36 | 0- 2 | 3- 7 | 2- 4 | 5 | 3 | 0 | 1 | 3 | 8 |
| McCants, c | 30 | | 4- 6 | 7-11 | 8 | 0 | 1 | 0 | 1 | 15 |
| Lewis, g | 39 | 3- 5 | 7-16 | 6- 9 | 8 | 0 | 0 | 0 | 1 | 23 |
| Stephens, g | 31 | 0- 1 | 4-10 | 0- 0 | 3 | 8 | 0 | 1 | 4 | 8 |
| T.Jones | 13 | | 0- 1 | 0- 1 | 0 | 0 | 0 | 0 | 1 | 0 |
| K.Jones | 8 | | 1- 3 | 0- 0 | 3 | 0 | 0 | 0 | 0 | 2 |
| Arnold | 15 | | 3- 6 | 0- 0 | 5 | 0 | 1 | 1 | 0 | 6 |
| Scheffler | 1 | | 0- 0 | 0- 0 | 0 | 0 | 0 | 0 | 0 | 0 |
| Fisher | 1 | | 0- 0 | 0- 0 | 0 | 0 | 0 | 0 | 1 | 0 |
| Team | | | | | 2 | | | | | |
| Totals | | 3- 8 | 28-60 | 18-30 | 40 | 12 | 2 | 4 | 13 | 24 | 77 |

## Indiana 88

| | M | 3FG | AFG | FT | R | A | B | S | F | Pts |
|---|---|---|---|---|---|---|---|---|---|---|
| Thomas, f | 16 | | 3-10 | 3- 4 | 8 | 1 | 0 | 1 | 0 | 4 | 9 |
| Calloway, f | 29 | | 6-14 | 0- 0 | 5 | 2 | 0 | 5 | 1 | 3 | 12 |
| Garrett, c | 29 | | 7-11 | 0- 0 | 10 | 1 | 5 | 0 | 3 | 3 | 14 |
| Alford, g | 39 | 2- 5 | 8-18 | 13-15 | 6 | 5 | 0 | 0 | 2 | 2 | 31 |
| Smart, g | 31 | 0- 1 | 3-12 | 2- 2 | 4 | 5 | 0 | 2 | 0 | 5 | 8 |
| Eyl | 26 | | 4- 4 | 2- 2 | 7 | 1 | 0 | 0 | 0 | 1 | 10 |
| Meier | 10 | | 0- 0 | 0- 0 | 0 | 0 | 0 | 0 | 0 | 3 | 0 |
| Freeman | 2 | | 0- 0 | 0- 0 | 0 | 0 | 0 | 0 | 1 | 1 | 0 |
| Hillman | 16 | | 0- 1 | 4- 5 | 1 | 1 | 0 | 0 | 2 | 4 | 4 |
| Smith | 1 | | 0- 0 | 0- 0 | 0 | 0 | 0 | 0 | 0 | 0 | 0 |
| Sloan | 1 | | 0- 0 | 0- 0 | 0 | 0 | 0 | 0 | 0 | 0 | 0 |
| Team | | | | | 1 | | | | | |
| Totals | | 2- 6 | 31-70 | 24-28 | 42 | 16 | 5 | 8 | 9 | 26 | 88 |

| SCORE BY HALVES | | | 3FG | AFG | FT |
|---|---|---|---|---|---|
| Purdue (16-3, 7-2) | 35 | 42—77 | .375 | .467 | .600 |
| Indiana (17-2, 8-1) | 36 | 52—88 | .333 | .443 | .857 |

**Officials**—Tom Rucker, Eric Harmon, Sam Lickliter.
**Attendance**—17,310 (sellout).

to give the Hoosiers a 34-32 lead. Illinois' Lowell Hamilton scored the first basket of the second half, and a beautifully competitive game was on. Back and forth the teams jousted without ever allowing the other the kind of point run common to the sport. Neither team ever led by more than four points. With just over two minutes to play and Indiana leading 64-62, Smart lost the ball to a steal by Tony Wysinger and Glynn Blackwell's layup tied the game.

Indiana ran off most of the 45-second shot clock before Smart got a pass to Garrett for a short jump hook shot that put Indiana up 66-64. It was a clutch shot taken and made by a player who, only a couple of weeks ago, had been put on a restricted shooting diet by Knight. Times had changed.

What hadn't changed was Garrett's ability to get especially psyched for big challenges. Everyone on the club had let him know he had one against Illinois: all-America candidate Ken "The Snake" Norman, who bit Indiana for 44 points in the two tight 1985-86 games. Nominally, Norman was a forward, but his most devastating work came inside, which meant that Thomas and Garrett would be dividing duty on him. "Joby (Wright) was telling me about Ken Norman and how tough he was — NBA prospect and all that," Garrett said. Thomas, who had gone head-to-head with Norman the year before, also had plenty to say, but this was more like the Pervis Ellison situation than the ones that sent Garrett against Will Perdue of Vanderbilt or Brian Rowsom of North Carolina-Wilmington. "I'd *heard* of Norman," Garrett said, "and I knew it was a big game for us. I was just pumped up to play."

After Garrett's tie-breaking basket, Illinois went for the lead with a three-point shot by Doug Altenberger. He missed but retrieved his own rebound, and the Illini got the ball to Norman in his prime operating area: low post, right side. Norman spun in the air and fired, but Garrett blocked the shot and recovered the rebound, giving Indiana possession of the ball with a lead and 47 seconds to go. With 30 seconds left, Blackwell got overeager and fouled the one man Illini coach Lou Henson didn't want to see at the free-throw line: Alford.

In the Louisville game, at a similarly crucial time, Alford shot a glance to Knight that asked for a timeout before taking the shot, to catch his breath. Knight hoards timeouts, and he declined, figuring even an exhausted Alford would hit the free throws. He missed. This time, when Alford asked, Knight called timeout. It's called icing when a coach takes a timeout in front of an opponent's clutch free throw. This was self-icing, and Alford coolly made it work by hitting both free throws — for a 68-64 lead, and the game-winning points, as things worked out. Two free throws by Hamilton at 0:12 and one by Garrett (giving him his first 20-point game as a Hoosier) at 0:11 put Indiana up 69-66 and gave Illinois a chance to catch up with a three-point shot.

It was the same situation Henson had faced in the Purdue game a week earlier, when critics said he blew the obvious choice: an intentional foul, giving the trailing opponent no chance to put up a three-pointer. Henson took his chances with defense and lost. Knight took exactly the same chance and won, when first Altenberger and then Norman missed — barely — from three-point range. "I still think it's a 50-50 call," Henson said. "Indiana played it the way we did. You're not going to make many of those."

The three-point shot has stayed in the game, so it's an issue that will continue. TV analyst Dick Vitale is adamant and fellow analyst Billy Packer only a little bit less certain that a foul is the right play, since it requires the trailing team to hit both free throws, then steal the ball back to have a chance to win. DePaul's Dallas Comegys showed another option in the Blue Demons' NCAA tournament victory over St. John's. Comegys intentionally missed a free throw, banging it hard off the rim and fielding the long rebound, con-

verting it into a game-tying basket. Late in a game, the Comegys ploy seems a lot more likely than the Vitale idea that teams trailing by two would try to make a free throw and gamble on a steal, especially since long rebounds benefit the shooting team, with the top defensive rebounders assigned to inside spots on the lane. Some day a team up three points will follow the Vitale theory with two seconds left, foul, and watch the opponent hit a free throw, then Comegys-style clang a hard shot off the rim, retrieve it — and win with a three-point shot. It's gotta happen.

Indiana had no mental problem at all in moving from the important victory over Illinois to the next game. Indiana-Purdue games rarely catch either team flat. If this one had gone overtime, it wouldn't have surprised anybody. The teams entered the game 16-2 overall, 7-1 in the Big Ten, tied for fourth in the most recent Associated Press poll. Just the season before, their game at Assembly Hall had gone overtime, and research showed something hard to believe: it was the first overtime in the 147-game history of one of the sport's most intense rivalries.

This one left the launching pad in a hurry. Indiana controlled the tip, Keith Smart brought the ball into the front court, sailed a quick pass to Alford lurking deep on the left wing, and Alford's three-point shot put Indiana up with only eight seconds gone. "It wasn't exactly a planned play, but it was something I wanted to do," Alford said. "Before the game, I was thinking that would be a great way to get started. I knew the fans would be pumped and excited, and I think that really got them into the game right away. Today might have been the best crowd we've had since I've been here. On the road, playing Indiana, everybody's going to be hyped up and excited. We're going to get their best, and we get the best from their crowds, too. So it's neat to be able to play somewhere where, hey, they *like* you."

> ## *It's neat to be able to play somewhere where, hey, they like you.*
> — Steve Alford

## Milestone

When Steve Alford set an Assembly Hall record with 42 points against Michigan State Feb. 4, he became the 10th Indiana player to score as many as 40 points in a game. Jimmy Rayl, who has the Indiana record with 56 (achieved twice), had five 40-point games; Don Schlundt, four; George McGinnis and Steve Downing, two each, and Mike Woodson, Walt Bellamy, Dick Van Arsdale, Scott May, Ted Kitchel and Alford, one each.

### IU's 40-point games

| | | |
|---|---|---|
| Jimmy Rayl vs. Minn., '62, ot | 56 |
| Jimmy Rayl vs. Mich. St., '63 | 56 |
| Mike Woodson vs. Illinois, '79 | 48 |
| Don Schlundt vs. Ohio St., '54 | 47 |
| Don Schlundt vs. Ohio St., '55 | 47 |
| Steve Downing vs. Ky., '72, 2ot | 47 |
| Geo. McGinnis vs. No. Ill., '71 | 45 |
| Jimmy Rayl vs. Wisconsin, '62 | 44 |
| Jimmy Rayl vs. Mich. St., '63 | 44 |
| Walt Bellamy vs. Illinois, '60 | 42 |
| Dick Van Arsdale vs. N.D., '64 | 42 |
| Steve Alford vs. Mich. St., '87 | 42 |
| Don Schlundt vs. N.D., '53 | 41 |
| Don Schlundt vs. SMU, '55 | 41 |
| Jimmy Rayl vs. DePaul, '72 | 41 |
| Geo. McGinnis vs. San Jose, '71 | 41 |
| Steve Downing vs. Illinois, '73 | 41 |
| Scott May vs. Wisconsin, '76 | 41 |
| Ted Kitchel vs. Illinois, '81 | 40 |

### Assembly Hall's biggest games

| | |
|---|---|
| Steve Alford vs. Mich. St., '87 | 42 |
| Steve Downing vs. Illinois, '73 | 41 |
| Terry Furlow, Mich. St., '76 | 40 |
| Ted Kitchel vs. Illinois, '81 | 40 |
| Isiah Thomas vs. Michigan, '81 | 39 |

*Purdue played extremely well the last 10 minutes of the half. Boy! It almost got away.*

— Bob Knight

The 17,310 at The Hall saw a lot they liked as Indiana moved from the game-opening outside strike to a frontcourt attack that paid off in a 19-10 jump. Then foul problems began. Whenever possible, Knight tries to avoid getting a third foul on any player before halftime. Garrett drew his second with less than three minutes gone in the game, but that was too early for Knight to get conservative. When the score was 26-13 with 9:49 to go in the half, he pulled Garrett for Todd Meier and left him on the bench till halftime. Thirteen seconds later, Thomas drew his second and Calloway, after a two-minute rest break, replaced him. With 5:16 to go in the half, Keith Smart drew his second foul (on a three-point play by Melvin McCants, cutting Indiana's lead to 32-24) and Tony Freeman replaced Smart. All three — Garrett, Thomas and Smart — sat on the bench while the 17,310 got growingly restive. The lead reached 34-24, then started to melt. Purdue shooter Troy Lewis scored to make it 34-30; Indiana patiently ran its offense and got Alford open, but he missed. Lewis scored again to make it 34-32; Indiana screens freed Alford again, and he missed. With 33 seconds left, Purdue forward Doug Lee drove to a three-point play that lifted Purdue ahead for the first time, 35-34. Two seconds before the halftime buzzer, Calloway scored for a 36-35 Indiana lead, and even Master Coach Knight, in the arena where outside critics say he can do no wrong, had second-guessers all over the building for the 13-point lead that had flitted away in the interest of preserving fouls.

"I didn't even think about (re-inserting Garrett, Thomas or Smart)," Knight said. "I didn't think we could come out the second half with one of them involved with three fouls. I had no illusions about being up by 12 or 13 at the half, but I was hoping we could be up by 5 or 6. Purdue played extremely well the last 10 minutes of the half. Boy! It almost got away."

Purdue's closing rush didn't come without a price. In the midst of it, standout junior forward Todd Mitchell was called for a charging foul, his third, on a play that very well could have gone the other way and been a three-point play for Purdue. Coach Gene Keady had to lift Mitchell then, and he already was in the foul plight Knight had avoided for his three benched players.

A half-minute into the second half, Thomas was charged with a foul. Not quite two minutes later, Smart fouled; 31 seconds after that, Garrett fouled. All three were able to stay in the game, a silent answer to the second-guessing. The rest of the answer came on the scoreboard, when Smart scored a basket that put Indiana up 49-45 and Thomas followed with two free throws for 51-45 command. It was 53-50 when Indiana ran in eight points in a row, on baskets by Calloway and Garrett (off Alford passes), Alford, and Eyl (rebounding an Alford miss). Purdue got within five once after that, but another late-game Indiana run — nine points, seven by Alford — buried the Boilermakers 78-61 and the Hoosiers coasted in, 88-77.

Alford had his best Purdue game ever: 31 points, an uncharacteristic 6 rebounds, 5 assists. Garrett came on in the second half for 14 points, 10 rebounds and 5 blocked shots

Feb. 4, Assembly Hall

## Michigan State 80

| | M | 3FG | AFG | FT | R | A | B | S | T | F | Pts |
|---|---|---|---|---|---|---|---|---|---|---|---|
| Carr, f | 36 | 1- 1 | 8-11 | 8- 9 | 6 | 3 | 1 | 2 | 5 | 3 | 25 |
| Worthington, f | 18 | | 1- 3 | 0- 0 | 6 | 1 | 0 | 1 | 1 | 2 | 2 |
| Fordham, c | 28 | | 0- 2 | 0- 0 | 1 | 0 | 1 | 1 | 3 | | 0 |
| Johnson, g | 33 | 0- 1 | 9-14 | 3- 3 | 0 | 5 | 0 | 1 | 5 | 4 | 21 |
| Manns, g | 23 | 1- 3 | 5- 8 | 0- 0 | 2 | 2 | 0 | 1 | 4 | 1 | 11 |
| Wright | 21 | | 0- 1 | 0- 0 | 3 | 4 | 2 | 0 | 2 | 2 | 0 |
| Valentine | 17 | | 5- 9 | 0- 1 | 3 | 0 | 1 | 0 | 1 | 1 | 10 |
| Papadakos | 12 | | 2- 2 | 0- 1 | 5 | 0 | 0 | 0 | 0 | 3 | 4 |
| Wolfe | 7 | 1- 1 | 3- 3 | 0- 0 | 0 | 0 | 0 | 0 | 1 | 0 | 7 |
| Redfield | 5 | | 0- 0 | 0- 0 | 1 | 0 | 0 | 0 | 0 | 0 | 0 |
| Team | | | | | 1 | | | | | | |
| Totals | | 3- 6 | 33-53 | 11-14 | 28 | 15 | 4 | 5 | 17 | 22 | 80 |

## Indiana 84

| | M | 3FG | AFG | FT | R | A | B | S | T | F | Pts |
|---|---|---|---|---|---|---|---|---|---|---|---|
| Thomas, f | 40 | | 8-21 | 4- 5 | 8 | 0 | 1 | 2 | 3 | 3 | 20 |
| Calloway, f | 28 | | 3- 5 | 0- 0 | 3 | 4 | 0 | 0 | 2 | 3 | 6 |
| Garrett, c | 21 | | 2- 6 | 2- 3 | 5 | 2 | 3 | 0 | 0 | 3 | 6 |
| Alford, g | 38 | 4- 5 | 12-19 | 14-15 | 0 | 0 | 0 | 3 | 3 | 0 | 42 |
| Smart, g | 7 | | 1- 2 | 0- 0 | 1 | 0 | 0 | 0 | 1 | 2 | 2 |
| Hillman | 30 | | 2- 4 | 0- 4 | 2 | 0 | 1 | 2 | 3 | 4 | 4 |
| Eyl | 27 | | 2- 2 | 0- 0 | 4 | 1 | 0 | 2 | 0 | 1 | 4 |
| Smith | 9 | | 0- 0 | 0- 0 | 1 | 0 | 0 | 0 | 1 | 0 | 0 |
| Team | | | | | 1 | | | | | | |
| Totals | | 4- 5 | 30-59 | 20-23 | 26 | 10 | 4 | 8 | 11 | 16 | 84 |

| SCORE BY HALVES | | | 3FG | AFG | FT |
|---|---|---|---|---|---|
| Michigan St. (8-12, 3-7) | 31 | 49—80 | .500 | .623 | .786 |
| Indiana (18-2, 9-1) | 44 | 40—84 | .800 | .508 | .869 |

**Officials**—Rich Weiler, Ted Hillary, Phil Robinson.
**Attendance**—16,868 (sellout).

and Calloway had 12 points plus 5 steals. One other set of numbers stood out. Eyl played 26 minutes as a reserve, hit all four shots he took, both free throws he was given, and totaled 10 points plus 7 rebounds. "I'd say the seniors were the difference today," Keady said. "Thomas did a good job (9 points and 8 rebounds, though limited to 16 minutes by fouls). Alford did a super, super job. And Eyl did a good job for them. I'm not sure if Eyl is a senior, but he sure as hell played like one." He was a junior, but a complimented one.

Garrett's reward for two big games was selection as the league's player of the week — for 34 points, 19 rebounds and 11 blocks. "He seems to be asserting himself much more defensively than he did in our game," said Michigan State coach Jud Heathcote as he sized up the Hoosiers for a Wednesday game at Assembly Hall. The Hoosiers, at 17-2, were boosted past weekend losers Iowa and North Carolina into second

place in the AP poll, behind Nevada-Las Vegas. "I think the big difference in Indiana from the first time we saw them is Garrett's improved play and maybe the continuity of the five playing together — plus Eyl's contribution from the bench," Heathcote said. "I felt all along the improvement of the junior college players was going to be a key to Indiana's continued success."

The Purdue game completed the first half the league schedule for Indiana, and the Hoosiers were on top. Just before Indiana took the floor against Purdue, Michigan completed a 100-92 victory over Iowa at Ann Arbor. Michigan State went into the second half the season with a 3-6 record in league play — and a habit of playing better over the years at Assembly Hall than any team in the league. In fact, Michigan State seniors Darryl Johnson and Barry Fordham went into the game with a chance for an unprecedented career record: 4-0 against Indiana at The Hall. Michigan State had won on the

**Michigan State's Barry Fordham, Vernon Carr hem in Daryl Thomas**

Larry Crewell

last three visits to give the Spartans a 5-10 record there. No other team has beaten Indiana more than three times in its 16-year-old arena.

The Johnson-Fordham record meant Alford was 0-3 against the Spartans in his favorite arena, although usually he had played well against them. His first 30-point game at Indiana came in a 57-54 loss to Michigan State at Assembly Hall his freshman year. Three years later, when his IU career ended, he had fourteen games of 30 or more points. In those games, Indiana was 13-1, the lone loss that first-time 30-point game against Michigan State.

This time, he threatened to reach 30 before halftime. A three-point basket with 1:24 left in the half did give him 24, and Indiana went to the break ahead 44-31. Michigan State hit its first eight shots of the second half, and the race was on. Alford's last of 12 field goals put the Indiana lead at 74-63 with 5:52 to play, but four straight Hoosier misses let Michigan State pull within 74-69. When Alford turned the ball over, Michigan State got it to guard Ed Wright for a breakaway layup that would have tightened the game to a three-point margin. Driving in uncontested, Wright took an extra step and lost the basket to a traveling call. In the last 70 seconds, Michigan State fouled Alford four times and he delivered eight points — none too many, it worked out, because Michigan State hit three-point shots on its last three possessions to chop the final margin to 84-80.

Alford had 42 points: his career high, and an Assembly Hall record. In the building's second year of use, Big Ten MVP Steve Downing had 41 points for Indiana against Illinois. Alford's previous Indiana high was 38 at Wisconsin his junior year.

Heathcote didn't really begrudge the points to him, except for the game-closing free throws. "We're telling our kids to grab anybody — *don't foul Alford.*' Maybe we weren't specific enough.

"It certainly was the Steve Alford show."

Knight admits to talking about

his players in a considerably different way after they have graduated, compared to when they are playing. Alford's outstanding performance started easing him into a post-graduate's honor spot with Knight. He hadn't really waited till the 42-point game. After pulling Alford to let him get a standing ovation late in the Purdue game, Knight walked to Alford on the sidelines and gave him a warm embrace. Later, in a room off the lockerroom that Knight uses as a postgame gear-down area, he told Alford he knew how hard he had played on a day when he had a severe cold, and told him how proud he was to be his coach. He went public with the feeling after Michigan State.

"The kid has just been a great player for us, and I probably haven't talked nearly enough about him over the years that he's been here. He's an all-America; he played like an all-American tonight. Without Alford, Michigan State wins going away." He declined to call it Alford's best IU game. "Steve's played that way ever since he was a freshman. It may be the most points he has scored, but he has made so many big baskets and taken charge of so many things."

Heathcote called Alford "very, very good, but I thought he played better tonight than at any time we've played him before. He scored 33 against us the first game. Maybe if we could play him one more game, he'd score 50 or 60. I saw Dominique Wilkins (of the NBA Atlanta Hawks) score 54 last night, an unbelievable performance, but he did it on athletic ability. Steve Alford does it on smarts, intelligence, constant movement on offense, and just a great, great, great shooting touch." In his record game, that touch made him 12-for-19 from the field, including 4-for-5 on three-point shots, and 14-for-15 at the free throw line.

Alford, author of the warning to Smart about how future opponents would be the first to take notice of a big scoring performance, had used the names of Gary Grant and Antoine Joubert. By chance, they were

*We're telling our kids to grab anybody — don't foul Alford! Maybe we weren't specific enough.*

— Jud Heathcote

John Terhune

**Steve Alford eludes Gary Grant, pulls a 2,000-point trigger**

Larry Crewell

**Bob Knight – Sweater's up**

**Dean Garrett goes up and over Kentucky's Richard Madison, Purdue's Melvin McCants**

Phil Whitlow

**Rick Calloway (20), Dean Garrett play volleyball with Iowa's Roy Marble**

John Terhune

**Bob Knight's ribbon of triumph**

Rick Calloway, Dean Garrett counter Dennis Hopson

Larry Crewell

Fond farewell for Steve Alford

John Terhune

**Seniors Todd Meier, Daryl Thomas, Steve Alford – Not-quite-last hurrahs**

**Daryl Thomas – A Senior Day star**

**Steve Alford – At home in the 'Dome**

**Fairfield's A.J. Wynder learns about Indiana screens**

**A Bob Knight hug and high-fives for Keith Smart**

Larry Crewell

**Bob Knight has victory in stride at Hoosier Dome**

Larry Crewell

**A firm grip for Steve Eyl**

Next page: More than 34,000 jam the Hoosier Dome to see Indiana meet Auburn in the second round of the NCAA tournament

Phil Whitlow

A Cincinnati welcome for Regional hero Rick Calloway

Trainer Tim Garl gives Rick Calloway a checkout in Duke game

**Rick Calloway – Soaring and scoring in hometown**

**Keith Smart, Ron Felling chat**

Larry Crewell

**Keith Smart dips inside for two against LSU**

Larry Crewell

John Terhune

With the score as a backdrop, Steve Alford attacks the Cincinnati nets

Larry Crewell

Leaders of different title teams, Quinn Buckner and Steve Alford, share tears and joy

Band-aid for Hoosiers at New Orleans

Freddie Banks, unstoppable from 3-point range, gets a wave from Keith Smart

Keith Smart coils, then rockets upward and out to elude 7-foot Rony Selkaly for a homestretch basket

Bob Hammel

'Everybody gets to take a shot at Bobby; why not the President of the United States?'

Bob Hammel

Steve Alford – From the champions to you, Mr. President

the guards coming up next for him, and he didn't have to give himself any warnings. "I loved playing against Grant," Alford said when his Indiana career was over. "That was probably the biggest challenge I had. He's the best defensive player I played against in college. He has such long arms and big hands and he's quick. It took me a long time to figure out how to beat him."

Alford went into the Sunday game with a plan, but he waited patiently to set it up. After nine minutes, he had taken just one shot and missed it. Grant was winning the individual battle on TV, and the game was 15-15. With 10:40 to go in the half, Alford surprised Grant and drove for the basket, pulling up for a short jump shot that put Indiana ahead. A Garrett rebound basket made the Hoosier lead 19-15, and Alford followed with a three-point shot for a 22-15 lead. In the last six minutes of the half, Alford scored eight more points and Indiana led at halftime, 41-29. The lead grew to as much as 24 points — within flirting range of the 28-point Michigan margin in 1986 — before winding up at 83-65. Indiana had completed its "must" sweep of the four mid-season home games.

Alford, 10-for-15 shooting, had 30 points — 103 for the last three games, the first time as a Hoosier he strung as many as three 30-point games. His Anti-Grant Plan? What scouting reports have said all along he couldn't do: drive the ball to the basket. And quickly. "You can't mess around with the ball. You've just got to catch it and go. You can't let him square up on you. If you're open, you shoot; if not, you've got to make him play the drive."

One other set of numbers stood out. Dean Garrett had 15 points — 13 in the second half — and 14 rebounds. Early in the game, he missed five tries from in close. "The kid has a really good personality," Knight said. "I just told him at the half to keep taking the shots that he had. He got carried away with one or two after that . . . and I think he made one of those."

Jim Rider

Feb. 8, Assembly Hall

## Michigan 67

| | M | 3FG | AFG | FT | R | A | B | S | F | Pts |
|---|---|---|---|---|---|---|---|---|---|---|
| Rice, f | 35 | | 5-17 | 3- 4 | 10 | 0 | 2 | 0 | 0 | 2 | 13 |
| Joubert, f | 31 | 0- 2 | 3-11 | 2- 3 | 1 | 1 | 0 | 0 | 2 | 1 | 8 |
| Hughes, c | 24 | | 3- 5 | 1- 2 | 10 | 2 | 0 | 1 | 0 | 3 | 7 |
| Grant, g | 29 | | 5-11 | 3- 4 | 3 | 3 | 0 | 0 | 3 | 4 | 13 |
| Thompson, g | 33 | 1- 4 | 6-10 | 0- 0 | 0 | 1 | 0 | 0 | 3 | 4 | 13 |
| Vaught | 20 | | 3- 6 | 0- 0 | 7 | 1 | 1 | 0 | 1 | 3 | 6 |
| Griffin | 14 | | 1- 3 | 0- 0 | 2 | 1 | 0 | 0 | 0 | 4 | 2 |
| Kramer | 8 | 1- 1 | 2- 2 | 0- 0 | 1 | 2 | 0 | 0 | 0 | 2 | 5 |
| Oosterbaan | 4 | | 0- 1 | 0- 0 | 0 | 2 | 0 | 0 | 0 | 0 | 0 |
| Stoyko | 2 | | 0- 0 | 0- 0 | 1 | 0 | 0 | 0 | 0 | 0 | 0 |
| Team | | | | | 2 | | | | | | |
| **Totals** | | 2- 7 | 28-66 | 9-13 | 37 | 13 | 3 | 1 | 9 | 23 | 67 |

## Indiana 83

| | M | 3FG | AFG | FT | R | A | B | S | F | Pts |
|---|---|---|---|---|---|---|---|---|---|---|
| Thomas, f | 34 | | 5-11 | 1- 2 | 3 | 1 | 0 | 4 | 2 | 3 | 11 |
| Calloway, f | 26 | | 4- 9 | 2- 2 | 3 | 2 | 0 | 1 | 2 | 3 | 10 |
| Garrett, c | 30 | | 6-13 | 3- 5 | 14 | 2 | 2 | 0 | 2 | 3 | 15 |
| Alford, g | 38 | 4- 5 | 10-15 | 6- 7 | 2 | 1 | 1 | 0 | 0 | 0 | 30 |
| Smart, g | 16 | | 2- 4 | 2- 2 | 2 | 2 | 0 | 0 | 0 | 3 | 6 |
| Eyl | 31 | | 2- 3 | 0- 2 | 6 | 4 | 0 | 1 | 2 | 1 | 4 |
| Meier | 8 | | 1- 1 | 2- 2 | 3 | 1 | 0 | 1 | 0 | 0 | 4 |
| Hillman | 5 | | 0- 0 | 0- 0 | 0 | 0 | 0 | 0 | 0 | 0 | 0 |
| Sloan | 5 | | 1- 1 | 0- 3 | 1 | 0 | 0 | 0 | 0 | 2 | 2 |
| Smith | 2 | | 0- 1 | 0- 0 | 0 | 0 | 0 | 0 | 0 | 0 | 0 |
| Freeman | 2 | | 0- 0 | 0- 1 | 0 | 0 | 0 | 0 | 0 | 0 | 0 |
| Pelkowski | 1 | | 0- 0 | 0- 0 | 0 | 0 | 0 | 0 | 0 | 0 | 0 |
| Minor | 1 | | 0- 1 | 0- 0 | 1 | 0 | 0 | 0 | 0 | 0 | 0 |
| Oliphant | 1 | | 0- 0 | 1- 2 | 1 | 0 | 0 | 0 | 1 | 0 | 1 |
| Team | | | | | 4 | | | | | | |
| **Totals** | | 4- 5 | 31-59 | 17-28 | 40 | 13 | 3 | 7 | 9 | 13 | 83 |

| SCORE BY HALVES | | | 3FG | AFG | FT |
|---|---|---|---|---|---|
| Michigan (15-8, 6-5) | 29 | 38—67 | .286 | .424 | .692 |
| Indiana (19-2, 10-1) | 41 | 42—83 | .800 | .525 | .607 |

**Officials**—Jim Bain, Ron Winter, Malcolm Hemphill.
**Attendance**—17,241 (sellout).

A surprise for Gary Grant: shooter Steve Alford as a driver, too, in Indiana's 83-67 victory.

## 7 Challenge met

In retrospect, it could be said that Bob Knight saw it coming — a slump, right behind his team's best sustained play of the year.

Yes, Knight said as he looked ahead to a game at Northwestern, the Hoosiers had played well in the consecutive victories over Illinois, Purdue, Michigan State and Michigan — better even, in his mind, than people who felt the four-point winning margin over Michigan State represented something of a slipoff. "I thought we played well, to the point where we were ahead 64-49," he said. "I was very pleased with that. That was not a four-point game." The three three-pointers in the last 45 seconds came when the issue was decided, he was saying. And, yes, he felt the Hoosiers "played well" in the Michigan game. "Michigan is a damned good basketball team. They handled Iowa and Syracuse.

"But we may be horseshit Wednesday night, how do I know? If I could figure all that out, boy, I'd really be smart. Who knows where we go from here? If you could answer the question why you can't play at a maximum all the time, you'd be the best person ever involved in athletics.

"We've got a whole lockerroom full of good kids. And I say, 'God dammit, you're not playing hard.' I think that they probably feel they are playing hard. I know they're not. It's really hard for coaches to convince kids that they aren't playing hard when they aren't, because if it's a good kid, he always thinks he's playing hard."

Steve Alford, college basketball's prototypical "good kid" of 1986-87, knew exactly what his coach meant.

"*Many* times in my four years, he has jumped on me — kicking me out of practice or sitting me down and just ripping into me. Maybe, at the moment when I'm emotional and he's emotional, I haven't really understood what he's been trying to say or why he's saying that. But every time I think he's wrong and I'm right, if I look at the films, it's amazing the times that he's right."

Alford and the Hoosiers, however, were caught in a difficult mental situation. They were playing their best basketball of the year, the best basketball of Alford's four Indiana seasons. They were going to Northwestern to play a team they had down 33-6 and beat 95-43 at a time when they themselves — the one-sided winners — weren't playing as well as they had in their last four or five games. Sure, any Big Ten team can beat you, but . . .

With a minute and a half to go before a pleasantly surprised and wild crowd at Northwestern's Welsh-Ryan Arena, No. 2-ranked Indiana was in trouble. The Hoosiers led just 72-68, and they had a half-minute to find a shot or risk giving the ball back one more time to the super-charged Wildcats. Daryl Thomas, who had been foul-troubled the last few weeks and had enjoyed just one good game in the previous five, saw an opening and drove to a basket with 1:09 left to cleave open a 74-68 lead. Northwestern got the points right back, but Keith Smart hit both halves of a one-and-one with 41 seconds to go for a 76-70 lead and the Hoosiers were fairly safe. A three-point basket by 1985 Indiana "Mr. Basketball" Jeff Grose of Warsaw with one second left made the final score a bit tighter than the game was, 77-75, but no tighter than

Northwestern deserved. Shon Morris, the Wildcats' 6-10 junior scoring leader, polished sections of the floor a half-dozen times with all-out dives in a marvelous, gamelong display of effort. The first Indiana-Northwestern game, he said wanly, "was maybe the longest night of my life. But tonight, I wanted it to last 10 seconds longer."

Knight was angry. Not to the Vanderbilt level, but angry and disappointed. He thought the Hoosiers had advanced beyond the stage of playing to their competition, but in the purest sense, they hadn't been able to compete with a team that was going nowhere. "What Northwestern did was outcompete us for 40 minutes," he snapped.

The game had begun with the spotlight firmly on Alford. Everyone in the building knew he had closed within 15 points of the Indiana career scoring record, one of the oldest in major college basketball. When the late Don Schlundt took possession of it, he was signaling the start of an all-new era. The record before Schlundt arrived was 792 points, by a splendid player: Bill Garrett, the first black player in Big Ten history, the last 6-2 all-America center in basketball history. Garrett's special role in Indiana basketball — including the starring role on

**Feb. 11, Evanston**

# Indiana 77

| | M | 3FG | AFG | FT | R | A | B | S | T | F | Pts |
|---|---|---|---|---|---|---|---|---|---|---|---|
| Thomas, f | 37 | | 9-16 | 14-16 | 11 | 1 | 2 | 2 | 3 | 2 | 32 |
| Calloway, f | 32 | | 4- 5 | 6- 8 | 1 | 3 | 0 | 2 | 6 | 3 | 14 |
| Garrett, c | 21 | | 1- 3 | 1- 2 | 3 | 1 | 0 | 2 | 3 | 3 | 3 |
| Alford, g | 40 | 3- 7 | 4-13 | 4- 4 | 3 | 4 | 0 | 0 | 3 | 3 | 15 |
| Smart, g | 32 | | 5- 5 | 3- 4 | 2 | 3 | 0 | 0 | 4 | 4 | 13 |
| Eyl | 15 | | 0- 0 | 0- 0 | 2 | 0 | 1 | 0 | 0 | 4 | 0 |
| Smith | 16 | | 0- 0 | 0- 0 | 2 | 2 | 0 | 1 | 0 | 0 | 0 |
| Meier | 7 | | 0- 0 | 0- 0 | 1 | 0 | 0 | 0 | 0 | 1 | 0 |
| Team | | | | | 0 | | | | | | |
| **Totals** | | 3- 7 | 23-42 | 28-34 | 25 | 14 | 6 | 5 | 18 | 20 | 77 |

# Northwestern 75

| | M | 3FG | AFG | FT | R | A | B | S | T | F | Pts |
|---|---|---|---|---|---|---|---|---|---|---|---|
| Morris, f | 31 | | 8-14 | 4- 5 | 7 | 2 | 1 | 0 | 5 | 5 | 20 |
| Buford, f | 24 | | 3- 5 | 1- 2 | 3 | 3 | 0 | 0 | 1 | 1 | 7 |
| Ross, c | 16 | | 1- 2 | 1- 2 | 3 | 0 | 2 | 0 | 1 | 5 | 3 |
| Fullen, g | 32 | 0- 2 | 4-13 | 8- 9 | 4 | 3 | 0 | 0 | 1 | 2 | 16 |
| Watts, g | 36 | | 1- 4 | 0- 0 | 0 | 3 | 0 | 1 | 1 | 2 | 2 |
| Pitts | 29 | | 3- 3 | 3- 4 | 1 | 2 | 0 | 0 | 2 | 4 | 9 |
| Wyss | 13 | | 0- 2 | 2- 2 | 3 | 3 | 0 | 0 | 3 | 2 | 2 |
| Grose | 19 | 4- 5 | 6- 8 | 0- 0 | 1 | 0 | 2 | 2 | 2 | 0 | 16 |
| Team | | | | | 4 | | | | | | |
| **Totals** | | 4- 7 | 26-51 | 19-24 | 25 | 17 | 3 | 3 | 16 | 21 | 75 |

| SCORE BY HALVES | | | 3FG | AFG | FT |
|---|---|---|---|---|---|
| Indiana (20-2, 11-1) | 34 | 43—77 | .429 | .548 | .824 |
| Northwestern (6-16, 1-11) | 32 | 43—75 | .571 | .510 | .792 |

**Officials**—George Solomon, Ralph Rosser, Jim Bain.
**Attendance**—8,117 (sellout).

John Terhune

**Steve Alford, Daryl Thomas scraped through in a few**

> *I'm telling you now, this is not a very good basketball team, and Northwestern proved it tonight.*
>
> — Bob Knight

little Shelbyville High School's surprise state high school championship team in 1947 — was half the reason the arrival of Dean Garrett as Indiana's new center carried such a note of fated appropriateness. Bill Garrett was Indiana's first black all-America player; Everett Dean was Indiana's first all-America player. Both were centers. The Californian arrived unknowingly carrying *two* revered Indiana basketball names.

Bill Garrett's hold on the career scoring record ended late in Schlundt's sophomore year. Two years later, Schlundt had moved it into a 1980s neighborhood: 2,192. And nobody touched it until Alford came along.

Bill Garrett died of a heart attack in his 40s. Schlundt died of cancer in the fall of 1985. Already by then he knew where his record was headed. "I never met him in person," Alford said, "but he wrote me when he was in the hospital. He wished me a lot of luck and said he always knew the record would be broken some day and he hoped it would be a person like me. I was grateful for that."

From the Michigan game through departure for Evanston, the Schlundt record that seemed within such easy range for him — especially, the thinking went, against Northwestern — was all that Alford heard about from interviewers and from friends. The full house at Northwestern showed up more red-clad as purple. Northwest Indiana fans traditionally jump on the game early as their one chance to see Indiana play, and this one, with its special Alford significance, became something rare around Evanston: a scalper's game.

Alford began the game with the patience that had worked so well in several other games. He took one early shot, missed, and contented himself with the same early role he played so successfully just a few days before against Michigan. When Northwestern took a 14-13 lead, he popped a three-point shot, then followed with two free throws for an 18-

14 Indiana lead. The game moved along, and he seemed so determined to be team-conscious and not record-conscious that he forgot his primary role: leading the team by scoring. At halftime, he had taken just five shots, including a desperation try at the end of the half, and Indiana led just 34-32. He missed the only two shots he got in the first eight minutes of the second half, and Indiana was hanging on, 47-44.

Down the stretch, he delivered a couple of times: a basket at 3:05 to boost the lead to 68-60, two free throws at 2:42 for a 70-62 lead. He couldn't get away from senior guard Shawn Watts for anything more, and he ended his off-game with 15 points — exactly even with Schlundt, and in Knight's disfavor. For one of the rare times in his coaching career, Knight was explicit with his displeasure. "Alford was horrendous," he said. "We got nothing from him in the way of leadership. It's his responsibility to get people ready to play a ball game."

Alford never will want for defenders in Indiana. The common response to the criticism in general was "How could he?" and, to the part about responsibility to get people ready: "I thought that was the coach's job." It is, of course. Alford,

### Feb. 16, Madison

# Indiana 86

|  | M | 3FG | AFG | FT | R | A | B | S | T | F | Pts |
|---|---|---|---|---|---|---|---|---|---|---|---|
| Thomas, f | 41 |  | 7-10 | 3- 5 | 9 | 0 | 0 | 2 | 4 | 5 | 17 |
| Calloway, f | 28 |  | 3- 5 | 1- 1 | 4 | 3 | 0 | 1 | 1 | 5 | 7 |
| Garrett, c | 46 |  | 9-17 | 3- 4 | 11 | 0 | 2 | 1 | 3 | 3 | 21 |
| Alford, g | 55 | 2-11 | 4-19 | 3- 4 | 4 | 2 | 1 | 4 | 1 | 1 | 13 |
| Smart, g | 32 |  | 4-10 | 7- 8 | 2 | 3 | 0 | 3 | 2 | 3 | 15 |
| Eyl | 30 |  | 3- 4 | 2- 3 | 4 | 3 | 0 | 1 | 0 | 0 | 8 |
| Hillman | 5 |  | 0- 1 | 0- 0 | 0 | 0 | 0 | 0 | 2 | 2 | 0 |
| Meier | 8 |  | 2- 4 | 1- 3 | 4 | 1 | 0 | 1 | 0 | 2 | 5 |
| Freeman | 23 |  | 0- 1 | 0- 0 | 2 | 7 | 0 | 0 | 3 | 1 | 0 |
| Smith | 7 |  | 0- 0 | 0- 0 | 0 | 0 | 0 | 0 | 0 | 0 | 0 |
| Team |  |  |  |  | 2 |  |  |  |  |  |  |
| Totals |  | 2-11 | 32-71 | 20-28 | 42 | 19 | 3 | 13 | 16 | 22 | 86 |

# Wisconsin 85

|  | M | 3FG | AFG | FT | R | A | B | S | T | F | Pts |
|---|---|---|---|---|---|---|---|---|---|---|---|
| Portmann, f | 16 |  | 1- 3 | 0- 0 | 2 | 0 | 1 | 0 | 2 | 4 | 2 |
| Molaski, f | 53 |  | 1- 2 | 2- 2 | 3 | 7 | 0 | 0 | 3 | 4 | 4 |
| Weber, c | 45 |  | 8-14 | 4- 6 | 10 | 5 | 3 | 5 | 3 | 5 | 20 |
| Heineman, g | 50 | 3- 6 | 7-13 | 3- 3 | 6 | 6 | 0 | 0 | 4 | 4 | 20 |
| Jackson, g | 46 | 1- 1 | 7-10 | 3- 4 | 1 | 1 | 0 | 1 | 4 | 2 | 18 |
| Ripley | 34 | 1- 1 | 3- 4 | 3- 5 | 3 | 2 | 0 | 1 | 0 | 1 | 10 |
| Smith | 17 | 1- 1 | 3- 6 | 0- 2 | 1 | 1 | 0 | 0 | 2 | 1 | 7 |
| Jones | 13 |  | 1- 2 | 2- 2 | 2 | 1 | 0 | 0 | 1 | 3 | 4 |
| Schubring | 1 |  | 0- 0 | 0- 0 | 0 | 0 | 0 | 0 | 0 | 0 | 0 |
| Team |  |  |  |  | 3 |  |  |  |  |  |  |
| Totals |  | 6- 9 | 31-54 | 17-24 | 31 | 23 | 4 | 7 | 19 | 24 | 85 |

| SCORE BY HALVES | | | 3FG | AFG | FT |
|---|---|---|---|---|---|
| Indiana (21-2, 12-1) | 31 31 8 9 7—86 | | .182 | .451 | .714 |
| Wisconsin (11-15, 1-12) | 32 30 8 9 6—85 | | .667 | .574 | .708 |

**Officials**—Gary Muncy, Mike Stockner, Ted Valentine.
**Attendance**—9,164.

of all people, knew that it was his, too, as the captain and chief liaison between coach and players. It was the classic case Knight had mentioned on Sunday: Good kids always think they're playing hard.

Daryl Thomas kept the Hoosiers from being in even worse shape. Playing back home in Chicagoland, he had the best scoring night of his career, 32 points, plus 11 rebounds. "If we don't have Daryl Thomas, we don't have a chance to win the game," Knight said. Northwestern coach Bill Foster put it another way: "Give Indiana credit: We play Alford, they get the ball inside to Thomas. They took what we gave them and Thomas made us play. He played a great game."

Knight was in no mood to give Indiana any sort of credit. At the press conference, he said, "I've told a few of you people we are not a very good basketball team, and you laughed at me. I've forgotten more basketball than any of you will ever know, and I'm telling you now this is *not* a very good basketball team, and Northwestern proved it tonight."

It was the kind of game another coach, almost any other coach, would have taken with a "Whew!" and gone on to other thoughts. As Knight rode home from Evanston, not at all happy but not really seething, he knew that would have been the standard response, and maybe the realistic response, given the first-game score between the two teams, the demands of the four previous games and all — including an exceptionally good and gutty performance by Northwestern. He couldn't bring himself to make that response, nor did he really want to.

He did expect his team to realize that if Northwestern was capable of a 50-point margin shrinkage from one game to another, Wisconsin certainly was. Wisconsin had played almost everyone in the league close, except for its one-sided disaster in Bloomington. Wisconsin hadn't beaten Indiana since 1980, but not because it hadn't competed, hard, in several near-misses. Alford knew better than any other Hoosier that

the Badgers always would be ready as long as he was around, because that also meant Wisconsin guard Mike Heineman would be there. Heineman was no Gary Grant in ability, but he yielded to no one in determination. It was Heineman who, with brother Chris — now a starter at Davidson — had led Connersville to the state championship that Alford wanted so much for his dad. It was the Heinemans and Connersville who ended the Alford dream, beating New Castle in the state tournament's quarterfinals.

Mike Heineman and Alford worked camps together in the summer and became good friends. Every time Wisconsin played Indiana, Heineman got primary defensive duties on Alford, and he scrapped with everything he had. Knight had such admiration for Heineman's competitiveness that when Heineman left the first Indiana-Wisconsin game in the final minutes, he sent word to public address system announcer Chuck Crabb to make note that it was Heineman's last appearance in Assembly Hall. The Hoosier crowd responded with a warm standing ovation, and Heineman — who stood and waved — was touched. "It was a nice gesture," Wisconsin coach Steve Yoder said, and Heineman's parents waited outside the Indiana dressing room to tell Knight directly how much they appreciated it.

Neither Yoder nor Heineman nor any other Badger had any nice gestures in mind when Indiana arrived for another of ESPN's late-late shows — this one later than Indiana's other one (at Michigan). By Indiana time, the game began at 9:42 p.m.

It seemed as if it would never end.

Wisconsin pulled ahead 22-12 early, but the penalty killers played their usual role for Indiana closing out the first half. Wisconsin native Todd Meier, who had a history of playing well in the Badgers' arena, replaced Garrett with 9:17 to go in the half after the center picked up his second foul. Indiana trailed at the time by the 22-12 score. Meier had two rebound baskets and

Steve Eyl was a problem right to the end for native Hoosier Kim Zurcher.

Larry Crewell

Joe Hillman, after losing his starting job the first month of the season, developed into an off-the-bench leader for the Hoosiers

Phil Whitlow

Thomas did the rest of the scoring as Indiana pulled within 32-31 at the half.

Alford had taken care of the record business by sinking a three-point shot barely five minutes into the game for a 7-4 lead. He didn't shake the shooting slump that had begun with his 4-for-13 game at Northwestern. And neither could Indiana shake Wisconsin, although three quick Garrett baskets let the Hoosiers jump ahead 39-34 early in the second half. In just two trips downcourt, Wisconsin tied the game again, Heineman hitting a three-point shot. With the game tied 51-51, Indiana committed four straight turnovers — two by Smart, two by Tony Freeman. Wisconsin converted two into baskets, then capitalized on a Smart miss by breaking another Indiana native, Shelton Smith of Indianapolis Cathedral, free for a layup and a 57-51 lead, with four minutes to play.

Alford, just 1-for-8 in a 25-minute stretch, halved the margin with a three-point play, and Smart cut it to 57-56 with a basket at 3:10. Wisconsin steadied and led 60-58 when the Badgers posted 6-5 Tom Molaski low against Alford. Alford tried to get around Molaski on the left to front him, but a pass freed Molaski to roll to the basket. An official ruled he had pushed Alford aside to get the pass, and Alford used the free throws awarded him to tie the game, 60-60, with 1:42 to go. At 1:10, Eyl stole a pass and drove to a dunk that put Indiana ahead, but Rod Ripley tied the game for Wisconsin with a jump shot at 0:46. Everyone knew what Indiana would do: run the clock down and let Alford fire. He fired. He missed.

Overtime.

Smart picked up the pace in the first overtime, hitting two free throws at 3:22 for a 66-65 lead and boosting it to 68-65 with a basket at 2:20. Heineman faked Rick Calloway into the air, drew a foul and somehow hit his shot for a three-point play that tied the game again, 68-68. It was 70-70 when Smart drove the middle for a shot at 0:45. He missed, but Eyl came out with the rebound and Indiana set up one more time in its get-Alford-open-late offense. He fired again, missed, and Eyl got a tip up, but . . .

Double overtime.

Down 76-75 with just over a minute left, Alford worked open for a three-point try but missed. Eyl came out with the rebound, drew a foul and hit both halves of a one-and-one for a 77-76 lead with 1:18 to go. Wisconsin freshman Danny Jones missed with a pass at 0:46, and when Alford hit Calloway cutting through the middle for a layup and a 79-76 lead with 28 seconds to go, Indiana appeared in good shape. Wisconsin looked for a three-point chance but couldn't find one. Trent Jackson started up with a desperation try, but Alford slapped the ball away and almost stole it, but it rolled out of bounds in the left corner to stay in Wisconsin possession at 0:13. Knight used a timeout to set up a special anti-three-point defense: Don't worry about backcuts to the basket, stay with anyone beyond the three-point line.

With eight seconds to go, Ripley found himself wide open, paused just a second, then fired the three-point basket that tied the game. Alford got a shot up at the buzzer but missed.

Triple overtime.

Wisconsin had an 83-82 lead with 1:15 to go when Garrett fielded Calloway's miss, went back up and scored — but lost the basket to a charging call. Wisconsin worked the clock down to 0:48 before Ripley was fouled, and he hit two free throws for an 85-82 lead. Smart hurried into the middle of the Wisconsin defense and drew a one-and-one that he sank, cutting the lead to 85-84 with 37 seconds left. At 0:26, Yoder took timeout to set his team up for the game-closing stall. The Badgers never got to use it. Wisconsin's Smith and Indiana's Hillman bumped before the mid-court pass-in, and it was ruled an intentional foul: two shots. Smith missed both, Alford claimed the rebound, and Indiana set up for its last victory try.

Alford had gone almost 19 minutes without a basket, 18 minutes without a point — on this, his record night. He worked to the left wing to try for one more opening, but when the defense converged on him, he dropped a pass to Hillman, open in the left corner. Hillman fired.

He overshot. The ball missed the rim, an air ball, but it glanced off the backboard, Garrett reached over Ripley to take the rebound, and he laid it in at 0:03 for the shot that made Indiana an 86-85 winner in the first triple overtime in 87 years and 1,833 games of Indiana basketball.

Knight couldn't forget the defensive breakdown by Smart and Calloway that left Ripley open to tie the game with his second-overtime three-pointer. He wasn't happy with officiating, and Yoder wasn't, either. But Knight warmed up most in postgame comments when the subject of the late-night TV contract

with ESPN came up. It wasn't, of course, ESPN's fault. Knight's Big Ten coaching colleagues begged their way onto the network when there were no legitimate openings. The league created Monday play to supply a game and satisfy the coaches. Knight knew all that and covered it all by saying:

"It's just ridiculous that we're leaving here to go home to get kids in class and won't get home till 3 o'clock in the morning. This Monday night television is just absolute bullshit. If the people in this conference can't think enough of these kids to get them in a situation where they miss as little class time as possible . . . It's time the presidents or somebody stepped in and laid some rules down on when these teams can play and when they can't, and how much class they're allowed to miss, and to hell with God-damned ESPN or whatever it is, getting

Dean Garrett, swooping in after a loose ball that Minnesota's Richard Coffey is about to corral, was a last-minute hero twice in a week

Larry Crewell

on television, because this is an absolutely ridiculous thing to put a college student through."

College student Garrett was one who didn't really mind. He could have flown home without an airplane after a season-high 21 points, 11 rebounds — and the first game-winning shot of his career. "I've never done anything like that in my life," he said. "You always dream of something like that. I still don't remember going up with the shot. I knew it went in, but I still don't remember grabbing the ball. We were kinda lucky. If I had been thinking about it, it never would have happened. It just kinda went so fast."

Alford was 4-for-19, the most shots he ever had missed in a college game; 8-for-32 for two games, two harrowing escapes. But the Hoosiers were 21-2 and still leading the league by a game, with the Iowa game not far away.

All that was in between was Minnesota, 2-10 in the league, 0-5 on the road, a 24-point loser to the Hoosiers four weeks before on their home court, a loser by 32 points at Iowa, 27 at Michigan, 22 at Illinois, 27 at Purdue.

With 55 seconds to go, the score was tied, Alford broke open for a three-point shot — and Indiana native Kim Zurcher (Wawasee High) rebounded the miss to give the Gophers a victory shot. At 0:46, first-year coach Clem Haskins took timeout. Minnesota had to shoot with at least 10 seconds to go, and Haskins' instructions were to run the shot-clock down, then "clear Kim for a jump shot, backscreen for him and get a shot from him in the corner. He's won two games for us. Against Wisconsin, he won the game with a three-pointer."

Zurcher got the ball and started to go up, but Alford swatted the ball away and out of bounds — the same play he had made in the second overtime at Wisconsin. The quick decision officials had to make was whether Alford had blocked a shot or knocked the ball away before a shot. Unlike pro ball, where a shot has to

hit the rim to take off shot-clock pressures, any college shot — even one quickly aborted — counts. Officials said Zurcher hadn't shot, so Minnesota had the ball out of bounds at 0:16, with six seconds left on the shot clock. The ball came in to Zurcher again, and Steve Eyl, four inches taller, blocked his shot, then saved the ball before it could go out of bounds. Alford hurried downcourt to get a shot away, and his miss wound up in Garrett's hands. This time, he didn't get a basket, but he was fouled as he shot, and at 0:03, he hit both free throws for a 72-70 victory.

"I've never done that in my *life*," Garrett said. "Now twice in one week . . ."

However wobbly the victory, however worried he might be getting with shooter Alford 7-for-20 this game and 15-for-52 over three, Knight had the eight-game winning streak that he had asked of his players, from Iowa to Iowa. "It's not the way we *wanted* to go into the game," said Thomas, who had another big game with 24 points, but the Hoosiers had met Knight's challenge — and they were still a game ahead in the league.

## It's not the way we wanted to go into the (Iowa) game
— Daryl Thomas

**Feb. 19, Assembly Hall**

# Minnesota 70

| | M | 3FG | AFG | FT | R | A | B | S | T | F | Pts |
|---|---|---|---|---|---|---|---|---|---|---|---|
| Burton, f | 26 | | 3- 6 | 0- 0 | 7 | 3 | 2 | 0 | 2 | 4 | 6 |
| Coffey, f | 31 | | 5-11 | 3- 3 | 6 | 0 | 0 | 0 | 0 | 3 | 13 |
| Shikenjanski, c | 21 | | 3- 7 | 0- 1 | 7 | 0 | 0 | 0 | 2 | 4 | 6 |
| Woods, g | 24 | 1- 3 | 6-10 | 0- 0 | 4 | 0 | 0 | 0 | 1 | 4 | 13 |
| Gaffney, g | 36 | | 4-11 | 3- 4 | 3 | 2 | 0 | 1 | 5 | 2 | 11 |
| Hanson | 22 | 0- 2 | 2- 5 | 0- 0 | 0 | 1 | 0 | 2 | 1 | 1 | 4 |
| Zurcher | 22 | | 4- 8 | 3- 4 | 3 | 6 | 1 | 0 | 2 | 1 | 11 |
| Smith | 18 | | 2- 3 | 2- 3 | 3 | 1 | 1 | 0 | 1 | 3 | 6 |
| Team | | | | | 5 | | | | | | |
| Totals | | 1- 5 | 29-61 | 11-15 | 38 | 13 | 4 | 3 | 14 | 22 | 70 |

# Indiana 72

| | M | 3FG | AFG | FT | R | A | B | S | T | F | Pts |
|---|---|---|---|---|---|---|---|---|---|---|---|
| Thomas, f | 40 | | 6- 9 | 12-13 | 7 | 1 | 0 | 0 | 0 | 4 | 24 |
| Minor, f | 10 | | 1- 2 | 0- 0 | 1 | 2 | 0 | 0 | 2 | 1 | 2 |
| Garrett, c | 34 | | 5- 8 | 7- 8 | 8 | 0 | 1 | 1 | 0 | 2 | 17 |
| Alford, g | 39 | 3- 9 | 7-20 | 0- 0 | 2 | 3 | 0 | 1 | 1 | 1 | 17 |
| Smart, g | 20 | 0- 1 | 1- 6 | 2- 4 | 1 | 4 | 0 | 0 | 1 | 2 | 4 |
| Calloway | 32 | | 3- 9 | 0- 1 | 5 | 3 | 0 | 0 | 2 | 2 | 6 |
| Eyl | 16 | | 0- 0 | 0- 0 | 1 | 2 | 1 | 0 | 0 | 2 | 0 |
| Freeman | 4 | | 0- 0 | 0- 0 | 0 | 1 | 0 | 0 | 1 | 1 | 0 |
| Meier | 3 | | 1- 1 | 0- 0 | 0 | 0 | 0 | 0 | 1 | 2 | 2 |
| Hillman | 2 | | 0- 0 | 0- 0 | 0 | 1 | 0 | 0 | 0 | 0 | 0 |
| Team | | | | | 7 | | | | | | |
| Totals | | 3-10 | 24-55 | 21-26 | 32 | 17 | 2 | 2 | 8 | 17 | 72 |

| SCORE BY HALVES | | 3FG | AFG | FT |
|---|---|---|---|---|
| Minnesota (9-14, 2-11) | 34 36—70 | .200 | .475 | .733 |
| Indiana (22-2, 13-1) | 36 36—72 | .300 | .436 | .769 |

**Technical foul**—Indiana.
**Officials**—Tom Rucker, Eric Harmon, Sam Lickliter.
**Attendance**—16,693.

# Damon 'Stated' his own case

No basketball player ever arrived in high school to such pressure as, thanks to a nationally popular book, Damon Bailey did. That made freshman Bailey's outstanding season all the greater.

Bob Knight's two visits to watch Bailey play as an eighth-grader and his impressed reaction afterward became the most charming, most remembered anecdote in *A Season on the Brink*. That section was included in *Sports Illustrated*'s excerpt, and the magazine went farther by naming Bailey the national freshman of the year, before he had ever played a high school game.

He has played 27 of them now, and the kid who came into the season with the biggest buildup ever delivered the biggest season an Indiana high school freshman ever had. With all those eyes watching, with newspapers and magazines and TV stations giving his team's games a carnival air, Bailey led Bedford North Lawrence to the state's Final Four. Of all the players there, he had the highest scoring average (23.6) *and* (at 6-2) the most rebounds (243 — 9.0 per game).

There, Bailey showed maybe a trace of nerves. So did Oscar Robertson in his first Final Four, as a junior. Bailey had early shooting trouble, third-quarter foul problems. He missed almost a quarter of the game because of fouls. Against the Marion team that won its third straight state championship and sent its three top stars on to the Big Ten and ACC, Bailey had 20 points and 8 rebounds, and Bedford North Lawrence was anything but disgraced, 70-61. "The question I was most frequently asked the week of the State was, 'Are you afraid of being embarrassed?' " Bailey's coach, Danny Bush, said. "It made

*Sanford Gentry*

me mad. Our kids were not fazed in any way. We played the last five minutes of the third quarter without Damon and were one-down."

Bush prefers playing with Bailey. "It's a pleasure to coach him. And I'm fortunate I had a good group of kids to go with him, good players and good people. They readily accepted the situation as it was. They knew Damon would get the publicity. As long as he works hard, there's no problem. And there never was one. He amazed me, the way he handled things. He's just a good kid, with good parents.

"The first game of the year, we played Scottsburg, and he scored 20 points. He shot the ball six times. Scottsburg packed its defense in, and he didn't force things. That's the beauty of his game: He lets the game come to him. He does things that you can't coach. And he's just an old country boy, like the rest of us."

**For Damon Bailey and coach Danny Bush, a year in the spotlight went astonishingly well**

*Sanford Gentry*

# 8 Upward bound

Mental toughness. It was a phrase that kept coming up in comments by Indiana players and coach Bob Knight. It seemed at times more of a goal than a championship was, or any particular victory. It was a very private matter for the Hoosiers' three seniors — Steve Alford, Daryl Thomas and Todd Meier. They knew the roots of it all, roots that started in their greatest victory.

The three were freshmen when Indiana rocked the 1984 NCAA tournament by taking out No. 1-ranked North Carolina and all-America stars Michael Jordan and Sam Perkins, 72-68, at Atlanta. "At that point, it was definitely the biggest thrill that I've had — to beat the No. 1 team in the country," Alford said. It was a heady time, one when he saw the raw genius of Knight The Coach in a different light.

"It was funny," Alford said. "I don't know if we really did think of North Carolina as a super team. Coach prepared us that way that week. They were obviously a great team with great athletes. We were a good ballhandling team, a good passing team, and a team that could shoot the ball pretty well. Looking at the films just showed us all the openings there were (in the run-and-jump pressuring defense another master coach, Dean Smith, liked to use). We got confidence that week. We just never once heard a doubt from Coach. I don't know if we even knew we were playing the No. 1 team in the country. I think we forgot about that as the week went on." The approach was: "Here is what they do, and here is how we are going to beat them." Matter-of-factly, upbeat, the only emotion that sur-

faced a light and easy humor to take away any edge, not to build one.

It was an improbable, glorious victory, one of the rare times in his Indiana days when Knight was back in his customary Army role: sending an underdog team against far more noted athletes and a much more acclaimed team. And two days later, going against Virginia for the spot in the Final Four that once had been virtually conceded to North Carolina but now appeared Indiana's by conquest, the Hoosiers themselves were upset victims.

"That started the whole mental toughness deal — beating North Carolina and then getting beaten by Virginia," Steve Alford said. "We felt we were a better team than Virginia." Obviously, Knight did, too. It became the challenge he continually laid before the Alford-led teams of the next three years, by far the worst of those the one that followed immediately after the freshman-year peak-and-valley regional.

That 1984-85 season, Alford's sophomore year, was his roughest ever. "I think so, because that's when the team struggled the most. We lost all those games at home (five in a row, in a place where Indiana teams over the years have batted .900 — five league losses in a row at a time when a traditional roaring Indiana finish might have meant another championship).

"Problem after problem just seemed to pile upon itself that year. Giomi not going to class and him leaving, others not playing well. That was when I had a shooting slump, a slump I had never seen before and I didn't know quite how to handle it." Junior forward Mike Giomi, the team's leading rebounder at the time, was dropped from the squad

**Feb. 21, Assembly Hall**

# Iowa 75

| | M | 3FG | AFG | FT | R | A | B | S | F | Pts |
|---|---|---|---|---|---|---|---|---|---|---|
| Marble, f | 34 | 3- 4 | 7-15 | 3- 4 | 6 | 1 | 0 | 0 | 2 | 4 | 20 |
| Lohaus, f | 32 | 2- 5 | 7-13 | 0- 1 | 6 | 2 | 0 | 0 | 2 | 4 | 16 |
| Wright, c | 24 | | 1- 4 | 1- 2 | 8 | 2 | 2 | 0 | 1 | 4 | 3 |
| Armstrong, g | 26 | 0- 1 | 2- 6 | 5- 7 | 3 | 2 | 0 | 2 | 2 | 3 | 9 |
| Gamble, g | 27 | | 2- 5 | 2- 3 | 4 | 1 | 0 | 2 | 2 | 3 | 6 |
| Moe | 19 | 1- 3 | 5- 7 | 2- 3 | 0 | 0 | 0 | 0 | 1 | 3 | 13 |
| Jones | 13 | | 0- 2 | 0- 0 | 1 | 2 | 0 | 0 | 2 | 1 | 0 |
| Lorenzen | 9 | | 2- 2 | 0- 1 | 2 | 1 | 0 | 0 | 1 | 1 | 4 |
| Horton | 13 | | 1- 4 | 0- 0 | 3 | 1 | 1 | 0 | 1 | 2 | 2 |
| Hill | 2 | | 1- 2 | 0- 0 | 2 | 0 | 0 | 0 | 0 | 0 | 2 |
| Reaves | 1 | | 0- 0 | 0- 0 | 0 | 0 | 0 | 0 | 0 | 0 | 0 |
| Team | | | | | 4 | | | | | | |
| **Totals** | | 6-13 | 28-60 | 13-21 | 39 | 12 | 3 | 4 | 14 | 25 | 75 |

# Indiana 84

| | M | 3FG | AFG | FT | R | A | B | S | F | Pts |
|---|---|---|---|---|---|---|---|---|---|---|
| Thomas, f | 32 | | 9-18 | 3- 5 | 5 | 0 | 0 | 0 | 3 | 4 | 21 |
| Calloway, f | 34 | | 3- 8 | 4- 5 | 5 | 2 | 0 | 0 | 3 | 3 | 10 |
| Garrett, c | 25 | | 2- 6 | 1- 3 | 9 | 3 | 3 | 1 | 0 | 4 | 5 |
| Alford, g | 37 | 4- 7 | 8-15 | 4- 4 | 0 | 3 | 0 | 0 | 3 | 3 | 24 |
| Smart, g | 27 | 1- 4 | 7-14 | 2- 2 | 6 | 5 | 0 | 0 | 1 | 4 | 17 |
| Hillman | 20 | 1- 1 | 2- 2 | 2- 2 | 3 | 4 | 0 | 0 | 1 | 2 | 7 |
| Eyl | 18 | | 0- 1 | 0- 1 | 3 | 1 | 0 | 1 | 2 | 2 | 0 |
| Meier | 4 | | 0- 0 | 0- 0 | 1 | 0 | 0 | 0 | 0 | 0 | 0 |
| Smith | 2 | | 0- 0 | 0- 0 | 1 | 0 | 0 | 0 | 0 | 0 | 0 |
| Sloan | 1 | | 0- 0 | 0- 0 | 0 | 0 | 0 | 0 | 0 | 0 | 0 |
| Team | | | | | 4 | | | | | | |
| **Totals** | | 6-12 | 31-64 | 16-22 | 37 | 18 | 3 | 2 | 13 | 22 | 84 |

| SCORE BY HALVES | | | 3FG | AFG | FT |
|---|---|---|---|---|---|
| Iowa (23-4, 11-4) | 27 | 48—75 | .462 | .467 | .619 |
| Indiana (23-2, 14-1) | 46 | 38—84 | .500 | .484 | .727 |

**Officials**—Richard Weiler, Ted Hillary, Phil Robinson.
**Attendance**—17,343 (sellout).

for good, winding up at North Carolina State for his senior season. The Alford slump wasn't relative — a slump for a player of *his* stature. It was a real one: 17-for-63 over a six-game stretch, a .270 percentage and 8.5 scoring average for an Olympian who was rolling along at .570 and 20.6 when it began.

One strong theory was Olympic burnout, accumulated weariness from the year that had taken him to the heights and depths at Atlanta, then almost directly into the Olympic Trials, then a summer of Olympic play climaxed by winning a gold medal. Probably, there was some truth to that theory, Alford admits now. "The strange thing about that was my first 10 games of my sophomore season statistically were really pretty good. I was shooting the ball well. We got home (from the Olympics) in August, and I had about 12 days at home and I had to turn around and come back to Bloomington and start everything all over again. I've always loved the game and grown up playing the game. I didn't think that would be any problem for me. But I think as the year got longer, I tired. I think that had to have an effect on my shooting. My

**Rebounding had a high priority with Daryl Thomas, in Iowa rematch**

John Terhune

John Terhune

**Big Ten shot-blocking leader Dean Garrett shows Iowa's B. J. Armstrong why**

legs were practically gone." The fourth game of that mystifying skid was the one in which the one person who lived the Olympic experience more intensely than Alford, Knight, threw a chair onto the court against Purdue. Those were not fun times around The Hall. In his entire life, Steve Alford never wanted a season to end, never could wait for the next one to begin. "If there *was* a season I was glad to put behind, it was probably that one," he said.

If it did represent something of an Olympic pricetag, Alford doesn't regret the golden payment. "Oh, no. I'd never trade that summer for anything."

His junior year, things improved considerably, but there still was the disappointing ending: the loss at Michigan, the first-round upset by Cleveland State. One more time, the mental toughness specter hung over a full squad but mostly the three veterans of the Atlanta experience and all that came afterward.

Now, the critical games of the entire season had arrived: Iowa, at Purdue, at Illinois, Ohio State. Three games against Top 10 regulars, the fourth against a likely NCAA tournament team. And Alford's shooting was off. The mental toughness problem was not only his but the whole ball club's, starting with seniors Thomas and Meier.

This was a team that had grown up believing its No. 1 solution to problems was getting Alford open. That hadn't been a cure-all these last three frustrating games, when teams the Hoosiers had beaten by a cumulative 114 points the first time around had cut that to a skinny 5.

"What was discouraging was when we went on the Northwestern and Wisconsin road trip and really struggled," Thomas said. "I really felt we could be a good team, but we didn't understand what was going on. Was it us, or was it the other teams just playing outstanding basketball against us? Then we'd look at the films and we'd see, 'Man, we *are* playing bad.' And they *were* playing good.

"We just wanted to hold together and we said, 'Whatever happens, we just can't lose.' Steve wasn't shooting well, so everyone else had to be conscious of scoring. We didn't know exactly *when* Steve was going to come out of his slump. We knew he *was* going to come out, but we just couldn't fold."

And very suddenly the clouds seemed to part. Iowa, the team the Hoosiers respected most, came into Assembly Hall and got bashed. The 84-75 final score didn't reflect the Indiana dominance, but it did suggest how uneasy the quick-striking Hawkeyes kept the Hoosiers in a game Indiana led 46-27 at halftime and by 21 points with less than five minutes to go. If things never really got scary for Assembly Hall's roaring 17,343, they stayed edgy.

As for Alford? What slump? He hit 8 of 15 shots, including four three-pointers. He delivered one of the three-point baskets three seconds before halftime to send the Hawkeyes in on a downer. Iowa had, after all, spotted Illinois a 19-point lead at Champaign and won. Indiana showed the Hawkeyes it's not a good habit to develop. The final margin was the closest they got. "Some teams will give you great intensity for five minutes and then they'll fold up," Iowa coach Tom Davis said. "We've fought through that before, but we couldn't today. Indiana just sustained it. I don't know if that's as great as they have played, but they sure gave a tremendous effort."

Rarely have negative numbers meant as much as Iowa's 39-37 rebounding edge did to all the Hoosiers, primarily Thomas and Garrett. After the 46-19 whipping Indiana had taken in first-game rebounding, there was no doubt in Thomas' mind: "Our key was the boards. We really went out and played tough against them. When we beat Iowa, I really felt that when all things were going together for us as a team, we could be really good." Thomas had 21 points, giving him 94 for the four

games that spanned the Alford slump. Garrett had only five points, but that wasn't his priority. His nine rebounds led both teams.

Alford remained mystified by the three near-misses that preceded the strong performance against Iowa. "I don't think consciously we were looking ahead," he said. "When you do that, you end up getting beat. Obviously, we came close to doing that three times. I think you have to give all three of those teams credit for really playing well against us. And maybe there was a feeling of waiting for this, a revenge factor — not revenge against Iowa but just to revenge ourselves and not play as badly as we did at Iowa City."

The slump? "I *know* I can shoot the ball," Alford said. "I've got a pretty good frame of mind, mental toughness, especially when it comes to shooting." Knight felt his entire team had made a major stride in not just the Iowa game but the four-game package, including the squeakers. "I don't think in the last two years our team could have done what it did in the three games leading up to this one. We've played against some teams playing very well against us. Minnesota played very, very well and hit some big shots at crucial times. We had to play through those three games with Steve going 15-for-52. These kids have just done a great job."

The Indiana-Iowa game made the national news wires before it was played. On Tuesday of game week, *Washington Post* columnist John Feinstein, whose book, *A Season on the Brink*, had climbed to No. 1 on the non-fiction best-sellers list, called to ask Indiana sports information director Kit Klingelhoffer for credentials to cover the game. Klingelhoffer deals with a finite number of spaces — 80 maximum, even counting two folding chairs set up in each of Assembly Hall's four corners for *really* big games. "I told John I didn't think I could take care of him because we were out of space," Klingelhoffer said. "He said, 'I don't understand.' I told him I already had turned down Dan Barreiro of the

| AP poll | | |
|---------|--|--|
| **After weekend games Feb. 23** | | |
| 1. Nevada-LV (49) | 28-1 | 1258 |
| 2. North Carolina (6) | 25-2 | 1195 |
| 3. Indiana (9) | 23-2 | 1179 |
| 4. DePaul | 25-1 | 1062 |
| 5. Temple | 28-2 | 991 |
| 6. Purdue | 20-3 | 986 |
| 7. Iowa | 23-4 | 799 |
| 8. Georgetown | 21-4 | 786 |
| 9. Pittsburgh | 22-5 | 680 |
| 10. Alabama | 21-4 | 673 |
| • • • | | |
| 11. Syracuse | 22-5 | 617 |
| 14. Illinois | 19-6 | 493 |
| 17. Duke | 21-6 | 179 |

*Minneapolis Tribune* and a couple of other papers. He said, 'My boss isn't going to like this.' " *Post* sports editor George Solomon called Klingelhoffer on Wednesday and got the same report. "He was all right that time," Klingelhoffer said. "He asked if they could check back later in the week, in case anything turned up, and I said, 'Fine, but I have to tell you if something does, I feel like I should give the first one to Minneapolis because they're going to be here Thursday covering our game anyway, and they're in our league.' Solomon called back on Thursday and he was a little different that time. He said Knight was behind it, because of the book. I said he wasn't — I hadn't even talked to Knight about the situation. I also told him several years ago Bob threw Curry

Kirkpatrick (of *Sports Illustrated*) out of a press conference but we didn't stop issuing press credentials to him to cover the games." On Saturday morning, the *Post* ran a short sports page item that said "Indiana University has denied press credentials to John Feinstein . . ." — the five-paragraph story's unmistakable overtones that Knight was responsible for banning Feinstein. "The first time I even mentioned the situation to Bob was Friday," Klingelhoffer said. Neither the *Post* nor the *Minneapolis Tribune*, nor some other newspapers and TV stations in Indiana, received credentials, but the national perception left by the incident (carried by both newspaper wire services) was that Knight had intervened in petulance. Knight's faith in journalistic fairness and accuracy was not heightened — nor, in that specific instance, was Klingelhoffer's.

Iowa's loss to Indiana virtually eliminated the Hawkeyes (11-4 in the league to Indiana's 14-1, with three games left), and Illinois (10-5) was out. With two weeks to go, it was a two-team race. Purdue, next up for Indiana, had refused to drop back. The Boilermakers used a miracle finish or two of their own to get to their return game with Indiana 12-2. Three days before the Indiana game, Purdue trailed at Illinois by 16 points with 12 minutes to go but won in overtime.

Game plans were predictable. Both Purdue coach Gene Keady and Knight commonly try for an inside attack to accumulate fouls on the other team's front line. It had worked that way to Indiana's benefit in the first game. The second time around, fouls fouled up Indiana more. Because of fouls, the Hoosiers got only 59 minutes of play combined from Thomas, Garrett and Smart. Purdue did many things well, but Indiana's attrition was the key to the Boilermakers' solid 75-64 victory that reshaped the Big Ten race.

Calloway, who had averaged 14.3 a game his first 11 games after returning from the knee injury, had tailed off sharply in the next month.

**For Rick Calloway and Purdue's Doug Lee, a loose basketball has some attraction**

Jim Rider

He scored 15 against Purdue, and that was his highest total in nine games. He wasn't getting rebounds, either. Knight benched him and started Calloway's fellow Cincinnatian, Dave Minor, in the Minnesota game but went back to Calloway against Iowa. From little up, at all levels, Calloway always has been able to score. At Indiana, he came off the bench to hit his first seven collegiate shots and finished his freshman-year opener 10-for-11 with 23 points to earn a fast promotion to starter. He averaged 13.9 points and 4.9 rebounds and made every freshman all-America team. Suddenly, he couldn't score or rebound, and he was as mystified as anyone.

"That was the first time that ever happened to me," he said. "Last year, it happened a couple of times, but it wasn't as bad as this time. Nobody really said that much to me because I was so young and they figured, 'He's just going through something.' " If his knee injury was part of the problem, it was hard to say why he played so well the first few weeks back compared to the next few. "I guess maybe I was so excited about coming back I really didn't worry about the knee," Calloway said. "Once I got into it, I guess I started getting away from that and worrying about my leg. But I went three or four games without even scoring in double figures, and I was only getting, like, two rebounds. It did bother me, but I tried not to let it get to me totally. At times it did, but I just told myself, 'You can come out of this. Keep playing and playing hard.' " At Purdue, he played all 40 minutes and had 15 points, a season-high 9 rebounds and 6 assists. There were a couple of forced shots that Knight sternly deducted from his account, but the balance for the day still was Calloway's best in a while. "I felt a lot better," Calloway said.

The Purdue loss made the Sunday game at Illinois essential to the Hoosiers' Big Ten championship hopes. Purdue won at home against Ohio State, so the Boilermakers

Jeff Arnold of Purdue looks for a way out against Steve Eyl and Todd Meier

Jim Rider

**Feb. 26, West Lafayette**

# Indiana 64

| | M | 3FG | AFG | FT | R | A | B | S | T | F | Pts |
|---|---|---|---|---|---|---|---|---|---|---|---|
| Thomas, f | 21 | | 6-11 | 6- 6 | 2 | 2 | 0 | 1 | 1 | 5 | 18 |
| Calloway, f | 40 | | 6-14 | 3- 6 | 9 | 6 | 0 | 0 | 3 | 1 | 15 |
| Garrett, c | 16 | | 1- 3 | 0- 1 | 4 | 1 | 0 | 0 | 1 | 5 | 2 |
| Alford, g | 39 | 1- 2 | 7-15 | 0- 0 | 2 | 1 | 0 | 2 | 1 | 3 | 15 |
| Smart, g | 22 | | 3- 7 | 0- 0 | 0 | 0 | 0 | 0 | 1 | 5 | 6 |
| Meier | 28 | | 0- 2 | 2- 2 | 4 | 0 | 0 | 1 | 2 | 4 | 2 |
| Eyl | 11 | | 0- 1 | 2- 2 | 1 | 0 | 0 | 0 | 0 | 1 | 2 |
| Hillman | 13 | 0- 1 | 1- 3 | 2- 2 | 1 | 3 | 0 | 0 | 1 | 2 | 4 |
| Freeman | 8 | 0- 1 | 0- 1 | 0- 0 | 0 | 1 | 0 | 1 | 0 | 0 | 0 |
| Smith | 2 | | 0- 0 | 0- 0 | 0 | 0 | 0 | 0 | 0 | 0 | 0 |
| Team | | | | | 4 | | | | | | |
| **Totals** | | 1- 4 | 24-57 | 15-19 | 27 | 14 | 0 | 5 | 10 | 26 | 64 |

# Purdue 75

| | M | 3FG | AFG | FT | R | A | B | S | T | F | Pts |
|---|---|---|---|---|---|---|---|---|---|---|---|
| Mitchell, f | 28 | | 5- 8 | 7- 8 | 5 | 2 | 0 | 1 | 1 | 4 | 17 |
| Lee, f | 37 | 3- 7 | 4- 8 | 0- 1 | 3 | 2 | 0 | 0 | 0 | 3 | 11 |
| McCants, c | 28 | | 2- 6 | 0- 2 | 6 | 2 | 0 | 0 | 2 | 4 | 4 |
| Lewis, g | 38 | 2- 2 | 2- 6 | 12-14 | 6 | 4 | 1 | 1 | 3 | 0 | 18 |
| Stephens, g | 31 | 2- 2 | 4- 6 | 4- 5 | 4 | 5 | 2 | 2 | 5 | 1 | 14 |
| Arnold | 21 | | 4- 6 | 0- 0 | 2 | 2 | 0 | 0 | 2 | 4 | 8 |
| T.Jones | 12 | | 1- 1 | 1- 2 | 0 | 1 | 0 | 1 | 2 | 2 | 3 |
| K.Jones | 5 | | 0- 0 | 0- 0 | 1 | 0 | 0 | 0 | 0 | 0 | 0 |
| Team | | | | | 2 | | | | | | |
| **Totals** | | 7-11 | 22-41 | 24-32 | 29 | 18 | 3 | 5 | 15 | 18 | 75 |

| SCORE BY HALVES | | | 3FG | AFG | FT |
|---|---|---|---|---|---|
| Indiana (23-3, 14-2) | 28 | 36—64 | .250 | .421 | .789 |
| Purdue (22-3, 13-2) | 37 | 38—75 | .636 | .537 | .750 |

**Officials**—Jim Bain, Gray Muncy, Ron Winter.
**Attendance**—14,123 (sellout).

were 14-2 with just two games left: road games at Michigan State and Michigan. An Indiana loss at Illinois would drop the Hoosiers to 14-3 with one game left: at home against Ohio State.

And that's what happened. Illinois, which couldn't get a close game to come out its way against the top contenders until it was out of the race, gave senior stars Ken Norman and Doug Altenberger a winning home finale by beating Indiana, 69-67. Norman and Altenberger contributed immensely, Norman with 24 points including a brilliant first-half stretch and Altenberger with 20 points, including 6 fiendishly timed three-pointers.

Illinois jumped out 13-6, then heard some early disgust from its full house of loyalists by getting outscored 18-3 in a four-minute stretch to drop back, 24-16. Altenberger steadied the ship with a three-point basket, and then Norman showed Dean Garrett the rave reviews he had heard weren't overstated. In 5½ minutes, he burned Garrett and the Hoosiers for six field goals and Illinois went up 40-36 at halftime. The Illinois lead reached 50-40 after Norman struck for six more points in the first 2½ minutes of the second half, but Indiana

strung eight points — one field goal each by Keith Smart and Garrett, two field goals by Calloway — to tie the game, 57-57, with 7:30 to go. At 59-all, Altenberger hit a three-point basket. Calloway cut the Illini lead to 62-61 with two free throws, and Altenberger hit another three-pointer. Altenberger said the three-point baskets came after he muttered to himself, "Dammit, they're not going to *come* back." The Illini had let leads of 22 and 16 points get away in home losses to Iowa and Purdue.

Even after the two Altenberger shots, Indiana caught up at 65-65, on two free throws by Thomas and a basket by Alford at 2:39. The backbreakers for the Hoosiers didn't come from either senior. Seven-foot center Jens Kujawa, a red-shirt sophomore from West Germany, looped in a hook over Garrett to break the tie. After Calloway drove into traffic and missed a forced shot from in close, Kujawa cleared the rebound, got himself fouled, and sank both free throws to put the Illini up 69-65 with 1:47 to play.

After a timeout, Indiana pulled out a play that may have been a first in the Knight era: an alley-oop pass to a guard. Alford threw, Smart slipped in behind 5-10 Tony Wysinger and caught — high above the rim. Smart slammed home a dunk and the Illini lead was 69-67 with 1:32 to go. With 52 seconds left, Illinois lost the ball out of bounds, and Knight elected to go for sudden victory: Run the clock down and try to get an Alford three-point shot. Alford wound up trapped along the baseline in the left corner, and he had to squirm his way into two-point range even to get a forced shot up. It missed, freshman Steve Bardo rebounded, and Illinois was in.

Later, Knight ran and reran films of the play — for himself, his staff, then Alford and the team. When time came to kick in the offense, with about 10 seconds left on the shot clock, Alford had the ball at the top of the key. He looked left, and dribbled that way, looking for a screen. Calloway came out to try to

*Nobody said anything. Everybody was down. I was thinking, We blew it. Now it's not in our hands any more*

— Rick Calloway

**Trainer Tim Garl gives Rick Calloway's tender right knee one more checkout**

John Terhune

help but brought his man into an accidental double-team. The play never had a chance.

Back up the film. Give Alford a fake left, then a drive right. Kujawa had come up to support Altenberger on Alford, and Garrett was open behind him to roll to the basket. Or, drive Alford left, then reverse the ball to Smart. The left side of the court is jammed with Illini, and Smart is left to operate in open court against Wysinger — for a jump shot, maybe a three-pointer, if Wysinger backs off, for a drive if he doesn't. Each run of the film was a painful reminder that all the wrong choices were made, but the right options were there. The education of a team, even of its all-America player, went right up to the end.

Knight chose to ride back to Bloomington by car. The Hoosiers flew home, and the atmosphere in the airplane was no noisier than it would have been if Knight had been along. "Nobody said anything," Calloway said. "Everybody was down. I was thinking, 'We blew it. Now it's not in our hands any more.'" Purdue was in position to freeze the Hoosiers out by winning its two road games. "All I was thinking about was that we were ending the season on a down note again, just like last year." Inevitably, that dark thought

crossed every mind in the airplane. "We were 14-1 and all of a sudden 14-3 and no longer in first place in the Big Ten," Alford said. "For the first time all year, we had to get help from somebody else."

Purdue clinched a tie by winning Wednesday night at Michigan State. Indiana was preparing for Ohio State with a new lineup. For the second time in five games, Knight had decided Calloway — because of the knee or whatever — wasn't producing, and he prepared Kreigh Smith to start to offer an outside scoring threat. Knight works six or seven players with the red-shirted first unit in practice and occasionally mixes another player or two from the white-shirts. Calloway wasn't in the picture. "I was on the white team all week," he said. "Coach didn't say a word to me the whole week of practice. I'd rather have him yelling at me than not saying a word. I would make a bad play or a good play and he wouldn't say a word. I was just . . . kinda . . . out there."

Indiana's game with Ohio State was the first half of a final-day Big Ten TV doubleheader. CBS had opted to take Purdue-Michigan as the featured second game. For a rematch, Indiana-Ohio State had some new angles. The Hoosiers weren't going to escape taking on Buckeye star Dennis Hopson this time. No 4-point, 10-minute game for the man averaging 30. That also was some of the thinking involving Smith: He probably would do a better defensive job on Hopson than Calloway, although no one in the league had held him under 21 with any sort of defense. Smith did all right in that role. Early in the game, he stopped a two-on-one break, then stole a pass aimed for Hopson, who didn't score until Smith fouled him on a shot attmpt with 11:06 to go in the half. His free throws put Ohio State ahead, 16-15, and Calloway replaced Keith Smart in the Indiana lineup.

Smart, though respected considerably more by the Buckeyes this time, still had sliced through the

**March 1, Champaign**

## Indiana 67

| | M | 3FG | AFG | FT | R | A | B | S | T | F | Pts |
|---|---|---|---|---|---|---|---|---|---|---|---|
| Thomas, f | 22 | | 1- 2 | 2- 3 | 2 | 0 | 0 | 1 | 2 | 4 | 4 |
| Calloway, f | 35 | | 2- 7 | 4- 7 | 3 | 4 | 1 | 1 | 1 | 2 | 8 |
| Garrett, c | 40 | | 8-15 | 1- 2 | 8 | 0 | 4 | 0 | 2 | 3 | 17 |
| Alford, g | 40 | 1- 4 | 6-16 | 4- 5 | 3 | 8 | 0 | 1 | 4 | 2 | 17 |
| Smart, g | 40 | 1- 1 | 9-13 | 0- 0 | 6 | 3 | 0 | 1 | 4 | 2 | 19 |
| Eyl | 9 | | 1- 1 | 0- 0 | 1 | 1 | 0 | 0 | 0 | 1 | 2 |
| Hillman | 2 | | 0- 0 | 0- 0 | 0 | 0 | 0 | 0 | 1 | 1 | 0 |
| Pelkowski | 1 | | 0- 1 | 0- 0 | 0 | 0 | 0 | 0 | 0 | 1 | 0 |
| Smith | 11 | | 0- 0 | 0- 0 | 1 | 1 | 0 | 1 | 1 | 1 | 0 |
| Team | | | | | 2 | | | | | | |
| Totals | | 2- 5 | 27-55 | 11-17 | 26 | 17 | 5 | 5 | 15 | 17 | 67 |

## Illinois 69

| | M | 3FG | AFG | FT | R | A | B | S | T | F | Pts |
|---|---|---|---|---|---|---|---|---|---|---|---|
| Norman, f | 40 | | 10-17 | 4- 5 | 8 | 2 | 2 | 1 | 2 | 3 | 24 |
| Altenberger, f | 40 | 6-10 | 7-12 | 0- 0 | 4 | 0 | 1 | 1 | 2 | 1 | 20 |
| Kujawa, c | 26 | | 2- 5 | 2- 3 | 6 | 2 | 0 | 1 | 2 | 2 | 6 |
| Wysinger, g | 32 | | 4-12 | 2- 2 | 1 | 5 | 0 | 2 | 4 | 2 | 10 |
| Bardo, g | 37 | | 2- 5 | 1- 4 | 7 | 7 | 3 | 3 | 3 | 4 | 5 |
| Hamilton | 14 | | 1- 3 | 0- 1 | 4 | 0 | 2 | 1 | 2 | 5 | 2 |
| Blackwell | 9 | | 1- 5 | 0- 0 | 3 | 0 | 0 | 0 | 1 | 1 | 2 |
| Gill | 2 | | 0- 0 | 0- 0 | 0 | 0 | 0 | 0 | 0 | 0 | 0 |
| Team | | | | | 3 | | | | | | |
| Totals | | 6-10 | 27-59 | 9-15 | 36 | 16 | 8 | 9 | 16 | 18 | 69 |

| SCORE BY HALVES | | | 3FG | AFG | FT |
|---|---|---|---|---|---|
| Indiana (23-4, 14-3) | 36 31 | —67 | .400 | .491 | .647 |
| Illinois (21-7, 11-5) | 40 29 | —69 | .600 | .458 | .600 |

**Officials**—Joe Silvester, Jim Burr, Tim Higgins.
**Attendance**—16,793 (sellout).

**AP poll**

**After weekend games March 2**

| | | |
|---|---|---|
| 1. Nevada-LV (50) | 30-1 | 1244 |
| 2. North Carolina (13) | 27-2 | 1210 |
| 3. Purdue | 23-3 | 1118 |
| 4. Indiana | 23-4 | 946 |
| 5. DePaul | 25-2 | 945 |
| 6. Iowa | 25-4 | 935 |
| 7. Georgetown | 23-4 | 914 |
| 8. Temple | 29-3 | 848 |
| 9. Alabama | 23-4 | 799 |
| 10. Syracuse | 24-5 | 654 |
| • • • | | |
| 12. Illinois | 21-7 | 577 |
| 14. Duke | 22-7 | 360 |
| 20. Notre Dame | 19-7 | 104 |

*I think Hopson is the best player I've seen this year. I think Alford is the most valuable player in the Big Ten.*

— Bob Knight

## Milestone

This year's co-championship pulled Indiana and Purdue a little farther ahead of the rest of the Big Ten in the league's all-time standings. Indiana retains a tiny lead in won-lost percentages, the Hoosiers' working out to 58.04 to Purdue's 57.97. The two are at the top in other ways, too. Purdue retains an edge over Indiana in overall Big Ten basketball titles (17-16). Indiana shares the lead with Ohio State in outright league championships at 9. Purdue has won 8 titles outright and shared the other 9.

### All-time Big Ten standings

|           | W   | L   | Pct.  | Ch. | CC |
|-----------|-----|-----|-------|-----|----|
| Indiana   | 610 | 441 | .5804 | 9   | 7  |
| Purdue    | 629 | 456 | .5797 | 8   | 9  |
| Illinois  | 629 | 473 | .571  | 6   | 6  |
| Ohio State| 531 | 483 | .524  | 9   | 4  |
| Michigan  | 498 | 468 | .516  | 7   | 5  |
| Iowa      | 512 | 497 | .507  | 4   | 4  |
| Mich. St. | 279 | 295 | .486  | 2   | 3  |
| Minnesota | 526 | 567 | .481  | 4   | 3  |
| Wisconsin | 493 | 607 | .448  | 6   | 7  |
| No'western| 378 | 674 | .359  | 1   | 1  |
|           |     | ● ● ● |     |     |    |
| Chicago   | 168 | 296 | .362  | 4   | 2  |

Bucks for three field goals before being pulled. As soon as he sat down, trainer Tim Garl put an ice pack on his neck. Mystery deepened. "He was so excited," Knight said. "It's the first time that some members of his family have seen him play in person. He hyperventilated. We had a hell of a time getting him back into a position where he could play." Later, Knight said he didn't mean to link the two factors together: The family was there; he hyperventilated. Cause-and-effect not established. Smart linked them. "It was the first time my mother has *ever* gotten a chance to see me play," he said. "I didn't play in high school. I wanted to do everything so well right away, it just caught up with me. I got so tired. I couldn't breathe. I just got superoverheated. I had to settle down."

After his practice week, Calloway didn't expect such an early call. He scored two free throws two minutes after entering the game to break a 20-20 tie. Ohio State led 31-30 when the Buckeyes scored seven quick points, the last three on a long-distance shot by Hopson after Calloway had lost a basket to a traveling call. Suddenly, Indiana was down 38-30 in a game it had to win to have any Big Ten chance, and the Hoosiers' first-half closers struck again — a nine-point run, started by a three-point play, climaxed by a three-point shot by Smith. Ohio State regained the lead by halftime, 40-39, on two free throws by Jay Burson, but the Hoosiers were alive. They got critically ill again in a hurry in the second half. Ohio State restored the eight-point lead at 56-48 and still had it, 69-61, as the game entered the final 10 minutes.

In 2½ minutes, the game was tied, 71-71, on six points by Calloway and four by Thomas. A three-point play by Curtis Wilson put Ohio State up, 76-75, with 6:02 to go, but Alford answered with one at 5:27 for a 78-76 lead. The last tie was 78-78. Smart broke it with two free throws at 4:44. Garrett rebounded a Hopson miss and hit a free throw for an 81-78 lead. The Buckeyes were still

alive at 84-80 when Wilson tried to float a pass from out-of bounds to Hopson. Calloway anticipated the pass, made the interception with a leap, then drove to the Indiana end, two-on-one with Alford on the other side. For an instant, Calloway seemed to be pulling up to run some time off, then he accelerated again, drove to the basket and banked in a soft jump shot for an 86-80 lead. "That was a great, key play, made with confidence and ability," Ohio State coach Gary Williams said. Indiana got points from every player on-court in the last five minutes and won, 90-81.

The breathing room at the end gave Knight a chance to give the crowd one of the treats it had come for: the opportunity to give Alford a roaring, emotional, standing ovation when he came out of a game at The Hall for the last time. He came out with 13 seconds to go, as Smart was shooting two free throws, and Knight led the reception line on the sidelines, wrapping Alford in an embrace. The same break let Knight get Thomas off, to the same kind of cheers and the same sideline reception.

Hopson closed out his Big Ten scoring championship with 25 points, and Ohio State (19-12) moved on into the NCAA tournament. After the game, Knight chose his words carefully. "I think Hopson is an outstanding player, the best player I've seen this year. I think Alford is the most valuable player in the Big Ten because of what he has meant to our team. I think a most valuable player has to be on a team that has contended for or won a championship. But the only player I think I've seen who can do the things that Hopson can do so often was (Magic) Johnson at Michigan State — and he was not the shooting threat that Hopson is. Hopson is a great basketball player." Almost two months later, the votes came in and Knight had called it. Hopson won the league coaches' award as the outstanding player, but when voting was done for the silver basketball that goes to the Big Ten's Most

Valuable Player, Alford was the winner — Indiana's ninth player to do it and Knight's seventh. No other Big Ten school has had more than five recipients of the 42-year-old award.

Against the Buckeyes, Calloway had scored 20 points in 24 minutes to match his high for the year — achieved in the other Ohio State game. Smart had 14 points, including 8-for-8 on free throws. Garrett scored just nine points but had nine rebounds and four blocks to finish as the Big Ten's leader in blocked shots with 51, just three off the record (Randy Breuer, Minnesota, 1983).

The final home game at IU during the Knight era, however, has belonged to the seniors. The last game ends and no one leaves. Farewell talks by the senior players is as much a part of the tradition as is winning that last game for them. Only once in the building's 16 years was there a last-day loss. Naturally, it was in the 1984-85 season, but even that loss was honorable. The Hoosiers played one of their best games of the season but lost to already-crowned champion Michigan on a last-second shot by Gary Grant, 73-71.

Knight opened the ceremonies: "We've had some great players stand where these three kids are, some players who I think, both on the basketball floor and off the basketball court here in the university, and then later whether they were playing professionally in the NBA or in business or whatever endeavor they went into, have represented Indiana, Indiana University and Indiana basketball to the absolute highest degree.

"We have three kids here today who I think carry that on. I'm going to let them speak to you in reverse alphabetical order." There was laughter because of who that meant would be last. The Hall crowd's *piece de resistance.*

"Daryl Thomas will be speaking to you first. Where's Mrs. Thomas? We had a little problem getting Daryl going to class in November. I talked to Mrs. Thomas and Mr. Thomas

Larry Crewell

**Dennis Hopson looks for an opening in a 25-point performance against Kreigh Smith and Indiana**

about this up in Gary, and Mrs. Thomas just looked at me and said, 'Coach, you do whatever has to be done.' Mrs. Thomas, I think it has worked out pretty good, don't you?

"You've seen Todd Meier play the last two years on a couple of knees that are hard to walk on let alone play basketball on, and I think over the four years that he has played for us, Todd has made an incredible number of big plays in games that were very, very important. Todd's father is a Lutheran minister, and one thing for sure, he leaves Indiana with a much broader vocabulary than he brought here.

"And then, as I've said, there have been a lot of great kids, a lot of good players and a few great players that have been on this floor and in this position the last 15 years, and I really believe Steve is one of those great players." Prolonged applause agreed.

"There will probably be a time, Steve, when we're working on our defense, and we don't get back in to get the ball, and I might quickly say, 'Dammit, Alford would have had

| Big Ten | | |
|---------|---|---|
| **Final** | | |
| 1. Indiana | 15- 3 | 30- 4 |
| Purdue | 15- 3 | 25- 5 |
| 3. Iowa | 14- 4 | 30- 5 |
| 4. Illinois | 13- 5 | 23- 8 |
| 5. Michigan | 10- 8 | 20-12 |
| 6. Ohio State | 9- 9 | 21-13 |
| 7. Michigan State | 6-12 | 11-17 |
| 8. Wisconsin | 4-14 | 14-16 |
| 9. Minnesota | 2-16 | 9-19 |
| Northwestern | 2-16 | 7 21 |

**Ohioan Steve Eyl battles Buckeyes for a rebound**

John Terhune

March 7, Assembly Hall

# Ohio State 81

| | M | 3FG | AFG | FT | R | A | B | S | T | F | Pts |
|---|---|---|---|---|---|---|---|---|---|---|---|
| Hopson, f | 37 | 2- 6 | 9-21 | 5- 6 | 9 | 4 | 1 | 1 | 4 | 4 | 25 |
| Francis, f | 33 | | 7-10 | 0- 0 | 6 | 1 | 0 | 2 | 1 | 4 | 14 |
| Anderson, c | 28 | | 1- 6 | 4- 4 | 8 | 0 | 0 | 0 | 1 | 5 | 6 |
| Wilson, g | 33 | 1- 2 | 8-18 | 4- 5 | 4 | 2 | 0 | 0 | 3 | 4 | 21 |
| Burson, g | 28 | | 4- 5 | 2- 3 | 3 | 3 | 0 | 1 | 2 | 5 | 10 |
| White | 9 | | 0- 1 | 0- 0 | 3 | 0 | 0 | 0 | 0 | 1 | 0 |
| Wesson | 15 | | 0- 0 | 0- 1 | 1 | 1 | 1 | 0 | 0 | 2 | 0 |
| Lomax | 16 | 0- 1 | 2- 4 | 1- 2 | 2 | 0 | 0 | 0 | 2 | 4 | 5 |
| Martin | 1 | | 0- 0 | 0- 0 | 0 | 0 | 0 | 0 | 0 | 0 | 0 |
| Team | | | | | 2 | | | | 1 | | |
| **Totals** | | 3- 9 | 31-65 | 16-19 | 38 | 11 | 2 | 4 | 14 | 29 | 81 |

# Indiana 90

| | M | 3FG | AFG | FT | R | A | B | S | T | F | Pts |
|---|---|---|---|---|---|---|---|---|---|---|---|
| Thomas, f | 34 | | 5- 9 | 6- 7 | 10 | 1 | 1 | 1 | 1 | 3 | 16 |
| Smith, f | 22 | 2- 2 | 2- 6 | 0- 0 | 3 | 1 | 0 | 1 | 0 | 1 | 6 |
| Garrett, c | 28 | | 4- 8 | 1- 2 | 9 | 0 | 4 | 0 | 1 | 2 | 9 |
| Alford, g | 39 | 2- 7 | 6-13 | 8-10 | 2 | 3 | 0 | 1 | 0 | 0 | 22 |
| Smart, g | 35 | 0- 1 | 3-10 | 8- 8 | 5 | 5 | 0 | 1 | 4 | 3 | 14 |
| Calloway | 24 | | 6-14 | 8- 9 | 2 | 1 | 1 | 2 | 2 | 3 | 20 |
| Meier | 3 | | 0- 1 | 0- 0 | 0 | 0 | 0 | 1 | 0 | 2 | 0 |
| Eyl | 14 | | 1- 3 | 1- 1 | 2 | 1 | 1 | 0 | 1 | 2 | 3 |
| Hillman | 1 | | 0- 0 | 0- 0 | 0 | 0 | 0 | 0 | 0 | 0 | 0 |
| Team | | | | | 4 | | | | | | |
| **Totals** | | 4-10 | 27-64 | 32-37 | 37 | 12 | 7 | 7 | 9 | 16 | 90 |

| SCORE BY HALVES | | | 3FG | AFG | FT |
|---|---|---|---|---|---|
| Ohio St. (19-12, 9-9) | 40 | 41—81 | .333 | .477 | .842 |
| Indiana (24-4, 15-3) | 39 | 51—90 | .400 | .422 | .865 |

**Technical foul**—Burson.
**Officials**—Bob Showalter, Ed Hightower, Sid Rodeheffer.
**Attendance**—17,289 (sellout).

that.' I might have slipped up. I might have meant Randy Wittman and your name came out by mistake. But it will be because, Steve, you're on my mind as one of the truly great basketball players that we've had here."

Thomas stepped to the microphone with the eagerness of an entertainer. "I would like to thank the former players I've had an opportunity to play with. You've brought me along, taught me the ways of IU, the tradition, and all the coach's ways, of course. I'd really like to thank them, and most of all the players who are playing now, especially the newcomers who have really made a contribution and some of the young players who are going to have their time.

"I'd like to thank the coaches, of course, Coach Knight for giving me the opportunity to play here. I really think if I didn't come here, my abilities and my talents would not have been brought out the way they have been. I'm not saying I'm a great player, but I could have been a lot worse than I am now.

"I'd also like to thank you fans for your support. Keep it up like you always have. I'd like for you to bring these young guys along, because I don't know about a few of them.

"This has been my best year. I've really enjoyed it.

"I've saved the best for last — my parents. I love you, mom and dad."

Meier stepped up in a role different from the other two's. The knee problems Knight cited made Meier a reserve, one for whom Knight created a special role. Most of his playing time came late in the first half, when Knight was saving fouls on Garrett, and a trademark of the season was how frequently Meier, Steve Eyl, Joe Hillman and others in similar roles combined with a starter or two to give the Hoosiers a surge closing out the half. Meier also was the team's only husband and father. He married his high school sweetheart, and on Nov. 9, Sunday of the week that wound up with the Hoosiers making their debut against the Soviet Union, Kris Meier gave birth to daughter Morgan. Both were there, along with Meier's parents, and he started with them in spreading his thank yous around to include IU's Academic Counseling Department and coaches. "I've made a lot of friends here. I would have liked to have played more, but I couldn't. I thank the team for a great season, and I wish Steve and Daryl the best of luck."

It took a while before Alford could start. It was a date many in the stands had awaited, with some eagerness and some dread, almost since the day Alford began one of the most popular careers in IU athletic history.

He had a thank you list similar to the others: family, IU people, coaches. "Coach Knight has helped me an awful lot. I don't even have words to say appreciation and thanks . . . the Olympic Games, just being invited to the Olympic Trials was a special treat — for a 19-year-old freshman that meant everything. Going through the trials and being elected to that team meant an awful lot. He has opened up an awful lot of doors to me and designed an awful lot of things on the floor for me.

"Like Daryl, I'd like to thank all the former players. They've been tremendous. An awful lot of them have come back to support us, and I think that shows a loyalty to the program, the interest they have in the players here. I deeply appreciate all the former players that I had a chance to play with and even before, when the tradition really started.

"One thing Dan Dakich (a graduate assistant coach and a teammate of Alford's his first two seasons) told me was, 'Whatever you do, don't look up at your parents.' I just don't think I can do that, because of what they've meant to me and done for me. They know how much I love them. They know the support they've given me. I can't express that in words. I know my brother (Sean) is sitting over here. He knows how much I think of him . . . how much I care for him.

"Last and definitely most important, I just want to thank the Good

Lord for all the things that He has done for me.

"And finally, to all of you, I haven't really had the chance to say thank you, but it's been an unbelievable four years, the support that you've given us. We were undefeated here at home this year and I think you had an awful lot to do with it. This was a game we desperately needed and we wanted to play well in. Now, hopefully, we'll go into the NCAA on a good note. I didn't think I could ever make myself say this, but let's go home and root for Michigan."

By then, it was almost unnecessary. Ten minutes into the game, Michigan had a stranglehold on the Boilermakers and never let up in a 104-68 massacre. The Hoosiers — and their three senior captains who were so eager to avoid being Knight's first recruits to go four years without a title — had their co-championship. "Our big theme was not to let anyone win the title outright, even though some of our players were against Indiana getting a tie," Michigan coach Bill Frieder said in Ann Arbor. Loved, right to the end.

**Continuing a personal tradition, Bob Knight gives Ohio State star Dennis Hopson a few farewell words before the senior's last game against Indiana**

John Terhune

# 9 Hoosiers' Dome

**Trainer Tim Garl checks out an ankle problem that bothered Kreigh Smith from pre-season off and on through the season. Smith, a sophomore, got a starting assignment against Ohio State star Dennis Hopson in the last regular-season game.**

It didn't take long for the benefits of Senior Saturday to begin stacking up for Indiana's co-Big Ten champions. A day later, the NCAA's Tournament Committee released site assignments and pairings, and Indiana was the Midwest Regional's No. 1 seed. It meant several things, among them that in every game leading up to the Final Four, the Hoosiers would be wearing the white home uniforms in which they had gone 15-0 — 16-0, counting the pre-season game with the Soviet Union. It also meant they really would be the home team in the first two rounds, at the Hoosier Dome in Indianapolis.

It was an assignment that seemed to be destined for Purdue, right up to the Boilermakers' 104-68 crushing at Michigan on the final day of the season. Purdue wound up with the No. 3 seed in the East Regional, paired with Northeastern. Tournament committee chairman Richard Schultz, athletic director at Virginia and former basketball coach at Iowa, hinted broadly that Indiana and Purdue exchanged assignments, because of Purdue's loss. Purdue coach Gene Keady, upset with the NCAA when his team had to play early-round games against home teams at Memphis State and Louisiana State in two of the three previous tournaments, said he doubted that. Some way, he felt, the NCAA was going to figure out a way to get Indiana into the Hoosier Dome to try to sell as many as possible of the building's 43,000 tickets. More likely, the committee — anticipating a Purdue victory over Michigan that would have meant an outright Big Ten championship and, probably, No. 2 finish in the national polls — had Purdue sketched in at the Hoosier Dome, Indiana as the No. 2 seed in the West and Iowa as No. 3 in the East. When the Boilermakers lost, so badly, Indiana inherited the Hoosier Dome spot, but the No. 2 seed in the West stood a chance of running into Arizona on its Tucson court, and the Purdue outrage over its 1984 and '86 assignments ruled that out. So, Iowa and Purdue were swapped. No one from the Tournament Committee said that, but it's a justifiable guess.

In Bloomington, nobody cared about all that. Indiana was going to Indianapolis, its home away from home. Indiana has played at least one game in Indianapolis every year

Larry Crewell

since Market Square Arena opened in the 1974-75 season. The last five seasons, the Hoosiers have been hosts to the Hoosier Classic there. In the Bob Knight era, Indiana hasn't lost to a collegiate team in Indianapolis — a 19-0 record going into the tournament, counting a 1971-72 victory at Butler.

The eight teams gathered for the Indianapolis games didn't have to wait long to get an idea of the grip IU basketball has on the city. Each team was given an hour for an open practice in the Dome on Wednesday, the day before the tournament began. When Indiana's turn came, on late-afternoon of a normal Indianapolis work day, an estimated 15,000 people were in the stands. Mitch Buonaguro, an assistant to Rollie Massimino when Villanova won the 1985 NCAA championship, brought his Fairfield team into Indianapolis to meet Indiana in the first round and he said, "I've emphasized to my team we can't get caught up in the Indiana mystique." Asked for a definition, he gave 15,000. He had just come into the press room from the main arena with its red-sea turnout for Indiana's practice. "That's what I'm talking about," Buonaguro said. "That's the Indiana mystique. Indiana basketball is world-renowned. Bobby Knight is a great coach. He has a great program. He has great players. He wins every year. He has a 75 percent winning percentage. He produces first-round draft choices. He plays before 18,000 people every game. When you talk about the premier programs, Indiana is right there every year. I just hope our kids don't get caught up in that."

They didn't. The Stags, champions of the Metro Atlantic Athletic Conference tournament, just didn't have enough manpower. They came in 15-15, even with their three tournament victories. They never quit trying, but they were down 46-21 at halftime and lost, 92-58.

Calloway was back in the lineup, and he was determined to stay there. First time downcourt, he drove to an opening on the left baseline and sank a 10-foot jump shot. He hit his

first four shots to escort Indiana to a 10-6 lead. He went on to score 17 points with a team-high 9 rebounds. "Calloway hurt us," Buonaguro said. "He's a very good player. He's got to be one of the top players in the Big Ten when he's playing right. Tonight he was."

Fairfield's defensive priority was stopping Steve Alford. "I thought we contained Alford pretty good," Buonaguro said. Alford took only five shots in his 25 minutes on-court, hitting four — two-for-two from three-point range. He scored 13 points, Daryl Thomas 14 and Dean Garrett, the starter given most chance to play (32 minutes) 20 points, with seven rebounds. "Defensively, Fairfield had to make some decisions, as we all do," Knight said. "Their decision was to play Steve and Daryl as hard as they could. Ricky had openings and he took advantage of them, right off the bat."

Of the 14 Hoosiers who got in the game, only one didn't score. Todd

Larry Crewell

For freshman Tony Freeman, it was mostly a year to sit and wait — though not usually on the court. Freeman, whose 13 assists against Northwestern was this year's Big Ten high, played 17 minutes and scored 4 points in Indiana's tournament-opening victory over Fairfield.

## Milestone

Daryl Thomas's first basket in Indiana's NCAA tournament opener against Fairfield made him the 24th Hoosier to score 1,000 points. Thomas had 999 when he scored with 12:50 to go in the half, putting Indiana ahead 12-6 in a game the Hoosiers won, 92-58, Thomas scoring 14.

Jeff Gromos, a midwesterner (Joliet, Ill.), scored 21 points and claimed 11 rebounds, including this one over IU sixth-man Steve Eyl. Gromos couldn't keep his Fairfield team close in a 92-58 victory that started Indiana down the NCAA tournament trail.

Larry Crewell

Meier wasn't concerned about that. Long before, Meier had made peace with himself on the totally different role he would play as compared with the one he dreamed of as an all-state player at Oshkosh, Wis., Lourdes Academy. That was quite a year in Wisconsin. The first-five all-state team that year included Meier, who averaged 23 points and 14 rebounds; Joe Wolf, who went on to star at North Carolina, and J. J. Weber and Rod Ripley, three-year starters at Wisconsin. Each of the four was 6-foot-6 or better. Wisconsin ranks low in most evaluators' esteem for annual production of high school stars — in comparison with Indiana, Illinois, Michigan and Ohio, for example — but that one year turned out more good college front-court players than Indiana has for a good many years.

That was the reason why Knight went outside his usual Indiana, Ohio and Illinois recruiting base to bring Meier in, and it was the reason

**NCAA MIDWEST FIRST ROUND**
March 12, Indianapolis

# Fairfield 58

| | M | 3FG | AFG | FT | R | A | B | S | T | F | Pts |
|---|---|---|---|---|---|---|---|---|---|---|---|
| O'Toole, f | 24 | | 2- 7 | 3- 5 | 3 | 0 | 0 | 2 | 1 | 5 | 7 |
| Duncan, f | 25 | | 1- 3 | 0- 0 | 1 | 1 | 0 | 0 | 2 | 2 | 2 |
| Gromos, c | 39 | | 8-19 | 5- 8 | 11 | 2 | 0 | 1 | 3 | 3 | 21 |
| Wynder, g | 34 | 0- 2 | 4-12 | 7- 9 | 5 | 3 | 0 | 2 | 6 | 4 | 15 |
| Golden, g | 33 | | 5- 7 | 1- 1 | 5 | 3 | 0 | 0 | 5 | 3 | 11 |
| Bradford | 19 | 0- 2 | 0- 6 | 0- 0 | 1 | 0 | 0 | 0 | 1 | 2 | 0 |
| Woodtli | 14 | | 0- 1 | 0- 0 | 1 | 0 | 0 | 0 | 0 | 5 | 0 |
| Cook | 3 | | 0- 0 | 0- 0 | 0 | 0 | 0 | 0 | 0 | 1 | 0 |
| Walters | 5 | | 0- 1 | 2- 2 | 0 | 0 | 0 | 0 | 2 | 0 | 2 |
| Barry | 4 | | 0- 0 | 0- 0 | 0 | 0 | 0 | 0 | 0 | 2 | 0 |
| Team | | | | | 2 | | | | | | |
| Totals | | 0- 4 | 20-56 | 18-25 | 29 | 9 | 0 | 5 | 20 | 27 | 58 |

# Indiana 92

| | M | 3FG | AFG | FT | R | A | B | S | T | F | Pts |
|---|---|---|---|---|---|---|---|---|---|---|---|
| Thomas, f | 21 | | 6- 8 | 2- 2 | 2 | 0 | 1 | 1 | 2 | 2 | 14 |
| Calloway, f | 27 | | 6-11 | 5- 5 | 8 | 3 | 1 | 2 | 2 | 2 | 17 |
| Garrett, c | 32 | | 7-11 | 6- 8 | 7 | 0 | 2 | 2 | 3 | 2 | 20 |
| Alford, g | 25 | 2- 2 | 4- 5 | 3- 3 | 2 | 3 | 0 | 3 | 2 | 3 | 13 |
| Smart, g | 16 | 0- 1 | 1- 7 | 2- 2 | 2 | 2 | 0 | 1 | 0 | 3 | 4 |
| Smith | 5 | | 1- 1 | 0- 0 | 1 | 1 | 0 | 0 | 0 | 0 | 2 |
| Eyl | 13 | | 2- 4 | 0- 0 | 4 | 3 | 1 | 1 | 0 | 0 | 4 |
| Hillman | 13 | | 1- 1 | 0- 2 | 1 | 3 | 1 | 1 | 0 | 1 | 2 |
| Freeman | 17 | | 1- 1 | 2- 2 | 1 | 1 | 0 | 0 | 1 | 2 | 4 |
| Meier | 4 | | 0- 0 | 0- 0 | 2 | 0 | 0 | 0 | 1 | 2 | 0 |
| Pelkowski | 8 | | 1- 4 | 0- 0 | 3 | 1 | 0 | 0 | 2 | 2 | 2 |
| Sloan | 7 | | 1- 3 | 4- 4 | 3 | 0 | 0 | 0 | 1 | 0 | 6 |
| Minor | 7 | | 0- 1 | 2- 2 | 1 | 0 | 0 | 0 | 0 | 1 | 2 |
| Oliphant | 5 | | 0- 0 | 2- 3 | 3 | 1 | 0 | 0 | 0 | 1 | 2 |
| Team | | | | | 1 | | | | | | |
| Totals | | 2- 3 | 31-57 | 28-33 | 41 | 18 | 6 | 10 | 14 | 21 | 92 |

| SCORE BY HALVES | | | 3FG | AFG | FT |
|---|---|---|---|---|---|
| Fairfield (15-16) | 21 | 37—58 | .000 | .357 | .720 |
| Indiana (25-4) | 46 | 46—92 | .667 | .544 | .848 |

**Officials**—Jim Howell, Tom Fincken, Richie Ballesteros.
**Attendance**—29,610 (NCAA first-round record).

Knight later chose to add junior college players. Meier didn't hesitate, when given the chance to play at Indiana, and he was conscious even then of the possibility that things could some day work out for a national championship. "I felt coming to a program that had a tradition like this, the potential to win it was there every year," he said. "I felt coming here I'd have a chance to win some things. You put a good team together and you never know what's going to happen."

What happened to Todd Meier began that senior season in high school. "Toward the end of the season, my right knee started swelling a lot. I don't remember anything happening, twisting it or injuring it. It just started swelling. Basically, I rested it during the summer to see what would happen." On healthy legs, he was state Class B shot put champion and he placed third in the high jump. The knee wasn't any better when he reported to Indiana in the fall, so arthroscopic surgery was performed. "They found torn cartilage and it was removed. I was back in three or four weeks, and I started with everybody the first day of practice. It seemed to get better my whole freshman year. In fact, the last game of the year I didn't even wear the sleeve on my knee." Meier started six games that rookie season, including a 9-point performance in a late-season 78-59 victory at Purdue, over a Boilermaker team that was Big Ten co-champion.

As a freshman, he started the Hoosiers' NCAA tournament opener, a victory over Richmond. He didn't start the next game, the epic game — the upset of North Carolina — and he didn't score in the game. Still, it provided him with an unforgettable thrill, and a shirt. "A friend of mine was at the game. The North Carolina people were selling T-shirts after the game for $1 apiece. My friend was going to buy a whole bunch of them, but they found out he was from Indiana and they wouldn't sell him any more. He had the one, and he told me, 'I think you'll get more out of it than I ever

would,' so he gave it to me." And Meier did. The Carolina-blue jersey had the number 84, and the lettering that went with the number was brash: "1984 NCAA champions. North Carolina." At about 10 o'clock the night before every road game, Knight meets with his players briefly to answer any last-minute game-plan questions after the players have had their own session together looking one more time at film Knight and the staff had put together. The Hoosiers travel in coats and ties, but the night-before sessions are considerably more informal. To every one of those in the 1986-87 season, Meier wore the North Carolina shirt. "Up until the tournament. Then I wore my championship shirt that Coach gave us."

The North Carolina game represented a career highlight in more ways than victory. When Meier started basketball again as a sophomore, new problems developed in the knee. "It got progressively worse. They finally operated at the end of the year to smooth out the cartilage, where it was torn." That sophomore season was the one that was dismal on-court, too, and Meier couldn't contribute much. "There was a point during the year when it hurt to walk. I had two knee braces on. I got tendinitis in my left knee compensating for my right. My knees were so sore I didn't even want to get up in the morning."

After the postseason surgery, "I gave it a good two months rest. It didn't seem too bad starting my junior year, but it was real sore and it bothered me a lot." That's when he understood that he had to look at things differently. "I had to realize there were a lot of things I couldn't do. I was more limited physically. I couldn't play a real long time. I knew the time that I did put in would have to be quality time. I had to get used to not playing much, and when I did play, to try to do what I can well: to get people open to score, screen, rebound. This year, when the other guys were running for pre-season conditioning, I swam. When practice started, I only practiced every other

Cincinnati buddies Dave Minor and Rick Calloway enjoyed some pleasant bench time in mop-up minutes of Indiana's 92-58 tournament victory over Fairfield.

| UPI poll | | | |
|---|---|---|---|
| Final regular-season | | | |
| 1. Nevada-LV (39) | 33- 1 | 626 |
| 2. Indiana (2) | 24- 4 | 548 |
| 3. North Carolina | 29- 3 | 540 |
| 4. Georgetown | 26- 4 | 457 |
| 5. DePaul | 26- 2 | 395 |
| 6. Purdue | 24- 4 | 385 |
| 7. Iowa | 27- 4 | 364 |
| 8. Temple | 31- 3 | 355 |
| 9. Alabama | 26- 4 | 306 |
| 10. Syracuse | 26- 6 | 250 |

day and sometimes skipped two days, depending on how much it hurt. I think that really helped a lot. It didn't hurt as much as it did last year."

Meier saw the future when Dean Garrett arrived. Day after day, especially once the season began and Meier's practice pace returned to near-normal, the husky, 6-8 Meier bumped and jostled with 6-10 Garrett in the post area, getting him accustomed to Big Ten contact. "Playing against him, I'd try to help him out. I think everybody on the team did that: help each other do what was set up. Dean has really worked hard and improved. I remember the first day he came in last summer. He couldn't run the floor. Right away when practice started, you could see he could do a lot of things, especially defensively. At the beginning, his turn-around jump shot was more of a throw. Now, he's a real good turn-around jump shooter. He squares up. He rebounds. He plays good help defense. He has developed into a real good shot blocker. He has the potential to dominate games. He's *real* strong. He has those big shoulders. He's just a big factor in the development of this team."

Knight puts Meier in the same category. "Todd is as compelling a story as we've ever had here. No one will ever understand, not having played on Todd's knees, just how much he has endured. But in terms of a rebound, or a pass, or a basket, or a screen, he has made tremendous contributions. I know in the future I'll question how badly somebody was hurt, and you can bet I'll remember when we had Todd Meier playing for us and I knew he *was* hurt."

Meier was a somewhat anxious tri-captain entering the NCAA tournament. "There were times when we played real well in the Big Ten. We won those three games on the road in the beginning of the season, and we had that four-game home stand. I really started feeling confident in the team — I really felt good, up until the time we kinda stumbled. I wasn't

> ## *Todd (Meier) is as compelling a story as we've ever had here. He has made tremendous contributions*
> — Bob Knight

really worried about it, but I didn't have that feeling like I had in the first half of the Big Ten." One of the reasons may have been shooting. Alford wasn't the only Hoosier who finished the season a little chillier than he played most of the year. In its last six games, Indiana never shot .500, finishing four of those games at .422 or below.

That's not an item to pass over lightly. It was the longest string of sub-.500 games by any Knight team in 15 years. And it led right up to the tournament.

The Fairfield game signaled a step in a different direction. The Hoosiers shot .544.

Indiana moved from Fairfield into considerably swifter company. Auburn finished regular-season play just 17-12, but on its good days, it was astoundingly good. It had some one-sided victories over teams that made big impact on the NCAA tournament: 100-62 over Louisiana State, 115-93 over Austin Peay, 81-68 and 84-70 over Florida. Coach Sonny Smith's background included a stint in Richmond, Ind., as a high school assistant to Dick Baumgartner and another at the University of Tennessee working under former Knight assistant Don DeVoe. He had a good idea before he arrived in Indianapolis what kind of atmosphere he would encounter in Hoosierland and what kind of game Indiana would play.

The Tigers were ready. They stunned the largest crowd ever to see an NCAA first- or second-round session, 34,185, by storming out to a 24-10 lead in the first six minutes. It was awfully early, but it was farther behind than this Hoosier team ever had been and come back to win. Knight didn't think in those terms but he was concerned about how easily and quickly the points were going up for Auburn. "If they had continued to score like they did in the first six minutes, we'd have had to score 200 to win," he said. Knight replaced Daryl Thomas with Steve Eyl for a few minutes of pointed emphasis about what was happening and reinserted him 71

A game official warns Auburn center Jeff Moore to cool off during early strife in Indiana's 107-90 victory at the Hoosier Dome

Phil Whitlow

seconds later. Already by then, the Hoosiers were on their way to a thunderous turnabout that produced a 107-90 victory — which breaks down to 97-66 after the shocking start. In doing so, the Hoosiers shot .603, their best mark in two months. The point total was Indiana's first time over 100 in NCAA tournament play, and Knight made it clear it wasn't altogether by choice. "I didn't want to get into that kind of game," he said. "We wanted to start out with control and speed up the tempo in the second half. That shows you how much we were able to do what we wanted to at the start."

Alford, jostled around early as Auburn clamped on a rugged box-and-one defense, didn't score for the first 10 minutes. Then he scored 10 points in less than a two-minute stretch to zoom the Hoosiers within 38-37. Mike Jones, a 6-7 sophomore forward who had averaged 15 points a game, was doing similar things to Indiana, inside and outside. He scored 13 straight Auburn points during the period when Indiana was making its move, and he complicated things further for Indiana by

drawing a third foul on Garrett to force his exit with 5:52 to go in the half. Fourteen seconds later, Thomas pulled the Hoosiers even for the first time with a three-point play that tied the game, 40-40. Keith Smart drove through the Tigers for the basket that broke the tie and put Indiana ahead — for good, it developed.

Smart was doing lots of things. He just missed what might have been Indiana's first "triple double" — the combination that Magic Johnson has made commonplace in the NBA, double-figure performances in points, rebounds and assists in the same game. At game's end, Smart had 20 points, 9 rebounds and 15 assists — the last figure truly special. It gave him Indiana's one-game record for assists, topping such golden Hoosier names as Quinn Buckner, Bobby Wilkerson and Isiah Thomas, who had shared the mark with Stew Robinson at 14. More than that, it tied the NCAA tournament record — for any game at any level.

"I think he's an outstanding player," Smith said. The focus of Auburn's defense, of course, had been on Alford. Besides the box-and-one, the Tigers tried a triangle-and-two that included coverage of Thomas. They also used a couple of five-man zones. "I think the triangle helped Smart," Smith said, "because we weren't guarding him and that made his game more effective. That's not a negative for the young man. He was a big, big factor in the game, but the defenses we were using helped him, where they wouldn't help other people."

Smart felt Alford helped him more than any alteration of alignments by Auburn. "Steve really got his rhythm and my job was to penetrate into their zone and get him the ball. They were shading a side sometimes and giving me a lane, so I'd get in there and dump it down to either Daryl or Ricky." Alford said Smart "played exceptionally well. He did an excellent job of finding me — not only me but also our inside guys. We worked (the day before the game) on his timing, on getting me the ball on cuts and delivering it on time. He did an outstanding job."

Rhythm for Alford meant 31 points, on 10-for-17 shooting, 7-for-11 from three-point range. "We felt if we alternated people on him we'd be better off than if we let one guy guard him," Smith said. "He still had a great game. He's a great player. That's a great Indiana team."

Jones finished with 30 points but only nine in the second half. Knight credited assistant coach Kohn Smith for the defensive adjustment that slowed Jones, a switch worked out between Thomas and Garrett to get more pressure on Jones around the top of the key.

It was a rough game that came as close to breaking into a brawl as any Indiana game in years. Front-court players from both sides had to be pried apart several times, and even the pristine Alford bristled and glared a couple of times. Once, Auburn guard Gerald White gave Alford a shove, and the crowd reacted more hotly than Alford — barely. White's view: "I was getting the club together (during a free-throw lineup) to give instructions from the bench.

*After a near-brawl and some hot words, some warm words between Bob Knight and Auburn coach Sonny Smith*

He tried to get in there and listen to what was going on. He knows better than that. You don't do anything like that." Alford's view: "He pushed me away. I never stuck my neck in there at all. I was lined up there. I have every right to be there. It was like them taking a free timeout. The official said that. He told them it wasn't a timeout." As the free throw was being set up anew, White moved to a backcourt defensive position, and Alford walked back to talk to him, eye-to-eye. "I just told him, 'We don't need that. That's not part of the game.' I think he was trying to intimidate me a little."

Knight laughed at that idea. "White trying to intimidate Steve after Steve has played for me for four years is like a sparrow trying to rape an elephant."

Alford said the jostling with White was no problem. "I'm glad he did it. It got me into the game. It got everybody into the game. It was more (White's backup, Terrance) Howard than White. Howard didn't do anything but try to come out and push people around. He took a couple of cheap shots."

The temper flareups on the floor led to a midcourt confrontation between Knight and Smith. Asked at the postgame press conference what was said there, Smith's dry answer was: "I don't know who cussed first, to be honest with you. Hey, honestly, if I tried to tell you what we said . . . I can't even remember. I couldn't pass a lie detector test, either." At halftime, they met again, and Knight's recreation of that conversation ran:

Smith: "Hey, first of all, you know I wouldn't have anybody out there to do that."

Knight: "I know that, just like I wouldn't tell one of my kids to shove somebody. But I thought you did a real good job of settling things down, and I'd expect you to say something to me if one of my kids pushed somebody."

"That happens," Knight said. "That's basketball. I don't have any problem with that. And I had a lot of good feeling about Sonny's reaction, getting the whole thing settled down.

**NCAA MIDWEST SECOND ROUND**
March 14, Indianapolis

# Auburn 90

| | M | 3FG | AFG | FT | R | A | B | S | T | F | Pts |
|---|---|---|---|---|---|---|---|---|---|---|---|
| Jones, f | 36 | 1- 2 | 10-22 | 9- 9 | 9 | 1 | 0 | 1 | 2 | 1 | 30 |
| Morris, f | 22 | | 5-11 | 0- 1 | 4 | 2 | 0 | 0 | 0 | 5 | 10 |
| Moore, c | 33 | | 11-20 | 2- 2 | 10 | 1 | 0 | 1 | 0 | 4 | 24 |
| White, g | 37 | 4- 9 | 6-13 | 1- 1 | 1 | 10 | 1 | 1 | 4 | 2 | 17 |
| Ford, g | 28 | 1- 2 | 4-11 | 0- 0 | 3 | 0 | 0 | 0 | 0 | 5 | 9 |
| Howard | 19 | | 0- 4 | 0- 0 | 4 | 1 | 0 | 0 | 2 | 4 | 0 |
| Lynn | 13 | 0- 1 | 0- 4 | 0- 0 | 2 | 0 | 0 | 1 | 2 | 2 | 0 |
| Caylor | 10 | | 0- 0 | 0- 0 | 0 | 0 | 0 | 2 | 1 | 2 | 0 |
| Dennison | 2 | | 0- 1 | 0- 0 | 0 | 0 | 0 | 0 | 0 | 0 | 0 |
| Team | | | | | 1 | | | | | | |
| **Totals** | | 6-14 | 36-86 | 12-13 | 34 | 15 | 1 | 6 | 11 | 25 | 90 |

# Indiana 107

| | M | 3FG | AFG | FT | R | A | B | S | T | F | Pts |
|---|---|---|---|---|---|---|---|---|---|---|---|
| Thomas, f | 36 | | 9-14 | 9-10 | 8 | 0 | 0 | 3 | 4 | 1 | 27 |
| Calloway, f | 39 | | 7-12 | 4- 4 | 13 | 1 | 0 | 1 | 5 | 0 | 18 |
| Garrett, c | 16 | | 4- 6 | 1- 2 | 3 | 0 | 2 | 0 | 1 | 4 | 9 |
| Alford, g | 38 | 7-11 | 10-17 | 4- 5 | 3 | 5 | 0 | 0 | 2 | 2 | 31 |
| Smart, g | 39 | 0- 2 | 7-12 | 6- 7 | 9 | 15 | 0 | 1 | 5 | 3 | 20 |
| Eyl | 16 | | 0- 0 | 0- 0 | 5 | 2 | 0 | 0 | 1 | 3 | 0 |
| Meier | 9 | | 0- 0 | 0- 0 | 2 | 0 | 0 | 0 | 0 | 1 | 0 |
| Smith | 2 | | 0- 0 | 0- 0 | 0 | 0 | 0 | 0 | 0 | 0 | 0 |
| Hillman | 2 | | 1- 2 | 0- 0 | 0 | 0 | 0 | 0 | 0 | 2 | 2 |
| Sloan | 1 | | 0- 0 | 0- 0 | 1 | 0 | 0 | 0 | 0 | 0 | 0 |
| Freeman | 1 | | 0- 0 | 0- 0 | 0 | 0 | 0 | 0 | 0 | 0 | 0 |
| Minor | 1 | | 0- 0 | 0- 0 | 1 | 0 | 0 | 0 | 0 | 0 | 0 |
| Team | | | | | 1 | | | | | | |
| **Totals** | | 7-13 | 38-63 | 24-28 | 45 | 24 | 2 | 5 | 18 | 14 | 107 |

| SCORE BY HALVES | | | | 3FG | AFG | FT |
|---|---|---|---|---|---|---|
| Auburn (18-13) | 48 | 42— | 90 | .429 | .419 | .923 |
| Indiana (26-4) | 53 | 54— | 107 | .538 | .603 | .857 |

**Officials**—Rick Wulkow, Chuck Weinkauf, Rusty Herring.
**Attendance**—34,185 (NCAA second-round record).

I thought he handled it very well."

Smith spoke before Knight, and he didn't want to leave an impression of a continuing feud between the two.

"I don't want a big story about Coach Knight and I meeting at midcourt. Let me tell you a human-interest story that is of value to me. Yesterday I was blind in my left eye at practice, which is a common thing to me because of eye surgery that I've had a number of times. He (Knight) took time out from his practice to call and get the best doctor in town for me, and he stayed with me — he didn't even go out to his practice. I don't know if they were practicing, but they were supposed to be out there (on the Hoosier Dome court). To me, that is much more valuable in the coaching profession than books or what we said at midcourt, because what guys say at midcourt in the heat of battle has nothing to do with the way they feel. Yesterday was a very important thing to me because of the things that are written about different people. That was kind of a touching thing to me, for somebody to do that. I got a good doctor, and I was able to see what happened today."

Phil Whitlow

**Keith Smart heads for one of his IU-record 15 assists**

# 10 Cincinnati Kid

Joe Hillman didn't need even a minute of playing time to give the Hoosiers a vital Regional lift

John Terhune

It was amazing how sunny life looked to Rick Calloway, just nine days after the non-person status he had felt when the Hoosiers were getting to play their season finale against Ohio State. In just three games, he not only had recaptured his starting spot but also had proved to himself — and to others, with varying involvements and curiosities — that he really could play like the old Rick Calloway again.

He was reluctant to say that his benching the week before against Ohio State snapped him out of whatever late-season problems he had. "The Purdue game did that," he said. "I think I played pretty well in the Illinois game, but not as well as I could. I think the Purdue game really turned it around. Everybody was putting it around the fact that Coach Knight benched me in the Ohio State game. I didn't think so. I think my leg got stronger as the year went on, and I started not worrying about it and just going out and playing. I said, 'If I hurt it, I hurt it. No big deal.' "

However, he admitted that when his chance did come in the Ohio State game, maybe — just maybe — he did go after things with a little more determination and zeal. "I think I did. I had something to prove to myself and everybody else. People were asking 'What's wrong with you?' — if my knee was bothering me, or a girl, or whatever. I was really getting tired of people asking me. I just said, 'I'm going to try to get rid of this *today*.'

"And the Fairfield game was just as tough. I had to prove that I could do it again, and then the next game, and the next game."

The next game was coming up in

the perfect place for Rick Calloway: Cincinnati. Home. The city where he was a star at Withrow High and everyone was saying he was a Louisville kind of player when suddenly he signed with Indiana, plodding Indiana. Only Bob Knight knew that the future he had in mind for Indiana basketball was at a considerably faster pace than the Hoosiers could play with 7-foot-2 West German Uwe Blab at the hub of their offense. Calloway, he of the quick first step, represented a very quick first step for Knight in the new direction.

It paid off quickly. Calloway's 23 points in the 1985-86 opener was an IU record for a freshman in his debut, 11 more than Isiah Thomas, 11 more than Steve Alford, 13 more than Randy Wittman, 14 more than Quinn Buckner, 17 more than the record-bound Don Schlundt. The previous high for a debuting Hoosier freshman was 16 by Mike Woodson.

And now the Hoosiers had filled in some other spots, enabling them to bring a considerably quicker game with them to Cincinnati.

Calloway's return was one part of the developing story as the regional field gathered — the smaller part, by far, outside Cincinnati. The spotlight was on the matchup of coaches: Bob Knight of Indiana vs. Mike Krzyzewski of Duke. In a basketball sense, it was as much Father vs. Son as it was in January 1972 when 31-year-old Bob Knight brought his first Indiana team into Columbus to play Fred Taylor and Ohio State. Knight recruited Krzyzewski out of Weber High School in Chicago's Catholic League. Krzyzewski scored a lot of points there. He did a lot of guarding and setting up other people on Knight's Army team, and he did it so well the teams won and Krzyzewski was his captain. When Krzyzewski's military obligation was over, he entered a graduate program at Indiana and joined Knight's staff as a graduate assistant. A year later, he was the new head coach at Army, and 10 years after that he had his Duke team playing in the national championship game against Louisville — with Knight in the stands wearing a Duke button.

Duke didn't win the championship, but the sign of a program was there as the Blue Devils came back to win 22 games and return to the NCAA tournament. They whipped Texas A&M and Xavier at Indianapolis to make it to Cincinnati — and set up the first coaching meeting of Knight with one of his former players. Before even leaving the dressing room at Indianapolis, Krzyzewski warned his team about what would be coming. "I told them a lot is going to be said about Indiana and Duke, about Coach Knight and myself. I've never coached against another coach. I'm going to try to get them ready to play Alford, Smart, Thomas and the rest of those guys. Hopefully we'll see two very good basketball teams."

Billy King was a frontline reserve as a sophomore on the NCAA runnerup team. As a 6-6 junior, he had moved up to be a starter and Krzyzewski's designated defender, and he was in line to get the Steve Alford assignment. King didn't have to go back home for film-watching to have an early line on Alford. After the Xavier game, with the Indiana-Duke matchup set, he said: "I know a lot about him already. He gets a lot of picks, and you've got to stay right with him. Give him a second and it's two points . . . or three. And I can't allow myself to get overconfident if he doesn't score the first five or six minutes. He lets the ball come to him. The kind of player I compare him to is Larry Bird. He's so smart. He lets you make the mistakes."

King also had an early idea of what to expect from the Indiana coach. "I'm almost a fan of Indiana. I'm a big fan of Coach Knight. I respect him so much I'm really looking forward to this game. I've almost finished the book (*A Season on the Brink*). As soon as I finish it, I'm going to write him a letter and let him know how I feel. I don't think people realize how much he cares for his players." Both King and the one holdover Duke starter, Tommy Amaker, remembered that Knight had attended a Duke practice in Dallas the day before play began in the Final Four. They laughed when asked how Krzyzewski had introduced Knight, because they couldn't remember. "I don't think he needed an introduction," Amaker said. King remembered Knight's message. "Oh yeah, I listened. We all did. Coach Knight's got that aura about him. When he speaks, he's like E. F. Hutton. I was afraid to move."

By arrival in Cincinnati, Krzyzewski felt the media overkill on the coach vs. coach angle had peaked early in the week and faded as any sort of potential distraction for players. "That stuff is getting a little bit boring now," Krzyzewski said. "It's like, how many ways can I say 'I love you'? What you can expect from Duke is for us to do our best to beat Indiana. That's one thing I learned from him."

He learned well. He had seen in

Duke's Billy King, in an uncooperative mood on Rick Calloway's grand homecoming night

Larry Crewell

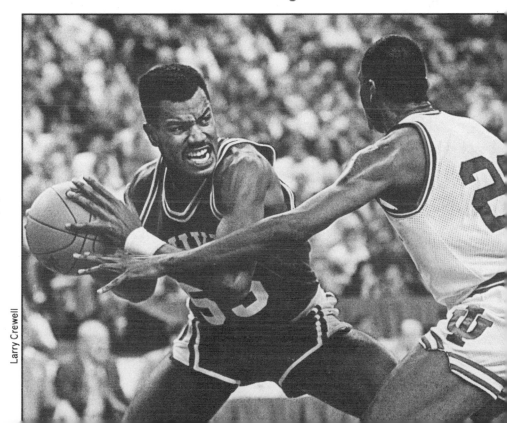

films that Purdue's victory key against Indiana was working Daryl Thomas and Dean Garrett into early foul problems. He went after the Hoosier big men from the start with 6-7 John Smith working a la the 1985-86 Thomas, with effective quickness inside. Smith had two early baskets, then six points in a row as Duke opened a 29-21 lead. Calloway, to the dismay of the home folks, was 0-for-3. Alford was 0-for-3, an indication that the King ploy was working. Except, it wasn't always King who was on Alford.

When King was on Alford, Knight wanted Alford to challenge King as he had Michigan's Gary Grant: as a ballhandler and setup man, with an occasional drive. Krzyzewski wanted his best man at pressuring the

basketball, Amaker, to take the primary ballhandler, capitalizing on Smart's inexperience as a setup man, if possible. Neither way worked out. The result was a coaching standoff: Amaker had to take ball-handler Alford. "I knew they wouldn't keep Smart in a ballhandling role," Krzyzewski said.

It was 31-24 when Alford sank his first basket of the night, then fed Calloway for a basket. Smith was called for an illegal screen and Thomas hit two free throws. Another Duke turnover blossomed into Alford's first three-point basket, and in less than two minutes the Hoosiers had gone from seven-down to a 33-31 lead. Then it was Calloway on a drive, Calloway on a 15-foot shot, Calloway on a one-and-one, Calloway on a short hook, Calloway on a jump shot. Ten minutes after appearing to be in trouble, the Hoosiers went to the dressing room up 49-39, and in the Riverfront Coliseum stands, Mother Calloway happily held up a sign, "Calloway Country."

Indiana continued to play well but couldn't shake the Blue Devils. Alford faked his way open for a jump shot that put Indiana up 76-66 with just over five minutes left. Ninety seconds later, 6-10 Danny Ferry

**Three late-game assists by high school quarterback Steve Eyl helped Indiana break away from Duke, 88-82**

John Terhune

### NCAA MIDWEST REGIONAL SEMIFINAL
March 20, Cincinnati

# Duke 82

| | M | 3FG | AFG | FT | R | A | B | S | T | F | Pts |
|---|---|---|---|---|---|---|---|---|---|---|---|
| Ferry, f | 37 | 4- 4 | 7-13 | 2- 3 | 7 | 4 | 0 | 0 | 4 | 3 | 20 |
| King, f | 28 | | 3- 5 | 0- 0 | 4 | 1 | 1 | 2 | 0 | 3 | 6 |
| Smith, c | 18 | | 4- 6 | 3- 4 | 0 | 1 | 0 | 0 | 4 | 5 | 11 |
| Amaker, g | 40 | 3- 3 | 8-17 | 4- 4 | 2 | 3 | 0 | 1 | 2 | 1 | 23 |
| Strickland, g | 32 | 1- 4 | 5-15 | 0- 0 | 6 | 1 | 1 | 1 | 2 | 5 | 11 |
| Snyder | 15 | | 0- 0 | 0- 0 | 2 | 1 | 0 | 1 | 3 | 0 | 0 |
| Brickey | 20 | | 3- 8 | 1- 2 | 5 | 0 | 1 | 1 | 0 | 3 | 7 |
| Abdelnaby | 7 | | 2- 3 | 0- 0 | 0 | 0 | 0 | 0 | 0 | 1 | 4 |
| Nessley | 3 | | 0- 0 | 0- 0 | 1 | 0 | 0 | 0 | 0 | 1 | 0 |
| Team | | | | | 3 | | | | | | |
| Totals | | 8-11 | 32-67 | 10-13 | 28 | 12 | 4 | 5 | 13 | 25 | 82 |

# Indiana 88

| | M | 3FG | AFG | FT | R | A | B | S | T | F | Pts |
|---|---|---|---|---|---|---|---|---|---|---|---|
| Thomas, f | 22 | | 6-10 | 3- 3 | 3 | 0 | 1 | 2 | 5 | 4 | 15 |
| Calloway, f | 39 | | 8-13 | 5- 6 | 8 | 2 | 0 | 0 | 3 | 2 | 21 |
| Garrett, c | 39 | | 4- 7 | 3- 5 | 9 | 0 | 3 | 0 | 0 | 2 | 11 |
| Alford, g | 38 | 1- 3 | 6-16 | 5- 7 | 2 | 5 | 0 | 0 | 2 | 2 | 18 |
| Smart, g | 30 | | 8-11 | 5- 6 | 7 | 3 | 0 | 1 | 3 | 3 | 21 |
| Meier | 4 | | 0- 0 | 0- 0 | 0 | 0 | 0 | 0 | 0 | 1 | 0 |
| Minor | 1 | | 0- 0 | 0- 0 | 0 | 0 | 0 | 0 | 0 | 0 | 0 |
| Eyl | 14 | | 0- 0 | 2- 4 | 5 | 3 | 0 | 1 | 0 | 1 | 2 |
| Smith | 1 | | 0- 0 | 0- 0 | 0 | 0 | 0 | 0 | 0 | 0 | 0 |
| Hillman | 12 | | 0- 0 | 0- 2 | 3 | 0 | 0 | 1 | 1 | 0 | 0 |
| Team | | | | | 2 | | | | | | |
| Totals | | 1- 3 | 32-57 | 23-31 | 38 | 16 | 4 | 4 | 14 | 16 | 88 |

| SCORE BY HALVES | | | 3FG | AFG | FT |
|---|---|---|---|---|---|
| Duke (24-9) | 39 43—82 | | .727 | .478 | .769 |
| Indiana (27-4) | 49 39—88 | | .333 | .561 | .742 |

**Officials**—Don Shea, Gene Monji, Jim Howell.
**Attendance**—16,902.

sank a three-point shot that cut the lead to 76-73.

Steve Eyl was a high school quarterback not far up the road from Cincinnati — at Badin High in Hamilton. Uncharacteristically for an Ohioan, he gave up football for basketball after his junior year, but he didn't give up passing. With Duke clawing for the ball, Eyl got a pass to Calloway for a basket (78-73) but Amaker answered with a three-point shot and it was 78-76, the closest Duke had been since Calloway's blitz closing out the first half. Again Blue Devils swarmed on the 6-6 Eyl as he handled the ball in the backcourt. Out of the swarm came a bounce pass that hit Alford on a tight cut through the middle and he banked in a layup. Kevin Strickland missed a three-point shot, Garrett rebounded, and Eyl delivered his third assist in a minute and a half — to Smart for a basket that opened an 82-76 lead with 1:50 to go. The crisis was over, and Indiana won, 88-82, with 11 points from Garrett, 15 from Thomas, 18 from Alford, and 21 each from Smart and Calloway. The Hoosiers were just three games into tournament play, and already all five starters had scored in the 20s at least once. "All five average in double figures," Krzyzewski said. "That's the nature of their team. I tried to tell everyone before the game it wasn't a case of just trying to stop Steve." He was right about the averages, but that was the first time all five reached double figures in the same game.

Knight enjoyed winning but felt a sense of loss for Krzyzewski. "I really didn't enjoy this game at all," he said. "I'm very, very happy for our players. But that was a tough ball game."

The NCAA's tournament format calls for a press conference on the day off between games. Knight attended, with Alford and Thomas, and the coach indicated he didn't quite agree with Calloway's theories on what had produced a sudden four-game, 19-point average for a player who had been slumping. "I think Calloway's improvement had a

John Terhune

lot to do with his being benched when we played Ohio State. You can talk about all the motivational speeches and phrases and devices in the world, but the greatest motivator of all is your ass on the bench. There is no better motivator. Ass meets bench. Bench retains ass. Ass transmits signal to brain. Brain transmits signal to body. Body gets ass off bench and plays better. It's a hell of a sequence of things that take place."

The victory moved the Hoosiers to the same point they had reached in

**Quin Snyder tries, but Steve Alford emerges with a three-point play**

**Cheerleader Jody Zima salutes a tournament triumph**

Larry Crewell

the seniors' freshman season: beyond North Carolina, approaching Virginia, with a Final Four trip at stake. The barrier this time was Louisiana State, which somehow lost 14 games but for the second year in a row kicked into gear in the tournament. LSU also was one victory away, from returning to Louisiana as the virtual home team in a Final Four at New Orleans.

LSU has an odd tournament history. Just before its surprise successes in the last two NCAA tournaments, the Tigers lost 10 straight postseason games — in the Southeastern Conference, the NIT, and the NCAA. That started with a 67-49 loss to Indiana in the national semifinals at Philadelphia in 1981. There was another thing about LSU and the NCAA tournament. Every LSU team that had ever won a game in the NCAA wound up losing to the eventual champion: Indiana in 1953, Michigan State in 1979, Louisville in 1980, Indiana in 1981, Louisville in 1986. It's still true.

Indiana, launched by a Calloway basket, rushed out to a 14-6 lead, but LSU came back quickly and Indiana led 18-17 when Daryl Thomas got the basketball in traffic in the post area. Thomas tried to find room to drive to the basket, couldn't, then tried to create some just as an official called him for a three-second lane violation. He also collided with a Tiger defender, but the violation came first. Play stopped for a TV timeout, and Knight wasn't sure what had been called: three seconds or a charging foul, which would have been No. 2 on Thomas. Rules say a captain can be sent on the court to get an answer to such questions. Normally, that would be Alford, but Alford had just sat down, Knight said later, and "I didn't want to get him up."

Official Tom Fraim was standing near the free-throw line in midcourt, at the Indiana end. From the Indiana huddle, Knight waved for Fraim's attention, then shouted, but in the noisy arena Fraim did not hear him and the official was looking straight ahead, downcourt. Knight stepped

from the huddle, then kept going. He had almost reached Fraim to ask his question when the red sweater looming up quickly on his left caught Fraim's attention. He turned and immediately signaled a technical foul, for Knight's leaving the assigned coaching area.

"In our league, it probably wouldn't have been a technical," Big Ten officiating supervisor Bob Wortman, an NCAA observer at the game, said. "Our guys are supposed to watch for something like that, where it's just a question of what was called. If he says one thing, yeah. Pop him. And I'm not saying Tom Fraim was wrong. He did not see him, and when he did, he almost had to call it."

Knight went from surprise to disbelief to anger. He argued his case with official Paul Houseman, then banged a fist on the table adjacent to the floor, beyond which sat official scorers and NCAA Tournament Committee representatives — notably, Notre Dame athletic director Gene Corrigan, to whom he addressed his remarks. In pounding his fist, Knight hit a telephone, the receiver popping in the air and making an eye-catching photograph for the national wires. A month later, the NCAA Tournament Committee took the unprecedented step of giving Knight a public reprimand and deducting $10,000 from Indiana's $1-million tournament share, chiefly for the national image conveyed by his hitting the telephone.

It was hardly the first time an upset coach hit the officials' booth (*e.g.*, Al McGuire, Marquette, 1974 finals, 1976 regional) or went straight to the tournament committee with objections over officiating (*e.g.*, John Thompson, Georgetown, 1982, and Eddie Sutton, Kentucky, 1986). "I can't speak for past committees," tournament committee chairman Richard Schultz, Virginia athletic director and former Iowa coach, said, "but I think this committee feels a responsibility to protect the integrity of the game." Schultz said Corrigan verified that Knight used no profanity in stating his courtside case, which would confirm to *A Season on the Brink* readers that Knight wasn't *really* mad. Only Knight knew whether he was being absolutely straight or lacing every word with irony in a statement he made responding to the penalty: "The Tournament Committee is made of people each of whom has spent a lifetime making great contributions to the game of basketball. These men over their careers have made a tremendous impact on the game that I like so well. I cannot contest their right to make a decision, as outlined in the NCAA rules." Most likely, he resented being singled out for precedent-setting punishment, given tournament history, and his true reaction was more along the lines of his postgame reference to Fraim's assessment of the technical foul: "Maybe (by Knight's going onto the court) he's put in a position where he *has* to call it. I know a lot of *good* officials who would never have called it." The Tournament Committee did not include a whole lot of basketball names, although until Pervis Ellison of Louisville in 1986 Arnold Ferrin of Utah was the only freshman to win the Outstanding Player Award at the Final Four (1944), and Fred Schaus, athletic director at West Virginia, was a professional player and coach as well as Jerry West's college coach at West Virginia. Others were James Delany, commissioner of the Ohio Valley Conference; Cedric Dempsey, athletic director at Arizona; Roy Kramer, athletic director (and former basketball coach) at Vanderbilt; Richard Shrider, athletic director (and former basketball coach) at Miami of Ohio, and Frank Windegger, athletic director at Texas Christian.

For all the month-later hubbub, the incident made little impact on the game. Anthony Wilson hit one of the two free throws awarded for the technical foul, and the game continued, tied 18-18. Alford's 17th and 18th points of the half came on free throws with 1:19 left in the half and let Indiana go to halftime up 47-46.

**An ungranted appeal, then a $10,000 thump for Bob Knight**

In the second half, LSU coach Dale Brown switched from a triangle-and-two defense to a box-and-one that brought the two front men high, as additional help against Alford. The openings figured to be inside, but Indiana didn't find them. The Hoosiers went scoreless on eight straight trips downcourt, four of them ending in turnovers, and LSU — with 6-8 Nikita Wilson slipping inside Garrett twice for dunks and scoring over him two more times — raced out to a 63-51 lead.

During that 10-point run, Indiana lost Calloway. With 14:31 to play, he went down clutching the knee that he had hurt in the Montana State opener. Trainer Tim Garl came onto the court to check out the injury, then left the playing area with Calloway. Calloway Country was still. In less than two playing minutes, Calloway was back and playing. In the meantime, Garl had taken him into the halls outside the main arena to let Calloway test the knee with some sprints, some starts and stops, and some cuts. Satisfied there was no new damage, Garl started back with Calloway, and for a few seconds, they had a new problem. They couldn't find an unlocked door. "All the doors were blocked off," Calloway said. It took some door-banging.

Calloway and Garl were back when Garrett struck back with five straight Indiana points to cut the lead to 73-66. It was 75-66 with 4:38 to go when Calloway slipped through a baseline opening and went up to power home a dunk.

He missed.

Colossally.

The ball bounced off the rim so hard that it came down out of bounds, a body blow for the Hoosiers at a time when comeback points were essential. A TV timeout coincided, and all through Calloway Country there were suspicions that Rick probably didn't look forward to his trip to the sidelines to meet with Knight. "He didn't say anything about that," Calloway said. "We didn't have time to sit there and worry about a missed dunk."

Scout's honor, Alford said. That's

the way it was. "Obviously Coach gets on us. But it wasn't so much yelling or chewing on one individual, it was more like, 'Hey, guys, we're all right. We've got time. You haven't done what's been set up. Now let's play the way I want you to play.' I think that really helped us, because when we got in *our* huddle, we said the same things: 'We've got plenty of time. Let's not try to get it all back at once. Let's go out and play a lot harder than they do the last five minutes and see what happens.' That's just what we did.

"It was strange. I never in the LSU game felt my career was going to end — or maybe I did subconsciously and said, 'Hey, it can't happen.' Maybe that's the feeling the other guys got from the seniors all through the tournament. We tried to tell them, 'It ends our career but it also ends your season. I think we really pulled together when we had to."

Indiana trailed 75-68 when Thomas intercepted a pass. Alford centered a break and gave Joe Hillman the ball driving in from the left. Bernard Woodside was back on defense for LSU, but Hillman got a shot over him and in, and it became a three-point play and 75-71 game when Woodside was charged with a foul, his fifth. Hillman had been in

> *He didn't say anything about that. We didn't have time to sit there and worry about a missed dunk.*
>
> — Rick Calloway

**NCAA MIDWEST REGIONAL FINAL**
**March 23, Cincinnati**

# Louisiana State 76

| | M | 3FG | AFG | FT | R | A | B | S | T | F | Pts |
|---|---|---|---|---|---|---|---|---|---|---|---|
| Woodside, f | 26 | 1- 1 | 6-10 | 0- 1 | 7 | 1 | 0 | 1 | 1 | 5 | 13 |
| Brown, f | 34 | | 3- 6 | 0- 2 | 7 | 8 | 0 | 3 | 0 | 2 | 6 |
| N.Wilson, c | 40 | | 9-16 | 2- 2 | 6 | 0 | 0 | 0 | 2 | 3 | 20 |
| A.Wilson, g | 40 | 2- 9 | 6-15 | 1- 2 | 4 | 1 | 0 | 0 | 1 | 2 | 15 |
| Joe, g | 21 | 1- 4 | 1- 7 | 1- 2 | 2 | 2 | 0 | 1 | 3 | 3 | 4 |
| Irvin | 22 | 2- 3 | 6- 7 | 0- 1 | 0 | 3 | 0 | 0 | 2 | 1 | 14 |
| Vargas | 17 | | 2- 4 | 0- 0 | 1 | 2 | 1 | 1 | 2 | 3 | 4 |
| Team | | | | | 4 | | | | | | |
| **Totals** | | 6-17 | 33-65 | 4-10 | 31 | 17 | 1 | 6 | 11 | 19 | 76 |

# Indiana 77

| | M | 3FG | AFG | FT | R | A | B | S | T | F | Pts |
|---|---|---|---|---|---|---|---|---|---|---|---|
| Thomas, f | 39 | | 5-11 | 6- 6 | 7 | 0 | 0 | 1 | 3 | 3 | 16 |
| Calloway, f | 37 | | 5-10 | 1- 2 | 5 | 5 | 0 | 1 | 2 | 4 | 11 |
| Garrett, c | 38 | | 8-10 | 1- 3 | 15 | 1 | 3 | 0 | 3 | 3 | 17 |
| Alford, g | 40 | 2- 4 | 4- 9 | 10-10 | 0 | 7 | 0 | 0 | 0 | 1 | 20 |
| Smart, g | 39 | 0- 1 | 4-10 | 2- 2 | 2 | 1 | 0 | 1 | 3 | 2 | 10 |
| Eyl | 5 | | 0- 1 | 0- 0 | 3 | 0 | 0 | 1 | 1 | 0 | 0 |
| Smith | 1 | 0- 1 | 0- 1 | 0- 0 | 1 | 0 | 0 | 0 | 0 | 0 | 0 |
| Hillman | 1 | | 1- 1 | 1- 1 | 0 | 0 | 0 | 0 | 0 | 0 | 3 |
| Team | | | | | 0 | | | | | | |
| **Totals** | | 2- 6 | 27-53 | 21-24 | 33 | 14 | 3 | 4 | 12 | 13 | 77 |

| SCORE BY HALVES | | | 3FG | AFG | FT |
|---|---|---|---|---|---|
| Louisiana State (24-15) | 46 30 | —76 | .353 | .508 | .400 |
| Indiana (28-4) | 47 30 | —77 | .333 | .509 | .875 |

**Technical foul**—Indiana.
**Officials**—Jim Burr, Tom Fraim, Paul Houseman.
**Attendance**—16,817.

the game just 53 seconds, and he left after the free throw for Smart. "Hillman made a hell of a tough play — the play of the game," Knight said. "That was like a pinch-hit home run in the ninth inning."

Brown had the Tigers in a clock-killing offense. "They only had four fouls, and we weren't going to shoot free throws. We felt we could bide time. If we would have been in the bonus at that point, we probably would not have done it because we're not a good free-throw shooting team."

With 50 seconds left, Darryl Joe hit a free throw for a 76-73 lead. He missed the second, and Smart rushed to a shot for Indiana. He missed but got his own rebound, and with 40 seconds left, he hit both halves of a one-and-one to tighten the game to 76-75. At 0:26, freshman Fess Irvin, on his best-shooting day of the year (6-for-7, by a .340 shooter), missed the front half of a one-and-one, Thomas rebounded, and Indiana had a victory chance.

Indiana went to work without a timeout, standard procedure under Knight. "They knew what we wanted to do," he said. First choice: get Alford open. The lessons of the Illinois finish, and the problems at the end of regulation time and all three overtimes at Wisconsin, had taught the Hoosiers that options were needed. Thomas screened for Alford, two LSU defenders jumped after Alford, and Thomas flashed into an opening in the middle. He caught a pass, 10 feet in front of the basket, spun and faked a shot. Jose Vargas of LSU went up, and Thomas "tried to draw a foul by jumping into him." It didn't work. Thomas forced a shot on up, "but I kinda pinched the ball. It dropped short."

It was Air Ball II, the Wisconsin miracle all over again. Calloway, cutting into the opening left by Vargas, pulled the ball out of the air and never came down with it, softly banking it in with six seconds to go. LSU got the clock stopped with a timeout, but the Tigers never got a shot away — in time. Steve Eyl, inserted for Alford to cover outside

shooter Anthony Wilson, cut him off from a pass. Joe dribbled the ball upcourt and got a pass into the post to Nikita Wilson, but officials said the shot he got away was too late. It missed.

The Hoosiers attacked each other, then the nets — the first set any of them had been able to cut down as collegians. A few strands hung from the hastily shorn rims, and Knight, ever the general, commanded, "Get every piece." Knight thought of the seniors' near-miss at Atlanta three years before and said, "It's been a hell of a road back. I have a tremendous feeling for these kids. They've found ways to win."

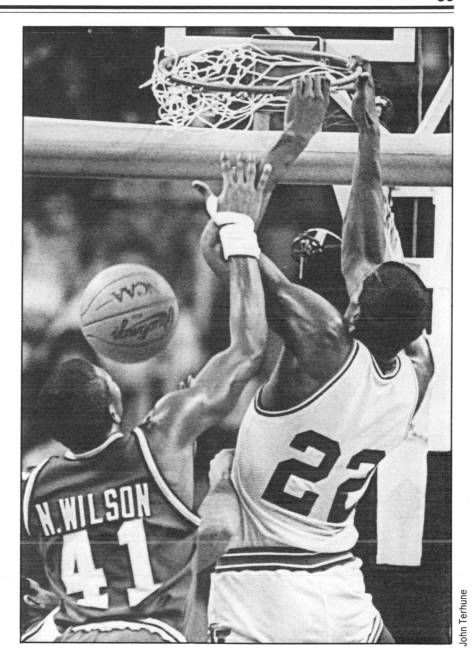

John Terhune

**Dean Garrett's dunk rebound started Indiana back from 75-66 deficit against LSU and star Nikita Wilson**

# 11 No. 1 task

**After a long wait and lots of frustrations, Steve Alford gets a chance to compete in Final Four**

Larry Crewell

Four teams made it to New Orleans for basketball's premier national event. Three of them made it there by Wednesday of Final Four Week. The fourth arrived Friday. Much was made during the year of how adaptable once-rigid Robert Knight had become, his team's junior college transfers and zone defense two items of proof offered up. The New Orleans arrivals were testimony that not everything had changed with Bob Knight — in reality, very little.

From the time he stopped thinking about LSU and focused in on his next opponent, which probably was about the time he walked off the floor in the pandemonium at Cincinnati, Knight figured on a Friday arrival. He had a mildly surprised look when asked why — given that the other three were approaching the trip differently. "As long as I've been involved in coaching, we have never, regardless of the game, gone to the site earlier than one day prior to the game. That's been my policy for 22 or 23 years now and that's the way we'll always do it. We're still in class. We'll miss a little class on Friday, and we'll get there in time to work out on Friday." Road game coming up? Get in all the practice you can at home, then go play. OK, so it's a little bigger road game than usual. Same basic thing. "I don't know *what* their thinking is," Knight said of his three coaching colleagues, in a tone not critical at all, just puzzled.

"I'm going to let the kids enjoy themselves," coach Jerry Tarkanian of No. 1-ranked Nevada-Las Vegas said. "We will definitely keep our team under close regimentation. We won't isolate them from the press. I think that's very important that they get the opportunity to talk to the press and the television people."

Young Rick Pitino, who pulled off a startling achievement by not just getting Providence to New Orleans but doing it with big winning margins over favorites Alabama and Georgetown in the Southeast Re-

gional, said he was taking his team in early because "I think it's just a great experience for all the kids — a once in a lifetime experience for all of them."

Jim Boeheim of Syracuse said, "We try to keep our practices as we've had them all year long, but I do want the kids to have some enjoyment. We want them to have a good time, but we expect that they're going to concentrate on playing well."

To each his own.

Knight felt he had a lot of preparation to do. Musing during Final Four week about his 1981 championship team, which lost nine regular-season games, Knight said he knew the team finally had meshed as the tournament arrived. "I just felt at that time if we played as well as we could play we'd win it. And we essentially did that. Other teams can obviously be like that. We could have gone right back through that tournament and been placed anywhere, and nobody would have come any closer to us. Then you're talking about an absolutely outstanding team. Of the teams that started in this tournament, I thought that the two teams that had the best chance to do that were Las Vegas and North Carolina."

Nevada-Las Vegas had been No. 1

**Pull back? 'No way, Joey,' Steve Eyl said on game-clinching three-point play against Jarvis Basnight and Nevada-Las Vegas**

**Armon 'The Hammer' Gilliam nailed IU for 32 points**

in the country since Ohio State's upset of Iowa. The Rebels entered the Final Four with a 22-game winning streak in which their average winning margin was 20 points. Iowa, which let a 19-point lead get away in losing in the regional finals to UNLV, 84-81, was the first team in 15 games to finish within 10 points of the Runnin' Rebels.

They were 37-1, the one loss (by a point at Oklahoma) controversial because of an officiating mistake on a three-point shot. "They were good — they deserved to be ranked No. 1," Daryl Thomas said. "For us, that was a milestone in itself, finally being underdogs.

"But we still had the white jerseys."

Nobody really noticed that little factor until the numbers started building. Thomas, Steve Alford and Todd Meier were on the team that had the poorest record in Assembly Hall's years (10-7 there in 1984-85, including a record five straight losses closing out the season). They also were on the team that had the best record there — 15-0 this season, the first unbeaten home season for an Indiana team since the '76 Hoosiers went unbeaten everywhere. They wore white in every one of

those games, plus the two they won in the Hoosier Classic at Indianapolis. NCAA tournament rules say the higher-seeded team is the home team in all regional and sub-regional games, so as No. 1 in the Midwest, the Hoosiers wore white in both games at Indianapolis and both at Cincinnati. That added up to 21-0, 22-0 counting the Soviet Union exhibition. The Hoosiers did not consider it a handicap when tournament rules said in case of equal seeding, the team that comes first in alphabetization is the home club.

UNLV made its basketball name for offense. The Rebels set an NCAA record by averaging 110 points a game in 1975-76. They averaged 107 a game when Tarkanian made his other Final Four trip with them in 1977. "Jerry has not really been understood as a coach as I feel he should be," Knight said. "I have always felt that basketball really begins and ends with defensive play. His teams have been extremely good defensively. Coaching is in evidence in how hard a team plays defensively and how consistently it plays hard defensively. I think you see that always on the floor in his teams."

The comments came on a na-

**Assistant coach Royce Waltman, making a point to the Hoosier bench, will be speaking in a different role next season. In May, Waltman was named head coach at DePauw University in Greencastle.**

tional midweek telephone press conference the NCAA set up, involving all four coaches. Tarkanian is the NCAA's *bete noire*. For Knight, recognized as perhaps the archfoe of cheating, to speak up for Tarkanian on the NCAA's line was a bit cheeky, which didn't really make it unappealing to him. Tarkanian let him know he sincerely appreciated the gesture. Clearly, the two — however far apart their philosophies — like each other.

On the same NCAA line, Tarkanian said, "I have great respect for Bobby. I sent him a letter before I knew him — when he had (1976 all-America center Kent) Benson and that group. I had never seen a team play as well offensively and defensively at the same time. At that time, Bobby was known as a defensive coach, but I thought his offense was the best that I'd ever seen. I like the fact that he's a tough guy. He's not a hypocrite. I think that's the biggest thing wrong with our profession today: it's full of hypocrites."

Knight even invited Tarkanian to go to dinner with him and a group of friends the night before the game. Tarkanian tentatively accepted, then had to withdraw for other plans. Knight's small group wound up in a chartered bus. Pete Newell was on it,

and coaches Mike Krzyzewski, Digger Phelps, Don Donoher, Hank Egan and Stu Starner. Quinn Buckner was there. And a doctor or two, a sportswriter or two, a Montana fishing pal or two, Knight's staff of assistants, trainer Tim Garl. Just an ordinary busful on an evening that shot the whole idea of a bunker mentality when Knight's at work.

Tarkanian's staff included a Hoosier — Mark Warkentien, the assistant who gained some notoricty for

A brief sideline chat for Bob Knight and UNLV guard Mark Wade, an unsatisfying view for Rebel coach Jerry Tarkanian

**NCAA SEMIFINAL**
March 28, New Orleans

# Nevada-Las Vegas 93

| | M | 3FG | AFG | FT | R | A | B | S | T | F | Pts |
|---|---|---|---|---|---|---|---|---|---|---|---|
| Paddio, f | 22 | 2- 8 | 2-13 | 0- 0 | 6 | 1 | 0 | 0 | 2 | 1 | 6 |
| Basnight, f | 22 | | 3- 4 | 0- 1 | 2 | 1 | 0 | 0 | 0 | 5 | 6 |
| Gilliam, c | 39 | | 14-26 | 4- 6 | 10 | 1 | 3 | 0 | 1 | 3 | 32 |
| Wade, g | 35 | 1- 6 | 1- 6 | 1- 2 | 4 | 18 | 0 | 4 | 0 | 4 | 4 |
| Banks, g | 35 | 10-19 | 12-23 | 4- 6 | 8 | 1 | 0 | 0 | 3 | 4 | 38 |
| Robinson | 5 | | 0- 0 | 0- 0 | 1 | 0 | 0 | 0 | 0 | 1 | 0 |
| Graham | 25 | 0- 2 | 0- 5 | 1- 4 | 2 | 0 | 0 | 0 | 2 | 4 | 1 |
| Hudson | 13 | | 3- 4 | 0- 0 | 5 | 1 | 0 | 1 | 0 | 2 | 6 |
| Willard | 4 | | 0- 1 | 0- 0 | 0 | 0 | 0 | 1 | 2 | 0 | |
| Team | | | | | 2 | | | | | | |
| Totals | | 13-35 | 35-82 | 10-19 | 40 | 23 | 3 | 5 | 9 | 26 | 93 |

# Indiana 97

| | M | 3FG | AFG | FT | R | A | B | S | T | F | Pts |
|---|---|---|---|---|---|---|---|---|---|---|---|
| Thomas, f | 18 | | 3- 5 | 0- 0 | 4 | 1 | 0 | 0 | 2 | 3 | 6 |
| Calloway, f | 40 | | 6-10 | 0- 0 | 6 | 6 | 0 | 1 | 3 | 3 | 12 |
| Garrett, c | 40 | | 7-10 | 4- 5 | 11 | 1 | 2 | 0 | 2 | 2 | 18 |
| Alford, g | 37 | 2- 4 | 10-19 | 11-13 | 4 | 2 | 0 | 0 | 2 | 4 | 33 |
| Smart, g | 23 | | 5- 7 | 4- 5 | 2 | 1 | 0 | 0 | 2 | 5 | 14 |
| Eyl | 20 | | 3- 3 | 1- 2 | 5 | 2 | 0 | 0 | 1 | 4 | 7 |
| Hillman | 17 | | 3- 4 | 1- 3 | 3 | 3 | 0 | 0 | 2 | 2 | 7 |
| Meier | 3 | | 0- 0 | 0- 0 | 3 | 0 | 0 | 0 | 0 | 0 | 0 |
| Smith | 2 | | 0- 2 | 0- 0 | 1 | 0 | 0 | 0 | 0 | 0 | 0 |
| Team | | | | | 3 | | | | | | |
| Totals | | 2- 4 | 37-60 | 21-28 | 42 | 16 | 2 | 1 | 14 | 23 | 97 |

| SCORE BY HALVES | | | 3FG | AFG | FT |
|---|---|---|---|---|---|
| UNLV (37-2) | 47 | 46—93 | .371 | .427 | .526 |
| Indiana (29-4) | 53 | 44—97 | .500 | .617 | .750 |

**Officials**—John Clougherty, Rusty Herring, Dick Paparo.
**Attendance**—64,959.

Larry Crewell

Larry Crewell

*We didn't plan
anything special.
We got the ball to
Steve, but we've
been doing that all
year. It's a good
idea.*

— Joe Hillman

## Milestone

Indiana's 97-93
victory over No. 1-ranked
Nevada-Las Vegas was
Bob Knight's 365th at
Indiana, the most ever by
a coach at a Big Ten
school. Knight went into
the game even with the
late Ward "Piggy"
Lambert of Purdue
(whose career started in
1917 and ended in
1945) and the late
Branch McCracken
(Indiana, 1938 to 1965)
at 364. With an 84-75
victory over Iowa at
Assembly Hall Feb. 21,
Knight reached 200 in
Big Ten victories. Only
Lambert (213) and
McCracken (210) had
done that.

### Big Ten's big winners

| | | |
|---|---|---|
| Bob Knight, Ind. | 366 119 | .755 |
| Ward Lambert, Pur. | 364 145 | .715 |
| BranchMcCracken,Ind. | 364 174 | .677 |
| Harry Combes, Ill. | 316 150 | .678 |
| Fred Taylor, Ohio St. | 297 158 | .653 |

### Big Ten games only

| | | |
|---|---|---|
| Ward Lambert, Pur. | 213 101 | .678 |
| BranchMcCracken,Ind. | 210 116 | .644 |
| Bob Knight, Ind. | 201 75 | .728 |
| Harry Combes, Ill. | 158 80 | .660 |
| Fred Taylor, Ohio St. | 158 102 | .608 |

getting himself declared the legal guardian of Lloyd Daniels, the widely traveled high schooler whose ventures never produced a diploma. Warkentien thought he had his ward on his way to collegiate eligibility when Daniels got picked up on a drugs charge. Warkentien isn't an Indiana graduate, but he was born in Huntington and raised in Fort Wayne before moving West. "My mother still lives in Fort Wayne," he said. "After we beat Iowa, I called her and she was excited. Then I asked her who she was going to root for in our game with Indiana. She said, 'It isn't going to be you.' Those Indiana fans are something."

From two schools of thought as far apart as the two schools are geographically, No. 1 Nevada-Las Vegas met No. 2 Indiana, and 64,959 people came out to watch. That probably wasn't the way Syracuse and Providence felt about it, but after the two Big East rivals' third game of the year wound up a dreary 77-63 Syracuse victory, No. 1 and No. 2 put on a show.

Indiana led early, but consecutive three-point shots by Gerald Paddio and Freddie Banks put UNLV up, 14-9. Keith Smart scored 10 points as Indiana shot ahead, 29-20. With 6:10 to go in the half, Alford sailed in a three-point shot and got himself whacked after it. His four-point play put the Hoosiers ahead, 41-27, and he reacted to the basket with uncharacteristic emotion. "That was a fun game to play in," Alford said later. "I really enjoyed that." He didn't mind letting his enjoyment show because he had formed an opinion about his role on the team. "The thing that's foremost in my mind is how my teammates will respond," he said. "A lot of times they react to the way my feelings are. If I come in tight and not really mentally into the game, that seems to be how the game's going to be played. I felt loose, and I think that was a big key."

Knight pulled Alford then — not because he had just picked up a second foul, Knight said later, but because he signaled that he was winded. He stayed out two minutes

and 47 seconds and returned with the lead down to 47-42. It was 53-47 at halftime, but Banks outside and Armon Gilliam inside was a combination no one had solved before and Indiana didn't in this one. Banks had such a day going from three-point range it impressed even him. "My shooting was tremendous," he said later. Gilliam may have been even more impressive. "Usually a strong guy bullies his way round, or a quick, agile guy finesses you," Thomas said. "He was both." A Banks three-point shot put Vegas up 59-57, and two Gilliam baskets inside kept them there through 63-61.

A TV timeout came right there, and after the way things went subsequently, Joe Hillman was asked what special planning went on inside the huddle. "We didn't plan anything special," Hillman said. "We got the ball to Steve, but we've been doing that all year. It's a good idea." Very. Alford hit two baskets, starting a 12-2 Indiana spurt that provided a 73-65 lead. And then he made nothing but history. With 8:28 to go, he missed both tries on a two-shot free throw —his first time ever, at Indiana. He was so shaken by the experience he hit eight straight in the last seven minutes, including two that made Indiana's lead a comfortable-sounding 88-76 with just 3:40 left. With 28 seconds to go, the lead was 92-88 and Banks — who had hit 10 three-point shots — was at the line for a one-and-one. He missed, Alford rebounded and got fouled, hitting the free throws. Banks missed a three-pointer, and Eyl grabbed the long rebound at full gallop and headed for the Indiana end. Hillman was behind Eyl heading down the court. "I heard Joe — he was about at the foul line," Eyl said. "I thought he said 'Pull it back out.' I said, 'No way, Joey.' We just needed a basket to seal it off." Eyl pounded a dunk through and got fouled for a three-point play that made the lead 97-88 with 13 seconds to go.

Alford and Eyl grabbed each other in a premature victory dance, and Hillman barked at them that the game wasn't over. In mentioning the makeup of the team, Thomas noted that the leadership he tried to give was "not by yelling and screaming, because that's not me. I don't think that was the personality of our team. We didn't have anybody who stood out that way, who could explain in a harsh tone just what had to be done — except for Joe Hillman."

Alford smiled Hillman off that time. "They couldn't catch us," he said. "They were out of timeouts." The final score was 97-93. UNLV used those last 13 seconds well.

Indiana won despite 70 points from Banks (38) and Gilliam (32), a two-man record against a Knight club. Alford countered the UNLV stars with 33, his best NCAA tournament total. Guard Mark Wade, who broke Smart's NCAA tournament record for assists with 18, had most of the duty against Alford and said: "Sometimes I thought I had him and I'd look around and he'd be somewhere else, and I'd say, 'Oh, my God. I've got to go through two or three more people to get to him.'" Wade called it "like trying to run through an offensive line."

Garrett had 18 points and 11 rebounds as Indiana — an unimpressive rebounding team all year, till the tournament began — topped the Rebels, 42-40. It was fitting that Garrett had a good day against UNLV. Knight had mentioned during the week that after he had signed Garrett last year, "I had had a lot of coaches tell me they didn't think Dean would really contribute much to our team. I had a chance to watch him play several days in the spring in two different junior college settings. I think Tark sensed that I had heard a lot of negative comments about Dean from West Coast coaches. Tark took me aside and said, 'Hey, just listen, this kid's going to play well for you and he's really going to do a good job for you.' I really appreciated that because I have great respect for Jerry as a person and as a coach. I think he was trying to pep me up at the time, but I also know that he felt that way about Garrett."

Larry Crewell

**IU cheerleaders celebrate a joyride into NCAA championship game**

# 12 The Shot

NCAA finals day offers a long time to think. Steve Alford had done some reading during the week, and he said, "I read where Joe Hillman said the reason why he came to Indiana was to win the national championship. I think in the back of our minds all of us felt that way. Now we have that opportunity."

Daryl Thomas remembered the days when he was making his final selection of Indiana over Notre Dame and Iowa. "In the back of your mind, when you think of Indiana, you think of Bob Knight and his success, and you think, 'If it can happen, it would be more likely to happen here.' That's exactly how I thought.

"Then once I got here, I didn't really think national championship as much as just wanting to play. You dream that you might win it all in your last year, but the odds are slim and none. Then, as things progressed, especially in the tournament, after the Duke game, I really felt like we could *play*. We had a good chance."

It was another time when a longed-for goal was in Alford's sight — like the state championship he wanted to give his Dad but couldn't, like the Final Four trip he thought was lined up his freshman year but wasn't, like the 1986 Big Ten championship his team played for on the final day and lost. A young man proud of his Christian faith admits during those times and the bleak sophomore year he wondered if he was being tested a bit. "Oh yeah," he laughed, "I didn't wonder. I *knew* something was going on. Dad always told me that those who work the hardest reap the most benefits, whether it happens on the day that

you work hard or down the road. My favorite Bible verse has always been James 1:12." In modern language, it begins: *Happy the man who remains steadfast under trial . . .*

The Hoosiers couldn't have wanted the victory one bit more than Syracuse. The Orangemen had the added problem of earning respect. Indiana had four national championship banners and a history of winning in the NCAA tournament. Syracuse had an outstanding pattern of regular-season success under coach Jim Boeheim, but a lack of tournament success kept Boeheim on the defense. When North Carolina and Dean Smith fell to the Orange in the East Regional final, the respect issue died. Beating Indiana and Bob Knight would bury it.

Surely, the burial will happen anyway, although the Hoosiers — or fate, or whatever — didn't let it happen. Indiana won and Syracuse lost, 74-73, in a finals that will live in memories for a long while for its decisive shot.

Boeheim opened the game with his team in a zone defense that lasted just two trips downcourt before he put a box-and-one defense on Alford, 6-foot Sherman Douglas on Alford most of the time. "Watching the (Indiana-UNLV) game and then watching the tape," Boeheim said, "I don't know if they are beatable when Alford plays the way he did. The games that he has played well, they just seem to beat anybody. A couple of games that we've seen during the course of the year when he didn't play so well, they were a little more beatable. I would compare him to a guy we played several times, Chrissy Mullen (of St. John's). Mullen is a little bigger, but he is the same kind of player. And we didn't have a whole lot of success against him."

Boeheim also didn't have Sherman Douglas on the clubs that Mullen shot up. Douglas earned the Alford assignment with strong defense all season long but a particularly outstanding performance in stopping Billy Donovan of Providence in the semifinal game. Donovan went into the game the highest scorer in the tournament. He managed just eight points, and the Orange defense also was able to confine Indiana transfer Delray Brooks to nine after Brooks, a popular favorite with his former teammates and coach, had an excellent first season as Donovan's backcourt partner.

Indiana wanted to work Thomas inside against 6-9 freshman Derrick Coleman and 6-10 center Rony Seikaly, hoping for foul trouble. Thomas had three of the Hoosiers' first four baskets, but the fouls didn't come. Alford's first two baskets were three-point shots, good for an 18-16 lead. Seikaly burned the Hoosiers with two straight fast-break dunks — one by accident, when Eyl deflected a pass — and Syracuse opened up a 29-24 lead.

One more time, Todd Meier came out to replace Garrett (who had two fouls) for the last five minutes of the half. Hillman came on in the absence of Calloway, who hadn't scored. And one more time, the Hoosiers used the final minutes of the half to make a move. It was 33-28 when Alford hit a three-point shot. Indiana got the ball back with less than 45 seconds to go and played for a last shot. Hillman brought Alford to him in the right corner and gave him enough of an opening with a screen that Alford's three-point shot went in a second ahead of the buzzer for a 34-33 lead that was reminiscent of a similar situation in the 1981 championship game. Indiana didn't lead against North Carolina until Randy Wittman's shot from the right baseline at the buzzer put the Hoosiers up 26-25 at halftime. Knight said he had a whole lot better feeling after

Wittman's shot in Philadelphia than after Alford's in New Orleans. "I thought we were playing well then. I honestly felt we were just kinda hanging on at halftime here."

The most dominant figure in the game wasn't scoring much. Coleman had just six points for Syracuse, but already he had 13 rebounds, 12 of them on defense.

Against North Carolina in '81, Indiana never lost that halftime lead. Syracuse reclaimed it immediately with two free throws by Seikaly. An Alford three-point shot opened a 41-37 lead, then Syracuse put together a 15-3 burst that redirected the game's flow. Early in the Orange charge, Keith Smart's lob pass misfired and Smart came out for Hillman. Smart remained out for 4½ minutes, and the Syracuse lead reached 52-44. It was 52-46 with 12:12 left when he returned.

He had been on court eight seconds when he drew a two-shot foul and hit one. After a three-point basket by Alford, Smart penetrated the Syracuse box and went over it to drop a pass to Thomas for a dunk that tied the game, 52-52.

Hillman stole the ball, and Smart went to work on the right baseline. His drive for the basket was cut off by Seikaly, who stepped out smartly — and was whipped, Smartly. Smart got Seikaly into the air and then leaped at almost a 45-degree angle to free himself for a twisting shot that he hit.

Back came Syracuse to go ahead 59-54, then 61-56 as Douglas showed some athletic skills, too — a drive that produced a two-shot foul, a three-point basket, then another drive for a finger-roll basket.

One more time Smart drove to set up a Thomas basket, then Smart lost freshman Steve Thompson with a quick move and scored to tie the game, 61-61.

Coleman scored on a rebound, but Smart back-doored Thompson and took a pass from Alford to score over Coleman. Smart tried to dish off one more time but Seikaly stepped in the way to intercept, but when Greg Monroe went for the Hoosier

---

*I kinda felt we were just hanging on at halftime.*

— Bob Knight

---

## Milestone

Indiana's NCAA tournament championship lifted the Hoosiers into first place, past UCLA, in all-time tournament won-lost percentage. Indiana (37-11) has a .771 mark; 10-time champion UCLA (56-17) is .767. No other school that has played as many as 10 tournament games has a .700 record.

**Leading NCAA Tournament teams**
**Minimum 10 games played**

| Tnys. | | W | L | Pct. | 1 | 2 |
|---|---|---|---|---|---|---|
| 15 | Indiana* | 37 | 11 | .771 | 5 | 0 |
| 23 | UCLA* | 56 | 17 | .767 | 10 | 0 |
| 5 | Loyola | 9 | 4 | .692 | 1 | 0 |
| 10 | Cincinnati | 20 | 9 | .690 | 2 | 1 |
| 5 | California | 11 | 5 | .688 | 1 | 1 |
| 12 | Georgetown* | 23 | 11 | .676 | 1 | 3 |
| 12 | Duke* | 25 | 12 | .676 | 0 | 3 |
| 14 | N.C. State* | 24 | 13 | .669 | 2 | 0 |
| 8 | Nevada-LV* | 16 | 8 | .657 | 0 | 0 |
| 6 | Michigan St.* | 12 | 6 | .667 | 1 | 0 |
| 21 | N. Carolina* | 43 | 22 | .662 | 2 | 4 |
| 9 | Oklahoma St.* | 15 | 8 | .652 | 2 | 1 |
| 6 | Virginia* | 11 | 6 | .647 | 0 | 0 |
| 32 | Kentucky* | 53 | 29 | .646 | 5 | 2 |
| 5 | Bradley | 9 | 5 | .643 | 0 | 2 |
| 15 | Ohio St.* | 25 | 14 | .641 | 1 | 3 |
| 17 | Kansas* | 30 | 18 | .625 | 1 | 3 |
| 7 | LaSalle | 10 | 6 | .625 | 1 | 1 |
| 18 | Louisville | 33 | 20 | .623 | 2 | 0 |
| 11 | Michigan* | 18 | 11 | .621 | 0 | 2 |
| 15 | San Francisco | 21 | 13 | .618 | 2 | 0 |
| 17 | Villanova | 27 | 17 | .614 | 1 | 0 |
| 8 | Wake Forest | 12 | 8 | .600 | 0 | 0 |

Larry Crewell

Syracuse freshman Derrick Coleman, who had 19 rebounds, defends as Daryl Thomas looks for an opening

jugular with a three-point shot and missed, Thomas rebounded and looped the ball to Alford for a fast-break layup and 65-65 tie.

A Triche free throw put Syracuse ahead; Smart answered with another basket. Garrett was too wrapped up in his own assignments to get the full impact of the very special performance that was taking place, but he has seen it since on film. "It was just all Keith, down the stretch."

All those self doubts of October and November, all the late-game turnovers of December and January

. . . Keith Smart down the stretch was a player for history.

Brilliant play after brilliant play didn't shake Syracuse. Seikaly put the Orange up 70-68, and Smart tied it again with a baseline drive and reverse layup — a 6-1 man inside with Seikaly and Coleman. Knight yelled for a foul when Thomas went down after a high and accidental Seikaly elbow, but Triche moved into the opening to put Syracuse up 72-70 with 57 seconds left. Smart worked the baseline for one more opening — but he missed, and re-

## Milestone

Indiana's record in one-point games under Bob Knight is 17-11, helped considerably by the 5-0 record in 1986-87 that included the regional final game and national championship game.

| | | |
|---|---|---|
| 1971-72 | Kentucky, n** | W 90-89 |
| | Minnesota, a | L 51-52 |
| | Purdue, a | L 69-70 |
| 1972-73 | Ohio State, a | L 69-70 |
| 1973-74 | Wisconsin, h | W 52-51 |
| | Purdue, h | W 80-79 |
| | Toledo, n* | W 73-72 |
| 1974-75 | Purdue, a | W 83-82 |
| 1976-77 | Michigan St., h | L 60-61 |
| 1977-78 | Notre Dame, h | W 67-66 |
| | Illinois, h | L 64-65 |
| | Purdue, h | W 65-64 |
| | Furman, n-T | W 63-62 |
| | Villanova, n-T | L 60-61 |
| 1978-79 | Pepperdine, n | L 58-59 |
| | Michigan, a | L 59-60 |
| | Purdue, n-NIT | W 53-52 |
| 1979-80 | Ohio State, a | L 58-59 |
| 1980-81 | Clemson, n | L 57-58 |
| 1981-82 | Illinois, a | W 54-53 |
| 1982-83 | Iowa, h | L 57-58 |
| 1985-86 | Purdue, h | W 71-70 |
| | Illinois, a | W 61-60 |
| 1986-87 | N.C.-Wilm., h | W 73-72 |
| | Michigan, a | W 85-84 |
| | Wisconsin, a*** | W 86-85 |
| | LSU, n-T | W 77-76 |
| | Syracuse, n-T | W 74-73 |

*Overtime periods; T, NCAA tournament

bounder Triche was fouled with 38 seconds left. He hit one free throw, for a 73-70 lead, but his second bounced hard and low, through the hands of Coleman in the second rebounding spot and into Smart's in No. 3. Instantly, Smart was in motion upcourt. Monroe was back to cut off a layup, but Smart drove right to him and leaped straight up for a soft 10-foot shot over Monroe for a basket that made the score 73-72 with 30 seconds to go.

Syracuse's primary concern was getting the ball in-bounds, so the Orange let Coleman take the ball out of bounds and brought Seikaly

**Inside Dean Garrett, Syracuse center Rony Seikaly prepares to go up for two points**

Larry Crewell

downcourt to field a lob pass. As soon as Seikaly touched the ball, Alford screamed from midcourt for Thomas to foul him, but Seikaly passed right back to Coleman, whom Smart attacked. At 0:28, Coleman was fouled, for a one-and-one.

Knight took a timeout — to freeze and to plan, Plan A if he makes both (look for a three-point shot or try to score quickly and get a timeout), Plan B if he makes one or none (rebound the miss and get into the offense — and don't call timeout).

The timeout was called late enough that Coleman and his teammates already were headed for the free throw line. When they returned, only Coleman was there. Boeheim, memory fresh of the Smart drive from a free-throw rebound to a fast-break basket, pulled everyone but shooter Coleman back to defend, conceding any rebound.

Deployment probably wouldn't have made any difference. Coleman's shot just grazed the rim and dropped into inside rebounder Thomas' hands.

Upcourt the Hoosiers came, facing the Wisconsin situation one more time, Illinois, LSU.

The Alford who forced the ball into traffic and put up a low-percentage last-gasp shot at Illinois felt that was his job as the team's shooter and most experienced player: somehow, get open and take the pressure shot. Even 120-plus games into a career, lessons are learned. "I had learned I didn't *have* to get the big bucket, and I didn't necessarily *have* to score 20 points to win. At Illinois, I just took the ball the wrong way. The whole setup in the Syracuse game was a lot better."

The setup was like LSU: try to screen for Alford, if possible, but don't force anything. The box-and-one was on, and Douglas moved with Alford on a baseline cut while Smart brought the ball up court. Alford read the court, saw Thomas posted low with Douglas behind him, saw Smart moving that way, and faked as if he would be popping out around Thomas, then cut back to the open right side of the court.

For an instant, he was wide open there; Douglas reacted to Smart first, then realized his mistake and raced to cover Alford. "Douglas was lost, all the way on the other side of the lane," Alford said. "But it would have been a real tough pass."

By then, Thomas had the ball, operating against Coleman. He had an opportunity to try the same forced shot he attempted against LSU. He tried a head fake. Rookie Coleman, well-schooled, "didn't budge," Thomas said. "I looked back at Keith." And the clock ticked, past :09, :08. Thomas passed back to Smart, who drove at him as Thomas screened off Coleman. Triche, the high man in the box on that side of the floor, raced at Smart and flailed across his face with a waving left arm.

But Smart's jumping skills took him out of reach. Fading slightly to his left but too high for Triche — six inches taller — to block, Smart sent a high 16-foot shot dead into the center of the basket.

The shot went through at :05. Nobody from Syracuse picked up the ball. Nobody in video view called timeout. The clock ran down to :01 before it was stopped, too late for anything but a prayer play.

Coleman took the ball out of bounds. Indiana ignored him, put-

**NCAA FINAL**
March 31, New Orleans

## Syracuse 73

| | M | 3FG | AFG | FT | R | A | B | S | T | F | Pts |
|---|---|---|---|---|---|---|---|---|---|---|---|
| Triche, f | 32 | | 3- 9 | 2- 4 | 1 | 1 | 0 | 0 | 0 | 4 | 8 |
| Coleman, f | 37 | | 3- 7 | 2- 4 | 19 | 1 | 3 | 1 | 2 | 2 | 8 |
| Seikaly, c | 34 | | 7-13 | 4- 6 | 10 | 1 | 3 | 1 | 3 | 3 | 18 |
| Monroe, g | 32 | 2- 8 | 5-11 | 0- 1 | 2 | 3 | 0 | 2 | 2 | 1 | 12 |
| Douglas, g | 39 | 2- 2 | 8-15 | 2- 2 | 2 | 7 | 0 | 1 | 4 | 3 | 20 |
| Brower | 9 | | 3- 3 | 1- 3 | 1 | 0 | 0 | 0 | 0 | 3 | 7 |
| Thompson | 17 | | 0- 2 | 0- 3 | 1 | 1 | 1 | 0 | 3 | 0 | 0 |
| Team | | | | | 0 | | | | | | |
| **Totals** | | 4-10 | 29-60 | 11-20 | 38 | 14 | 7 | 5 | 14 | 16 | 73 |

## Indiana 74

| | M | 3FG | AFG | FT | R | A | B | S | T | F | Pts |
|---|---|---|---|---|---|---|---|---|---|---|---|
| Thomas, f | 40 | | 8-18 | 4- 7 | 7 | 1 | 0 | 0 | 3 | 1 | 20 |
| Calloway, f | 14 | | 0- 3 | 0- 0 | 2 | 1 | 0 | 0 | 2 | 3 | 0 |
| Garrett, c | 33 | | 5-10 | 0- 0 | 10 | 0 | 3 | 0 | 0 | 4 | 10 |
| Alford, g | 40 | 7-10 | 8-15 | 0- 0 | 3 | 5 | 0 | 2 | 3 | 2 | 23 |
| Smart, g | 35 | 0- 1 | 9-15 | 3- 4 | 5 | 6 | 0 | 2 | 2 | 2 | 21 |
| Meier | 4 | | 0- 0 | 0- 1 | 1 | 0 | 0 | 0 | 0 | 0 | 0 |
| Eyl | 13 | | 0- 0 | 0- 0 | 1 | 1 | 0 | 0 | 1 | 2 | 0 |
| Smith | 1 | | 0- 0 | 0- 0 | 0 | 0 | 0 | 0 | 0 | 1 | 0 |
| Hillman | 20 | | 0- 1 | 0- 2 | 6 | 3 | 0 | 3 | 0 | 2 | 0 |
| Team | | | | | 4 | | | | | | |
| **Totals** | | 7-11 | 30-62 | 7-12 | 35 | 20 | 3 | 7 | 11 | 17 | 74 |

| SCORE BY HALVES | | | 3FG | AFG | FT |
|---|---|---|---|---|---|
| Syracuse (31-7) | 33 40—73 | | .400 | .483 | .550 |
| Indiana (30-4) | 34 40—74 | | .636 | .484 | .583 |

**Officials**—Joe Forte, Nolan Fine, Jody Silvester.
**Attendance**—64,959.

**Game hero Keith Smart goes rim-high for a rebound**

ting all five men at midcourt or beyond. Coleman plays as a pronounced left-hander, every move setting up his left hand for shots. The first basket of the game was a Coleman cut that could have produced a natural righthanded basket, but Coleman turned back to his left instead and forced a shot into and over Thomas.

The throw-in Coleman made was right-handed.

As everything else did in the last 12 minutes, it went right at Smart, who grabbed it, dribbled till he heard the buzzer, then threw the ball deep into the Superdome stands — a wild fling in the general direction of his parents' seat in the Indiana section. It was a prized trophy that was returned. It's part of Indiana's basketball treasurehouse now, just as the team that used it is a part of Indiana history.

Smart won the media vote for the Final Four's Outstanding Player Award. Knight, in the last of six special columns he wrote for 35 newspapers during the tournament, said the Hoosiers won "because Keith Smart made as many big plays in critical situations as anybody I've ever seen."

The national championship game in Louisiana had been won by the team's Louisianan, just as the championship game in Cincinnati had been won by its Cincinnatian, Calloway.

The game had been won on a shot from the left side of the court by a player wearing No. 23. In 1982, the only other NCAA championship game played at the Superdome was won by a shot from the left side of the same end of the court, by Michael Jordan of North Carolina, wearing No. 23.

And the Cincinnatian? The other starters who had been delivering such balance throughout the tournament did it again: Alford with 23 points, Smart 21, Thomas 20, Garrett 10 and 10 rebounds. Regional hero Calloway did not score a point in the game and played just 14 minutes. TV speculation was that his knee was sore, that the tipoff was he was wearing more tape than usual. He wasn't. The problem for Calloway was a broken right wrist, sustained when he lunged to stop a Seikaly shot in the post and fell, landing on the wrist. He played only 14 minutes.

Calloway was wearing No. 20. In 1976, Indiana lost a key starter to an injury in the opening minutes. Bobby Wilkerson didn't score a championship-game point. He wore No. 20.

There's a story to Smart's 23.

A year ago, when Indiana was preparing for the NCAA tournament, Smart made his decision to go to Indiana and talked with Knight by telephone. Knight mentioned that he liked to have players wear the number they preferred and asked what one could be held for him.

There was a long pause after Smart's answer.

"Uhhhh," Knight said, "I'll tell you what: We've got a guy in No. 12 right now. You take No. 11 this year and you can have 12 next year."

Smart still laughs at the one time he one-upped Knight. "Oh, sure, I knew Steve had No. 12," he said. "When I got here, I took No. 23 because Daryl had 24 and Dean took 22 so we were right in a row. That 12 thing was just a joke, really. Hey, I know there's no way they're going to give anybody Steve's number."

**Bob Knight has a quick sideline message for final-game official**

Larry Crewell

Larry Crewell

**Keith Smart is the man of the hour for Steve Alford, Steve Eyl and Indiana's celebrating fans**

Larry Crewell

# A couple of Giants in history

John Terhune

John Terhune

The shoes Steve Alford left behind at Indiana will be difficult to fill, but the uniform already is promised. Make that uniforms. Both numbers that Alford wore with such distinction during his IU years — the No. 12 that was his for four Hoosier seasons and the No. 4 that he wore for the 1984 U.S. Olympic team — are destined for the Hoosiers' two freshman recruits, who have worn them with a historic distinction of their own.

Lyndon Jones was No. 4 and Jay Edwards No. 12 through the three seasons that they led Marion to state high school basketball championships. Their 1987 title made Marion the first team in 65 years to win three Indiana championships in a row, and Jones and Edwards just the second and third players in Hoosier high school history to start on three championship teams. The other was the late Robert "Fuzzy" Vandivier, whose play at Franklin High School (1920-22) and Franklin College put him in the Naismith Basketball Hall of Fame.

Edwards and Jones made a joint announcement in October that they would sign Indiana tenders. They did it early to concentrate on the rare opportunity they, their teammates, and Coach Bill Green had. Saturday, March 28, was one of the greatest basketball days in the state of Indiana's rich history. At 11 a.m. Marion took on and defeated Bedford North Lawrence and renowned rookie Damon Bailey in the opening state tournament semifinal game; immediately afterward, Richmond made it an all-North Central Conference final game by defeating Gary Roosevelt; timing was perfect for the state's spotlight to shift to New Orleans and catch IU's fast and flashy Final Four semifinal victory over No. 1-ranked Nevada-Las Vegas; and then it was Marion's time to fulfill its legend by beating Richmond, 69-56, for championship No. 3.

Jones had 27 points and Edwards 22 in the victory over Bedford North Lawrence. Edwards had 35 points and Jones 23 in the championship game. They finished four-year careers with 3,571 points — 1,860 by Edwards and 1,711 by Jones. Edwards (6-5) led the team the last two years in rebounds; Jones (6-3) led the team the same two years in assists. Jones led "Sweet 16" scoring (the last two weekends of tournament play) in both 1985 and '86, the first player ever to do that. Edwards led it this year, and Jones was second.

For their dominance, they were named to share "Mr. Basketball" honors in the state, the first teammates to do that since Dick and Tom Van Arsdale of Indianapolis Manual (1961) and IU (1963-65).

Edwards and Jones became exposed to Indiana's intrastate following long before their high school careers ended. "There's a *lot* of IU fans in Indiana," Jones said. "When we go out of town, everywhere we go we're asked for autographs. People we don't even know come up and shake our hands. We were down for an IU game and on the way back we stopped at a cafeteria in Martinsville. The whole cafeteria came up, asking for autographs, shaking our hands, showing us all kinds of pictures of past IU teams and saying that we'd be hanging up on the wall one day."

# Epilogue

Todd Meier remembers the heady feeling of standing on the victors' platform at the Louisiana Superdome, holding the 49th NCAA tournament's championship plaque high. "There was nothing better than that — it was great. It's so hard to describe. You watch every year on TV and say, 'Boy, that's a neat thing.' Just sit in awe, thinking about what it would be like to be there. Then you're there and you win it. I can't believe it happened to us."

Rick Calloway remembers what it was like to snip the nets at New Orleans, and at Cincinnati. "A whole lot of things were going through my mind, a whole lot of joy." Dean Garrett can't remember that particular act because "I never got a chance to cut the net. I was running around too much. I never got a piece of the net at all." Not even at Cincinnati? "No, I sure didn't. I told Steve (Alford), 'We'll get ours in New Orleans.' I still never got it. I was just running around. When I saw them cutting it down, I ran over there but it was too late. It didn't even bother me, at the time." Surely a strand or two will be found.

To Daryl Thomas, the paramount feeling atop the ladder, in the dressing room afterward, celebrating later into the night, was, "Man . . . practice is over."

"I was happy we won, but it didn't really hit me right then and there that we had won it all. At that moment, it was just a feeling that all the monkeys were off our back. We got a piece of the Big Ten championship. We played really outstanding basketball in the tournament. And we capped it off with the championship. But it really wasn't until the next night . . . We got back to Bloomington (at about noon, ar-riving to a celebration that packed about 8,000 students into Assembly Hall) and back to our rooms after that. I went to sleep. I woke up about 6 to eat. I went to my night class. I came back and laid down again. I woke up around 3 o'clock in the morning, all slept out. I sat up. I turned on the television, and ESPN was showing highlights of the game.

"And that's when it *really* hit me, like 'Man! We're national champions!' I saw Keith's shot and I thought, 'I don't be-*lieve* this. I won the national championship!'

"I *couldn't* sleep then. I sat up and I was doodling on paper: 'NCAA Champs.' 'No. 1 — Indiana.' I wrote down the pairings. And the rankings. It was . . . great."

Meier had an equally strong reaction to watching a videotape of the game. "I *can't* watch it," he said. "I watched it one night and couldn't get to sleep that whole night again. It's almost worse than the game." He did watch closely enough to see what friends were kidding him about. As Smart's shot goes through, the CBS camera angle shows sore-kneed Todd Meier leaping straight in the air, high. "People have told me they didn't know I had that kind of vertical jump," Meier laughed. "I didn't realize I did it till I saw it in the tape. Holy cow!"

On Friday of game week, the Hoosiers were back together for a visit to Washington at President Reagan's invitation. Walking down Washington streets on a quick taste of tourism between capital commitments, Smart got an idea just what The Shot had done for his notability. Teenaged kids shouted his name — "Hey, Keith Smart!" — and ran up for autographs. Alford, of course, also was barraged. On the steps of

**Bob Knight — on top again**

the Lincoln Memorial, Bob Knight stopped to sign a couple of autographs and the holidaying crowd in town for Washington's Cherry Blossom Festival let even Mr. Lincoln wait for a moment and engulfed Knight in a quick circle. It was nothing new for Knight or Alford. "I can't believe it," Smart said of his instant fame. "I finally had to take my telephone off the hook to get some sleep. People have been calling all day and all night — people I don't even know. I came back from class and my suitemate had a list of people who first called — a whole long sheetful of names."

Reagan spoke to the Hoosiers at a Rose Garden reception, mixing together high praise and genial barbs. He referred to "the shy and retiring Bobby Knight" and said, "Everybody gets to take a shot at Bobby. Why not

the President of the United States?" His were soft shots, because "When all is said and done, Bobby is my kind of coach." Vice President George Bush was there, along with much of the Indiana congressional delegation. First Lady Nancy Reagan watched from a third-floor window and waved to the Hoosiers.

The Washington visit was by the President's invitation, but it was his Secretary of Health and Human Services' party. Dr. Otis Bowen, two-term governor of Indiana, met Knight and the team with a reception at Washington National Airport, then served as their host again at a larger reception. "There are some myths about him I want to put to rest," Bowen told reception guests. "The first myth is that he is tough on reporters. That is not so. Bob Knight is the reporter's best friend.

**Keith Smart was almost too hot to touch during portions of Indiana's NCAA championship drive, but Steve Alford and Magnus Pelkowski low-bridged him, anyway**

John Terhune

Larry Crewell

**Conversation for Todd Meier and coach Bob Knight, confrontation for Dean Garrett on a shot attempted in his area**

He has given the sports writers of America more stuff to write about than a barrelful of Babe Ruths. Myth No. 2: Bob Knight is one tough cookie and don't mess with him. That's wrong, too. I know personally he's the softest touch in town when it comes to giving his time and integrity to a good cause. Myth No. 3: Bob Knight is a law-abiding, up standing citizen. Wrong again. I had to use all of my powers as governor of Indiana to keep this man out of jail one time. This is true. You remember that little misunderstanding he had with the police in Puerto Rico . . .

"Finally, the basest charge of all: They say you have been known to use four-letter words, as if that were something. Heck, I use them, too. I'm going to use a couple of them right now to express how a lot of other folks from Indiana feel about what you and your people accomplished: 'Ya done good.' "

Alford gave the team response. "I'm sure all of you have heard numerous times how hard it is to play for Coach because he's demanding, he's tough, he's competitive . . . and, Dr. Bowen, that's *not* a myth."

Two weeks later, more than 3,000 people turned out at Assembly Hall for the IU Basketball Banquet, at which Alford became the first player in Big Ten history named MVP four years in a row by his team. The

John Terhune

night's 3,000, and a statewide TV audience, heard Knight use his previous IU national championship teams to put into perspective the reservations he had expressed about his last title team as it moved along during the season.

"I have never in any way meant to shortchange this basketball team. I have talked from Day 1 about this team being very, very tough to play against, when we play well, offensively. I have said on given nights during this year that nobody in the country could have beaten us that night.

**Steve Alford and Joe Hillman exchange a late-game greeting with another white-jerseyed victory in sight**

John Terhune

"What is greatness in a team? Greatness in 1976 was (Quinn) Buckner and (Bobby) Wilkerson not letting anybody come across mid-court. Greatness was (Scott) May being a tremendous defensive player, and the second-best defensive forward on our team, (Tom) Abernethy being the best. Greatness was (Kent) Benson playing in the middle. That was a team that was almost impossible to beat, because of its toughness, its strength, its size. In 1981, there was a greatness to that team. (Randy) Wittman was a tremendous all-round player. Isiah Thomas was as tough — with as much ability — as anybody who ever played his position in college basketball. (Ray) Tolbert and (Landon) Turner were the two best defensive forwards I've ever seen. (Ted) Kitchel was a tough, hard-nosed guy playing inside. That team over the year developed into a great basketball team.

"And there was a greatness to this team. It doesn't have the two greatest defensive guards or the two greatest defensive forwards. Its greatness was a lot more subtle.

"These seniors as freshmen gave us a great treat when they came within a step or two of going to the NCAA finals in Seattle, beating the No. 1 team in the country, North Carolina, along the way. It was an unexpected brush with greatness. They learned a lot about the real world the next year. They weren't as good as they thought they were, as many of you thought they were. They had to suffer through a season that was very, very tough on them. They had to wonder, 'What happened?' I'm not sure they had the answers. And then we made the trip around the world (in the summer of 1985), and they began to get a little better and a little better. The 1985-86 season was for them almost a single mission to become a better basketball team, and they did. The problems of the past crept up in their last two games. I think they still felt there were questions they had to answer. It was in that regard that I feel these three seniors have carved a considerable niche for themselves in Indiana basketball history.

"The greatness in this team may be a greatness no other team here has had, to the degree that this one did — almost a total resolve not to recognize or be a part of defeat. This team played the last five minutes of critical games as well as I've ever seen a team play."

In Bloomington two weeks later, Alford was in a swirl of activity. He had just completed a nine-stop tour of Indiana communities as the top attraction on a Big Ten all-star team that included his fellow Hoosier captains, Meier and Thomas, plus Doug Altenberger and Ken Norman of Illinois, Doug Lee of Purdue, Antoine Joubert of Michigan and Shawn Watts and Elliot Fullen of Northwestern. He made a videotape of the workout program he had stayed on since he and his dad worked it out the summer of his freshman year in high school. A month after the season, he was named the Big Ten's most valuable player, the eighth time in Knight's 16 seasons one of his players won the award.

The tribute that seemed to mean most to him, however, was the recognition Knight had given to him and his teammates on the one simple scoreboard: mental toughness.

"When we seniors sat down before the season, more than anything else, more even than winning any games, we felt we wanted to prove to him and to ourselves, individually, that we *had* grown mentally and we *were* mentally tough. We felt that would take care of winning ball games.

"And this has been unbelievable. We accomplished not only a national championship but also that goal of showing we were mentally tough.

"I know the sophomores and the freshmen had to get a lot out of it, but from the seniors' standpoint, it was four years of a lot of hard work. Unlike the Olympics, this was four years with a lot of valleys and peaks that you had to overcome. Being able, on the final day of your career, to be up there cutting the nets was a dream come true."

At Indiana's basketball banquet, Steve Alford became the first Big Ten player to be his team's MVP four years — and a few weeks later added the Big Ten MVP award.

# President Reagan

It's a pleasure to welcome you all to the White House to welcome the NCAA men's basketball champs from Indiana University.

We figured the Rose Garden would be an appropriate place to host you all. The dimensions are about the size you're used to. I apologize; we didn't have enough time to paint free-throw lines and put up baskets to make you feel really at home.

This has been a very special week for you all as players, for your coach, shy and retiring Bobby Knight, and for the people of Indiana.

I grew up just one state west of the Wabash River and I know a little something about Hoosier hysteria. In Indiana, babies aren't born with silver shoes in their mouth. They come equipped with basketballs and high-topped sneakers. I don't know how mothers there manage. Basketball is a way of life in Indiana that many people will never understand.

A movie out these days —you know, the one with the funny name, Hoosiers — along with your example will help explain this phenomenon. I have to say also I have a personal memory of that, because back in my days of athletics, playing and later broadcasting, Indiana was sort of the capital of basketball. Many of your high schools played about 40 basketball games a season and no football. Some of those came to the college where I was enrolled. When the football season was over and I, having played some basketball in high school, toyed with the idea of now going out for basketball, on the first day at the gym I took a look at those fellows and what they were doing with a basketball and I said, 'No, I think I will go into swimming.'

One measure of Indiana basketball is much like politics and government: statistics. Indiana was co-champion this year in the tough Big Ten conference; they won 30 games, including a rather important 7-game run at the end of the season. This is the fifth NCAA basketball championship for Indiana, but the numbers don't match the thrill you provided for millions of basketball fans here in America. You won tough victories from extraordinary teams — LSU, Nevada-Las Vegas, and of course a one-point, come-from-behind victory against Syracuse right before the buzzer. This was no series for the faint of heart, players or spectators.

But let me talk about some individuals who are with us today. Seniors Todd Meier and Daryl Thomas have played with heart, talent and determination for Indiana for four years, and came through when called for Monday night. Ricky Calloway, Dean Garrett, Steve Eyl and Joe Hillman each provided us with clutch performances and moments of brilliance.

Keith Smart, the tournament most valuable player. Keith wanted to play basketball so badly that after an accident his senior year in high school he decided to grow six inches and play as a walk-on at Garden City Junior College in Kansas. And play he did. Last year, Keith was a junior college all-American. This year Keith iced a 16-foot jump shot with four seconds on the clock to give Indiana its national title. That's what I call progress.

Then there is Steve Alford, one of those basketball babies I referred to a moment ago.

Indiana's Mr. Basketball in high school, an Olympic gold medalist, two-time all-American, the leading scorer in Indiana history and Indiana's team leader. That's just on court.

Off the court, Steve is a conscientious student and a model citizen whose values are as important as his field-goal percentage. He's my kind of basketball player and he's America's kind of student-athlete.

Finally, I'd be remiss if I didn't offer a few words of comment about coach Bobby Knight. Everybody gets to take a shot at Bobby; why not the President of the United States? Actually, I'll leave Bobby's critics to their own devices. Critics aside, one thing is certain: Bobby cares deeply about his players on and off the court. He seeks to produce the best in his players through hard work, excellence in execution, and selfless team play. When all is said and done, Bobby is my kind of coach.

But you know the stats as well as I do. Bobby Knight is the winningest coach in Big Ten history. He's won eight Big Ten titles. He's won America gold medals in the 1979 Pan American Games and the 1984 Olympic Games, and he's coached three Indiana teams to national titles, joining Adolph Rupp and Johnny Wooden in the elite three-and-over fraternity.

Hard work makes for winners on the court. Dedication in the classroom makes for winners throughout life. These two elements are certainly at the core of this Indiana team. And I congratulate you for living this example.

Now, I understand Doc Bowen has planned a little reception for you at his place, so I'll close with what I understand is a popular Indiana benediction: If I don't see you in the future, I'll see you in the pasture.

---

Mr. President, thank you very much for taking the time and allowing us to bring this group of young men to visit with you this afternoon. I have here on behalf of the team —really, not just from the team but from the state of Indiana, where I think you well know you have a tremendous amount of supporters— a jacket that represents both the state of Indiana and Indiana University, basketball being a big thing in our state. I also thought I'd make it in red, our color, when I brought it to you. So I'd like to give you this jacket on behalf of the state of Indiana.

As a basketball team, we took a lot of pride in the fact that we were a pretty tough team. We came from behind a lot in some critical situations. We talked about what we'd like to say that would be most appropriate to you on behalf of our players and coaches, and it would be this:

Mr. President, I think you have shown all of us across America what it's like to be tough in critical situations. We have a great appreciation for your mental toughness and your competitiveness in the situations in which you've been involved. I think all of us in this country appreciate that more than anything else. I would hope our basketball team reflects those same ideals that you have during the time you have been here in the presidency.

Thank you very much for giving us that.

# Bob Knight

Steve Alford    Don Schlundt

Mike Woodson    Kent Benson

Scott May    Randy Wittman

Archie Dees    Walter Bellamy

Ray Tolbert    Jimmy Rayl

Uwe Blab    Ted Kitchel

# Indiana basketball statistics

## ALL GAMES: WON 30, LOST 4

| | G | S | M | Hi | 40 | FG | Pct. | 3FG | Pct. | FT | Pct. | R | Av. | Hi | A | Bl | St | TO | PF-FO | Pts | Av. | Hi |
|---|---|---|---|---|---|---|---|---|---|---|---|---|---|---|---|---|---|---|---|---|---|---|
| Steve Alford | 34 | 34 | 1261 | 55 | 8 | 241-508 | .473 | 107-202 | .530 | 160-180 | .889 | 87 | 2.6 | 6 | 123 | 3 | 39 | 64 | 52-0 | 749 | 22.0 | 42 |
| Daryl Thomas | 34 | 34 | 1003 | 41 | 5 | 199-370 | .538 | 0-0 | .000 | 136-173 | .786 | 194 | 5.7 | 11 | 27 | 13 | 45 | 71 | 98-2 | 534 | 15.7 | 32 |
| Rick Calloway | 29 | 27 | 881 | 40 | 2 | 146-275 | .531 | 0-0 | .000 | 72-97 | .742 | 126 | 4.4 | 13 | 76 | 7 | 31 | 68 | 78-2 | 364 | 12.6 | 21 |
| Dean Garrett | 34 | 33 | 952 | 46 | 3 | 163-301 | .542 | 0-0 | .000 | 61-96 | .635 | 288 | 8.5 | 16 | 21 | 93 | 17 | 41 | 92-2 | 387 | 11.4 | 21 |
| Keith Smart | 34 | 31 | 892 | 40 | 1 | 148-286 | .517 | 12-33 | .364 | 74-88 | .841 | 100 | 2.9 | 9 | 109 | 2 | 30 | 74 | 101-4 | 382 | 11.2 | 31 |
| Steve Eyl | 34 | 1 | 570 | 31 | 0 | 35-54 | .648 | 0-0 | .000 | 31-46 | .674 | 116 | 3.4 | 8 | 41 | 7 | 16 | 27 | 45-1 | 101 | 3.0 | 10 |
| Joe Hillman | 32 | 5 | 395 | 30 | 0 | 28-58 | .483 | 1-5 | .200 | 23-31 | .742 | 37 | 1.2 | 4 | 66 | 2 | 11 | 29 | 45-0 | 80 | 2.5 | 8 |
| M. Pelkowski | 14 | 1 | 118 | 20 | 0 | 24-46 | .522 | 2-3 | .667 | 3-5 | .600 | 27 | 1.9 | 5 | 2 | 3 | 2 | 7 | 22-0 | 53 | 3.8 | 11 |
| Kreigh Smith | 25 | 1 | 192 | 22 | 0 | 12-24 | .500 | 7-8 | .875 | 6-7 | .857 | 19 | 0.8 | 3 | 14 | 0 | 4 | 6 | 12-0 | 37 | 1.5 | 8 |
| Tony Freeman | 16 | 0 | 166 | 23 | 0 | 10-24 | .417 | 1-4 | .250 | 14-20 | .700 | 14 | 0.9 | 4 | 38 | 0 | 10 | 19 | 16-0 | 35 | 2.2 | 11 |
| Brian Sloan | 17 | 1 | 126 | 18 | 0 | 13-29 | .448 | 0-1 | .000 | 9-18 | .500 | 19 | 1.1 | 5 | 8 | 4 | 4 | 7 | 15-0 | 35 | 2.1 | 6 |
| Todd Meier | 29 | 0 | 190 | 28 | 0 | 9-20 | .450 | 0-0 | .000 | 13-22 | .591 | 43 | 1.5 | 5 | 7 | 1 | 6 | 14 | 35-0 | 31 | 1.1 | 5 |
| Dave Minor | 18 | 2 | 111 | 15 | 0 | 5-20 | .250 | 0-0 | .000 | 5-7 | .714 | 15 | 0.8 | 7 | 10 | 0 | 0 | 13 | 9-0 | 15 | 0.8 | 4 |
| Jeff Oliphant | 2 | 0 | 6 | 5 | 0 | 0-0 | .000 | 0-0 | .000 | 3-5 | .600 | 4 | 2.0 | 3 | 1 | 0 | 0 | 1 | 1-0 | 3 | 1.5 | 2 |
| Indiana | 34 | | | | | 1033-2015 | .513 | 130-256 | .508 | 610-795 | .767 | 1189 | 35.0 | 48 | 543 | 135 | 215 | 449 | 622-11 | 2806 | 82.5 | 107 |
| Opponents | 34 | | | | | 937-2077 | .451 | 118-307 | .384 | 420-620 | .677 | 1179 | 34.7 | 52 | 448 | 83 | 179 | 519 | 735-28 | 2412 | 70.9 | 101 |

## BIG TEN GAMES: WON 15, LOST 3

| | G | S | M | Hi | 40 | FG | Pct. | 3FG | Pct. | FT | Pct. | R | Av. | Hi | A | Bl | St | TO | PF-FO | Pts | Av. | Hi |
|---|---|---|---|---|---|---|---|---|---|---|---|---|---|---|---|---|---|---|---|---|---|---|
| Steve Alford | 18 | 18 | 687 | 55 | 4 | 126-267 | .472 | 54-108 | .500 | 85-95 | .895 | 44 | 2.4 | 6 | 63 | 2 | 22 | 34 | 25-0 | 391 | 21.7 | 42 |
| Daryl Thomas | 18 | 18 | 536 | 41 | 3 | 102-188 | .543 | 0-0 | .000 | 83-105 | .790 | 106 | 5.9 | 11 | 17 | 7 | 19 | 34 | 63-2 | 287 | 15.9 | 32 |
| Rick Calloway | 18 | 16 | 548 | 40 | 1 | 86-166 | .518 | 0-0 | .000 | 46-64 | .719 | 64 | 3.6 | 9 | 49 | 3 | 21 | 43 | 53-2 | 218 | 12.1 | 20 |
| Dean Garrett | 18 | 18 | 487 | 46 | 1 | 85-159 | .535 | 0-0 | .000 | 30-47 | .638 | 139 | 7.7 | 14 | 12 | 51 | 6 | 23 | 49-1 | 200 | 11.1 | 21 |
| Keith Smart | 18 | 17 | 459 | 40 | 1 | 76-143 | .531 | 9-20 | .450 | 35-40 | .875 | 46 | 2.6 | 6 | 47 | 1 | 17 | 36 | 56-2 | 196 | 10.9 | 31 |
| Steve Eyl | 18 | 0 | 333 | 31 | 0 | 22-31 | .710 | 0-0 | .000 | 18-24 | .750 | 64 | 3.6 | 8 | 21 | 4 | 8 | 13 | 26-1 | 62 | 3.4 | 10 |
| Joe Hillman | 17 | 1 | 189 | 30 | 0 | 13-29 | .448 | 1-4 | .250 | 11-13 | .846 | 16 | 0.9 | 4 | 26 | 0 | 6 | 15 | 25-0 | 38 | 2.2 | 8 |
| M. Pelkowski | 6 | 0 | 40 | 20 | 0 | 10-17 | .588 | 1-2 | .500 | 0-1 | .000 | 9 | 1.5 | 5 | 1 | 3 | 2 | 1 | 5-0 | 21 | 3.5 | 9 |
| Tony Freeman | 11 | 0 | 109 | 23 | 0 | 6-16 | .375 | 1-3 | .333 | 7-11 | .636 | 8 | 0.7 | 4 | 30 | 0 | 6 | 9 | 10-0 | 20 | 1.8 | 11 |
| Todd Meier | 15 | 0 | 118 | 28 | 0 | 6-13 | .462 | 0-0 | .000 | 8-14 | .571 | 21 | 1.4 | 4 | 4 | 0 | 5 | 10 | 21-0 | 20 | 1.3 | 5 |
| Brian Sloan | 8 | 0 | 66 | 18 | 0 | 6-12 | .500 | 0-0 | .000 | 3-8 | .375 | 10 | 1.3 | 5 | 4 | 1 | 2 | 4 | 6-0 | 15 | 1.9 | 5 |
| Dave Minor | 6 | 1 | 27 | 10 | 0 | 3-6 | .500 | 0-0 | .000 | 2-2 | 1.000 | 5 | 0.8 | 2 | 3 | 0 | 0 | 3 | 2-0 | 8 | 1.3 | 4 |
| Jeff Oliphant | 1 | 0 | 1 | 1 | 0 | 0-0 | .000 | 0-0 | .000 | 1-2 | .500 | 1 | 1.0 | 1 | 0 | 0 | 0 | 0 | 0-0 | 1 | 1.0 | 1 |
| Kreigh Smith | 11 | 1 | 75 | 22 | 0 | 2-7 | .286 | 2-2 | 1.000 | 0-0 | .000 | 7 | 0.6 | 3 | 6 | 0 | 3 | 1 | 3-0 | 6 | 0.5 | 6 |
| Indiana | 18 | | | | | 543-1054 | .515 | 68-139 | .489 | 329-426 | .772 | 591 | 32.8 | 42 | 283 | 72 | 117 | 233 | 344-8 | 1483 | 82.4 | 103 |
| Opponents | 18 | | | | | 495-1061 | .467 | 63-160 | .394 | 253-350 | .723 | 607 | 33.7 | 46 | 249 | 45 | 94 | 272 | 387-11 | 1306 | 72.6 | 101 |

## NCAA TOURNAMENT GAMES: WON 6, LOST 0

| | G | S | M | Hi | 40 | FG | Pct. | 3FG | Pct. | FT | Pct. | R | Av. | Hi | A | Bl | St | TO | PF-FO | Pts | Av. | Hi |
|---|---|---|---|---|---|---|---|---|---|---|---|---|---|---|---|---|---|---|---|---|---|---|
| Steve Alford | 6 | 6 | 208 | 40 | 0 | 42-81 | .519 | 21-34 | .618 | 33-38 | .868 | 14 | 2.3 | 4 | 27 | 0 | 5 | 11 | 14-0 | 138 | 23.0 | 33 |
| Daryl Thomas | 6 | 6 | 176 | 40 | 1 | 37-66 | .561 | 0-0 | .000 | 24-28 | .857 | 31 | 5.2 | 8 | 2 | 2 | 7 | 19 | 14-0 | 98 | 16.3 | 27 |
| Keith Smart | 6 | 6 | 182 | 39 | 0 | 34-62 | .548 | 0-5 | .000 | 22-26 | .846 | 27 | 4.5 | 9 | 28 | 0 | 6 | 15 | 18-1 | 90 | 15.0 | 21 |
| Dean Garrett | 6 | 6 | 198 | 40 | 1 | 35-54 | .648 | 0-0 | .000 | 15-23 | .652 | 55 | 9.2 | 15 | 2 | 15 | 2 | 9 | 17-0 | 85 | 14.2 | 20 |
| Rick Calloway | 6 | 6 | 196 | 40 | 1 | 32-59 | .542 | 0-0 | .000 | 15-17 | .882 | 42 | 7.0 | 13 | 18 | 1 | 5 | 17 | 14-0 | 79 | 13.2 | 21 |
| Joe Hillman | 6 | 0 | 65 | 20 | 0 | 6-9 | .667 | 0-0 | .000 | 2-6 | .333 | 8 | 1.3 | 3 | 15 | 1 | 3 | 3 | 6-0 | 14 | 2.3 | 7 |
| Steve Eyl | 6 | 0 | 81 | 20 | 0 | 5-8 | .625 | 0-0 | .000 | 3-6 | .500 | 24 | 4.0 | 5 | 11 | 1 | 3 | 4 | 10-0 | 13 | 2.2 | 7 |
| Brian Sloan | 2 | 0 | 8 | 7 | 0 | 1-3 | .333 | 0-0 | .000 | 4-4 | 1.000 | 3 | 1.5 | 3 | 1 | 0 | 0 | 1 | 0-0 | 6 | 3.0 | 6 |
| Tony Freeman | 2 | 0 | 18 | 17 | 0 | 1-1 | 1.000 | 0-0 | .000 | 2-2 | 1.000 | 1 | 0.5 | 1 | 1 | 0 | 6 | 10 | 12-0 | 4 | 2.0 | 4 |
| M. Pelkowski | 1 | 0 | 8 | 8 | 0 | 1-4 | .250 | 0-0 | .000 | 0-1 | 1.000 | 3 | 1.5 | 3 | 2 | 0 | 0 | 2 | 2-0 | 2 | 2.0 | 2 |
| Kreigh Smith | 6 | 0 | 12 | 5 | 0 | 1-4 | .250 | 0-1 | .000 | 0-0 | .000 | 3 | 0.5 | 1 | 1 | 0 | 0 | 0 | 0-0 | 2 | 0.3 | 2 |
| Dave Minor | 3 | 0 | 9 | 7 | 0 | 0-1 | .000 | 0-0 | .000 | 2-2 | 1.000 | 2 | 0.7 | 1 | 0 | 0 | 0 | 1 | 1-0 | 2 | 0.7 | 2 |
| Jeff Oliphant | 1 | 0 | 5 | 5 | 0 | 0-0 | .000 | 0-0 | .000 | 2-3 | .667 | 3 | 3.0 | 3 | 1 | 0 | 0 | 0 | 0-0 | 2 | 2.0 | 2 |
| Todd Meier | 6 | 0 | 24 | 9 | 0 | 0-0 | .000 | 0-0 | .000 | 0-1 | .000 | 8 | 1.3 | 2 | 0 | 0 | 1 | 4 | 4-0 | 0 | 0.0 | 0 |
| Indiana | 6 | | | | | 195-352 | .540 | 21-40 | .525 | 124-156 | .795 | 234 | 39.0 | 45 | 108 | 20 | 31 | 83 | 104-1 | 535 | 89.2 | 107 |
| Opponents | 6 | | | | | 185-416 | .445 | 37-91 | .407 | 65-100 | .650 | 200 | 33.3 | 38 | 90 | 15 | 32 | 78 | 138-8 | 472 | 78.7 | 93 |

## IU's leading scorers

| | | | |
|---|---|---|---|
| 1. | Steve Alford | 1984-87 | 2,438 |
| 2. | Don Schlundt | 1952-55 | 2,192 |
| 3. | Mike Woodson | 1977-80 | 2,061 |
| 4. | Kent Benson | 1974-77 | 1,740 |
| 5. | Scott May | 1974-76 | 1,593 |
| 6. | Randy Wittman | 1979-83 | 1,549 |
| 7. | Archie Dees | 1956-58 | 1,546 |
| 8. | Walter Bellamy | 1959-61 | 1,441 |
| 9. | Ray Tolbert | 1978-81 | 1,427 |
| 10. | Jimmy Rayl | 1961-63 | 1,401 |
| 11. | Uwe Blab | 1982-85 | 1,357 |
| 12. | Ted Kitchel | 1980-83 | 1,336 |
| 13. | Tom Bolyard | 1961-63 | 1,299 |
| 14. | Joby Wright | 1969-72 | 1,272 |
| 15. | Steve Green | 1973-75 | 1,265 |
| 16. | Tom Van Arsdale | 1963-65 | 1,252 |
| 17. | Dick Van Arsdale | 1963-65 | 1,240 |
| 18. | Steve Downing | 1971-73 | 1,220 |
| 19. | Quinn Buckner | 1973-76 | 1,195 |
| 20. | Vern Payne | 1966-68 | 1,101 |
| 21. | Joe Cooke | 1968-70 | 1,099 |
| 22. | Bob Leonard | 1952-54 | 1,098 |
| 23. | Daryl Thomas | 1984-87 | 1,095 |
| 24. | Butch Joyner | 1966-68 | 1,030 |

## IU's NCAA leaders

### TOTAL POINTS

| | G | TP | Av. | Hi |
|---|---|---|---|---|
| 1. Steve Alford, 1984, '86, '87 | 10 | 217 | 21.7 | 33 |
| 2. Don Schlundt, 1953, '54 | 6 | 162 | 27.0 | 41 |
| 3. Kent Benson, 1975, '76 | 8 | 157 | 19.4 | 33 |
| 4. Isiah Thomas, 1980, '81 | 7 | 138 | 19.7 | 30 |
| 5. Quinn Buckner, 1973, '75, '76 | 12 | 130 | 10.8 | 16 |
| 6. Randy Wittman, 1981, '82, '83 | 9 | 126 | 14.0 | 22 |
| 7. Steve Green, 1973, '75 | 7 | 117 | 16.7 | 34 |
| 8. Scott May, 1975, '76 | 8 | 115 | 14.4 | 33 |

## NCAA coaching records

| | W | L | Pct. | Ch. |
|---|---|---|---|---|
| 1. Bob Knight, Indiana | 27 | 8 | .771 | 3 |
| 2. Dale Brown, LSU | 14 | 6 | .700 | 0 |
|    Norm Sloan, Florida | 7 | 3 | .700 | 1 |
| 4. Rollie Massimino, Villanova | 16 | 7 | .696 | 1 |
| 5. Denny Crum, Louisville | 27 | 12 | .692 | 2 |
| 6. Jim Valvano, N. Carolina St. | 13 | 6 | .684 | 1 |
| 7. John Thompson, Georgetown | 21 | 10 | .677 | 1 |
| 8. Dean Smith, North Carolina | 37 | 18 | .673 | 1 |
| 9. Jud Heathcote, Michigan State | 10 | 5 | .667 | 1 |
|    Bill Foster, Northwestern | 6 | 3 | .667 | 0 |
| 11. Jerry Tarkanian, UNLV | 23 | 13 | .639 | 0 |
| 12. Terry Holland, Virginia | 11 | 7 | .611 | 0 |
| 13. Gene Bartow, Ala.-Birmingham | 14 | 10 | .583 | 0 |
| 14. Hugh Durham, Georgia | 8 | 6 | .571 | 0 |

## At Assembly Hall

| INDIANA RECORDS | | | ATTENDANCE | |
|---|---|---|---|---|
| Year | W | L | Ranked by average | |
| 1986-87** | 15- | 0 | 1975-76* | 16,892 |
| 1974-75* | 14- | 0 | 1979-80* | 16,762 |
| 1972-73* | 12- | 0 | 1986-87** | 16,600 |
| 1975-76* | 12- | 0 | 1974-75* | 16,444 |
| 1977-78 | 13- | 1 | 1982-83* | 16,327 |
| 1979-80* | 13- | 1 | 1973-74** | 16,181 |
| 1981-82 | 13- | 1 | 1980-81* | 16,112 |
| 1982-83* | 13- | 1 | 1983-84 | 15,970 |
| 1971-72 | 10- | 1 | 1984-85 | 15,692 |
| 1973-74** | 10- | 1 | 1985-86 | 15,670 |
| 1980-81* | 14- | 2 | 1981-82 | 15,650 |
| 1985-86 | 13- | 2 | 1976-77 | 15,552 |
| 1978-79 | 12- | 2 | 1977-78 | 14,539 |
| 1983-84 | 12- | 3 | 1978-79 | 14,364 |
| 1976-77 | 9- | 4 | 1972-73* | 14,031 |
| 1984-85 | 10- | 7 | 1971-72 | 13,284 |

*Big Ten champion; **co-champion

# Big Ten champions

NCAA champions in capitals

| | Conference W | L | Pct. | All Games W | L | Pct. |
|---|---|---|---|---|---|---|
| 1987—INDIANA | 15 | 3 | .833 | 30 | 4 | .882 |
| Purdue | 15 | 3 | .833 | 25 | 5 | .833 |
| 1986—Michigan | 14 | 4 | .778 | 28 | 5 | .848 |
| 1985—Michigan | 16 | 2 | .889 | 26 | 4 | .867 |
| 1984—Illinois | 15 | 3 | .833 | 24 | 4 | .857 |
| Purdue | 15 | 3 | .833 | 22 | 6 | .786 |
| 1983—Indiana | 13 | 5 | .722 | 23 | 5 | .821 |
| 1982—Minnesota | 14 | 4 | .778 | 23 | 6 | .793 |
| 1981—INDIANA | 14 | 4 | .778 | 26 | 9 | .743 |
| 1980—Indiana | 13 | 5 | .722 | 21 | 8 | .724 |
| 1979—MICHIGAN STATE | 13 | 5 | .722 | 26 | 6 | .813 |
| Purdue | 13 | 5 | .722 | 27 | 8 | .771 |
| Iowa | 13 | 5 | .722 | 20 | 8 | .714 |
| 1978—Michigan State | 15 | 3 | .833 | 25 | 5 | .833 |
| 1977—Michigan | 16 | 2 | .889 | 26 | 4 | .867 |
| 1976—INDIANA | 18 | 0 | 1.000 | 32 | 0 | 1.000 |
| 1975—Indiana | 18 | 0 | 1.000 | 31 | 1 | .969 |
| 1974—Michigan | 12 | 2 | .857 | 22 | 5 | .814 |
| Indiana | 12 | 2 | .857 | 23 | 5 | .821 |
| 1973—Indiana | 11 | 3 | .786 | 22 | 6 | .786 |
| 1972—Minnesota | 11 | 3 | .786 | 18 | 7 | .750 |
| 1971—Ohio State | 13 | 1 | .929 | 20 | 6 | .769 |
| 1970—Iowa | 14 | 0 | 1.000 | 20 | 6 | .769 |
| 1969—Purdue | 13 | 1 | .929 | 23 | 5 | .821 |
| 1968—Ohio State | 10 | 4 | .714 | 21 | 8 | .724 |
| Iowa | 10 | 4 | .714 | 16 | 9 | .640 |
| 1967—Indiana | 10 | 4 | .714 | 18 | 8 | .692 |
| Michigan State | 10 | 4 | .714 | 16 | 7 | .696 |
| 1966—Michigan | 11 | 3 | .786 | 18 | 8 | .692 |
| 1965—Michigan | 13 | 1 | .929 | 24 | 4 | .857 |
| 1964—Michigan | 11 | 3 | .786 | 23 | 5 | .821 |
| Ohio State | 11 | 3 | .786 | 16 | 8 | .667 |
| 1963—Ohio State | 11 | 3 | .786 | 20 | 4 | .833 |
| Illinois | 11 | 3 | .786 | 20 | 6 | .769 |
| 1962—Ohio State | 13 | 1 | .929 | 26 | 2 | .929 |
| 1961—Ohio State | 14 | 0 | 1.000 | 27 | 1 | .964 |
| 1960—OHIO STATE | 13 | 1 | .929 | 25 | 3 | .893 |
| 1959—Michigan State | 12 | 2 | .857 | 19 | 4 | .826 |
| 1958—Indiana | 10 | 4 | .714 | 13 | 11 | .542 |
| 1957—Indiana | 10 | 4 | .714 | 14 | 8 | .636 |
| Michigan State | 10 | 4 | .714 | 16 | 10 | .615 |
| 1956—Iowa | 13 | 1 | .929 | 20 | 6 | .769 |
| 1955—Iowa | 11 | 3 | .786 | 19 | 7 | .731 |
| 1954—Indiana | 12 | 2 | .857 | 20 | 4 | .833 |
| 1953—INDIANA | 17 | 1 | .944 | 23 | 3 | .895 |
| 1952—Illinois | 12 | 2 | .857 | 22 | 4 | .846 |
| 1951—Illinois | 13 | 1 | .929 | 22 | 5 | .815 |
| 1950—Ohio State | 11 | 1 | .917 | 22 | 4 | .846 |
| 1949—Illinois | 10 | 2 | .833 | 21 | 4 | .840 |
| 1948—Michigan | 10 | 2 | .933 | 15 | 5 | .750 |
| 1947—Wisconsin | 9 | 3 | .750 | 16 | 6 | .727 |
| 1946—Ohio State | 10 | 2 | .833 | 16 | 5 | .762 |
| 1945—Iowa | 11 | 1 | .917 | 17 | 1 | .944 |
| 1944—Ohio State | 10 | 2 | .833 | 14 | 7 | .667 |
| 1943—Illinois | 12 | 0 | 1.000 | 17 | 1 | .944 |
| 1942—Illinois | 13 | 2 | .867 | 18 | 5 | .783 |
| 1941—WISCONSIN | 11 | 1 | .917 | 20 | 3 | .870 |

| | Conference W | L | Pct. | All Games W | L | Pct. |
|---|---|---|---|---|---|---|
| 1940—Purdue | 10 | 2 | .833 | 16 | 4 | .800 |
| INDIANA* | 9 | 3 | .750 | 20 | 3 | .870 |
| 1939—Ohio State | 10 | 2 | .833 | 16 | 7 | .696 |
| 1938—Purdue | 10 | 2 | .833 | 16 | 4 | .800 |
| 1937—Minnesota | 10 | 2 | .833 | 14 | 6 | .700 |
| Illinois | 10 | 2 | .833 | 14 | 4 | .778 |
| 1936—Indiana | 11 | 1 | .917 | 18 | 2 | .900 |
| Purdue | 11 | 1 | .917 | 16 | 4 | .800 |
| 1935—Illinois | 9 | 3 | .750 | 15 | 5 | .750 |
| Purdue | 9 | 3 | .750 | 17 | 3 | .850 |
| Wisconsin | 9 | 3 | .750 | 15 | 5 | .750 |
| 1934—Purdue | 10 | 2 | .833 | 17 | 3 | .850 |
| 1933—Northwestern | 10 | 2 | .833 | 15 | 4 | .890 |
| Ohio State | 10 | 2 | .833 | 17 | 3 | .850 |
| 1932—Purdue | 11 | 1 | .917 | 17 | 1 | .944 |
| 1931—Northwestern | 11 | 1 | .917 | 16 | 1 | .941 |
| 1930—Purdue | 10 | 0 | 1.000 | 13 | 2 | .867 |
| 1929—Michigan | 10 | 2 | .833 | 14 | 2 | .875 |
| Wisconsin | 10 | 2 | .833 | 15 | 2 | .882 |
| 1928—Indiana | 10 | 2 | .833 | 15 | 2 | .882 |
| Purdue | 10 | 2 | .833 | 15 | 2 | .882 |
| 1927—Michigan | 10 | 2 | .833 | 14 | 3 | .824 |
| 1926—Indiana | 8 | 4 | .667 | 12 | 5 | .706 |
| Iowa | 8 | 4 | .667 | 12 | 5 | .706 |
| Michigan | 8 | 4 | .667 | 12 | 5 | .706 |
| Purdue | 8 | 4 | .667 | 13 | 4 | .765 |
| 1925—Ohio State | 11 | 1 | .917 | 14 | 2 | .875 |
| 1924—Wisconsin | 8 | 4 | .667 | 11 | 5 | .688 |
| Chicago | 8 | 4 | .667 | 9 | 7 | .563 |
| Illinois | 8 | 4 | .667 | 11 | 6 | .647 |
| 1923—Iowa | 11 | 1 | .917 | 12 | 2 | .857 |
| Wisconsin | 11 | 1 | .917 | 12 | 3 | .800 |
| 1922—Purdue | 8 | 1 | .889 | 15 | 3 | .833 |
| 1921—Michigan | 8 | 2 | .800 | 16 | 4 | .800 |
| 1920—Chicago | 10 | 2 | .833 | 14 | 4 | .778 |
| 1919—Minnesota | 10 | 0 | 1.000 | 13 | 0 | 1.000 |
| 1918—Wisconsin | 9 | 3 | .750 | 14 | 3 | .824 |
| 1917—Illinois | 10 | 2 | .833 | 13 | 3 | .813 |
| Minnesota | 10 | 2 | .833 | 12 | 2 | .857 |
| 1916—Wisconsin | 11 | 1 | .917 | 20 | 1 | .952 |
| 1915—Illinois | 12 | 0 | 1.000 | 16 | 0 | 1.000 |
| 1914—Wisconsin | 12 | 0 | 1.000 | 15 | 0 | 1.000 |
| 1913—Wisconsin | 11 | 1 | .917 | 14 | 1 | .933 |
| 1912—Wisconsin | 12 | 0 | 1.000 | 15 | 0 | 1.000 |
| Purdue | 10 | 0 | 1.000 | 12 | 0 | 1.000 |
| 1911—Purdue | 8 | 4 | .667 | 11 | 4 | .733 |
| Minnesota | 8 | 4 | .667 | 10 | 4 | .714 |
| 1910—Chicago | 9 | 3 | .750 | 9 | 3 | .750 |
| 1909—Chicago | 12 | 0 | 1.000 | 12 | 0 | 1.000 |
| 1908—Chicago | 7 | 1 | .875 | 21 | 2 | .913 |
| 1907—Chicago | 6 | 2 | .750 | 22 | 2 | .917 |
| Minnesota | 6 | 2 | .750 | 13 | 3 | .867 |
| Wisconsin | 6 | 2 | .750 | 11 | 3 | .786 |
| 1906—Minnesota | 6 | 1 | .857 | 13 | 2 | .867 |

*Runner-up Indiana, which had defeated Purdue twice, was designated as the Big Ten's tournament entry and won the national championship.

# NCAA highs

| INDIANA |
|---|
| 41—Don Schlundt, vs. Notre Dame, 1953 |
| 34—Steve Green, vs. Oregon State, 1975 |
| 33—Kent Benson, vs. Kentucky, 1975 |
| 33—Scott May, vs. St. John's, 1976 |
| 33—Steve Alford, vs. Nevada-Las Vegas, 1987 |
| 31—Steve Alford, vs. Auburn, 1987 |
| 30—Don Schlundt, vs. Kansas, 1953* |
| 30—Isiah Thomas, vs. Purdue, 1980 |
| 29—Don Schlundt, vs. Louisiana State, 1953 |
| 29—Don Schlundt, vs. Louisiana State, 1954 |
| 29—Steve Downing, vs. Marquette, 1973 |
| 28—Archie Dees, vs. Notre Dame, 1958 |
| 27—Isiah Thomas, vs. Alabama-Birmingham, 1981 |
| 27—Steve Alford, vs. North Carolina, 1984 |
| 27—Daryl Thomas, vs. Auburn, 1987 |
| 26—Steve Downing, vs. UCLA, 1973 |
| 26—Scott May, vs. Michigan, 1976* |
| 26—Mike Woodson, vs. Furman, 1978 |
| 26—Ray Tolbert, vs. Maryland, 1981 |
| 25—Archie Dees, vs. Miami, 1958 |
| 25—Scott May, vs. Alabama, 1976 |
| 25—Kent Benson, vs. Michigan, 1976* |
| 24—Mike Woodson, vs. Villanova, 1978 |
| 24—Ted Kitchel, vs. Alabama-Birmingham, 1982 |
| 24—Steve Alford, vs. Cleveland State, 1986 |
| 23—Don Schlundt, vs. DePaul, 1953 |
| 23—Steve Downing, vs. Kentucky, 1973 |
| 23—Kent Benson, vs. Oregon State, 1975 |
| 23—Isiah Thomas, vs. North Carolina, 1981* |
| 23—Steve Alford, vs. Syracuse, 1987* |
| *Championship game |

| IU OPPONENTS |
|---|
| 38—Freddie Banks, Nevada-Las Vegas, 1987 |
| 36—Wayne Embry, Miami, 1958 |
| 32—Armon Gilliam, Nevada-Las Vegas, 1987 |
| 31—Tom Hawkins, Notre Dame, 1958 |
| 30—Mike Jones, Auburn, 1987 |
| 29—Bob Pettit, Louisiana State, 1953 |
| 29—John McCarthy, Notre Dame, 1958 |
| 29—Glen Combs, Virginia Tech, 1967 |
| 29—Kevin Stacom, Providence, 1973 |
| 27—Ron Feiereisel, DePaul, 1953 |
| 27—Bob Pettit, Louisiana State, 1954 |
| 27—Kelvin Johnson, Richmond, 1984 |
| 27—Clinton Ransey, Cleveland State, 1986 |
| 26—B.H. Born, Kansas, 1953* |
| 26—Sam Perkins, North Carolina, 1984 |
| 25—Dick Rosenthal, Notre Dame, 1954 |
| 25—Johnny Powell, Miami, 1958 |
| 25—Forest Grant, Robert Morris, 1982 |
| 24—Jeff Moore, Auburn, 1987 |
| 23—Jim Andrews, Kentucky, 1973 |
| 23—Ron Widby, Tennessee, 1967 |
| 23—Keith Herron, Villanova, 1978 |
| 23—Oliver Robinson, Alabama-Birmingham, 1982 |
| 23—Tommy Amaker, Duke, 1987 |
| 22—Tommy Curtis, UCLA, 1973 |
| 22—Mike Flynn, Kentucky, 1975 |
| 22—Earl Tatum, Marquette, 1976 |
| 22—Albert King, Maryland, 1981 |
| 21—Al Daniel, Furman, 1978 |
| 21—Jeff Gromos, Fairfield, 1987 |

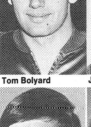

**Tom Bolyard** **Joby Wright**

**Steve Green** **Tom Van Arsdale**

**Dick Van Arsdale** **Steve Downing**

**Quinn Buckner** **Vern Payne**

**Joe Cooke** **Bob Leonard**

**Daryl Thomas** **Butch Joyner**

# Indiana's New Castle connection

## Steve Alford's record IU career

**Vern Huffman** — All-America, '36

**Marvin Huffman** — NCAA MVP, '40

**Butch Joyner** — 1,030 points, '66-68

**Kent Benson** — All-America, '76-77

### SENIOR

| | 3PFG | M | FG | FT | R | A | BS | St | TO | PF | TP | Total |
|---|---|---|---|---|---|---|---|---|---|---|---|---|
| Syracuse | 7-10 | 40 | 8-15 | 0-0 | 3 | 5 | 0 | 2 | 3 | 2 | 23 | 2438 |
| Nevada-LV | 2-4 | 37 | 10-10 | 11-13 | 4 | 2 | 0 | 0 | 2 | 4 | 33 | 2415 |
| LSU | 2-4 | 40 | 4-9 | 10-10 | 0 | 7 | 0 | 0 | 0 | 1 | 20 | 2382 |
| Duke | 1-3 | 38 | 6-16 | 5-7 | 2 | 5 | 0 | 0 | 2 | 2 | 18 | 2362 |
| Auburn | 7-11 | 38 | 10-17 | 4-5 | 3 | 5 | 0 | 0 | 2 | 2 | 31 | 2344 |
| Fairfield | 2-2 | 25 | 4-5 | 3-3 | 2 | 3 | 0 | 3 | 2 | 3 | 13 | 2313 |
| Ohio St. | 2-7 | 39 | 6-13 | 8-10 | 2 | 3 | 0 | 1 | 0 | 0 | 22 | 2300 |
| Illinois | 1-4 | 40 | 6-16 | 4-5 | 3 | 8 | 0 | 1 | 4 | 2 | 17 | 2278 |
| Purdue | 1-2 | 39 | 7-15 | 0-0 | 2 | 1 | 0 | 2 | 1 | 3 | 15 | 2261 |
| Iowa | 4-7 | 37 | 8-15 | 4-4 | 0 | 3 | 0 | 0 | 3 | 3 | 24 | 2246 |
| Minnesota | 3-9 | 39 | 7-20 | 0-0 | 2 | 3 | 0 | 1 | 1 | 1 | 17 | 2222 |
| Wisconsin | 2-11 | 55 | 4-19 | 3-4 | 4 | 2 | 1 | 4 | 1 | 1 | 13 | 2205 |
| No'western | 3-7 | 40 | 4-13 | 4-4 | 3 | 4 | 0 | 0 | 3 | 3 | 15 | 2192 |
| Michigan | 4-5 | 38 | 10-15 | 6-7 | 2 | 2 | 1 | 0 | 0 | 0 | 30 | 2177 |
| Mich.St. | 4-5 | 38 | 12-19 | 14-15 | 0 | 0 | 0 | 3 | 3 | 0 | 42 | 2147 |
| Purdue | 2-5 | 39 | 8-18 | 13-15 | 6 | 5 | 0 | 0 | 2 | 2 | 31 | 2105 |
| Illinois | 0-3 | 39 | 3-11 | 4-4 | 3 | 2 | 0 | 2 | 1 | 3 | 10 | 2074 |
| Minnesota | 4-8 | 36 | 7-16 | 6-6 | 2 | 1 | 0 | 2 | 2 | 0 | 24 | 2064 |
| Iowa | 5-8 | 39 | 6-11 | 4-4 | 0 | 3 | 0 | 0 | 2 | 2 | 21 | 2040 |
| No'western | 3-6 | 26 | 4-9 | 0-0 | 3 | 6 | 0 | 2 | 1 | 0 | 11 | 2019 |
| Wisconsin | 7-8 | 26 | 7-9 | 0-1 | 0 | 5 | 0 | 2 | 2 | 0 | 21 | 2008 |
| Michigan | 3-3 | 39 | 9-16 | 2-2 | 5 | 4 | 0 | 1 | 4 | 1 | 23 | 1987 |
| Mich.St. | 3-5 | 38 | 11-19 | 8-8 | 2 | 3 | 0 | 1 | 1 | 0 | 33 | 1964 |
| Ohio St. | 3-5 | 40 | 7-13 | 5-6 | 5 | 9 | 0 | 0 | 3 | 4 | 22 | 1931 |
| IllinoisSt. | 1-3 | 36 | 6-16 | 8-8 | 5 | 7 | 0 | 0 | 3 | 1 | 21 | 1909 |
| Princeton | 8-11 | 32 | 9-13 | 0-0 | 3 | 3 | 0 | 1 | 0 | 1 | 26 | 1888 |
| Louisville | 3-7 | 40 | 4-17 | 6-7 | 3 | 2 | 0 | 2 | 1 | 2 | 17 | 1862 |
| Morehead | 4-8 | 28 | 6-12 | 2-3 | 1 | 4 | 0 | 2 | 1 | 0 | 18 | 1845 |
| E.Carolina | 1-3 | 28 | 6-13 | 1-1 | 6 | 3 | 0 | 4 | 0 | 1 | 14 | 1827 |
| NC-Wilm. | 4-10 | 40 | 8-21 | 0-1 | 2 | 1 | 0 | 0 | 3 | 1 | 20 | 1813 |
| Vanderbilt | 4-5 | 40 | 9-17 | 6-6 | 2 | 5 | 0 | 0 | 2 | 1 | 28 | 1793 |
| Kentucky | 2-2 | 39 | 10-19 | 4-5 | 2 | 6 | 0 | 2 | 3 | 2 | 26 | 1765 |
| Notre Dame | 2-6 | 40 | 7-14 | 10-10 | 0 | 1 | 1 | 0 | 0 | 2 | 26 | 1739 |
| Montana St. | 3-5 | 33 | 8-18 | 5-6 | 5 | 1 | 0 | 1 | 6 | 2 | 24 | 1713 |

### JUNIOR

| | M | FG | FT | R | A | BS | St | TO | PF | TP | Total |
|---|---|---|---|---|---|---|---|---|---|---|---|
| Cleveland St. | 40 | 10-20 | 4-4 | 2 | 7 | 0 | 1 | 1 | 1 | 24 | 1689 |
| Michigan | 33 | 7-11 | 1-1 | 1 | 1 | 0 | 2 | 1 | 0 | 15 | 1665 |
| Mich. St. | 39 | 12-19 | 7-8 | 2 | 4 | 0 | 3 | 2 | 1 | 31 | 1650 |
| Iowa | 40 | 8-15 | 9-10 | 2 | 3 | 0 | 1 | 4 | 1 | 25 | 1619 |
| Minnesota | 26 | 9-14 | 4-5 | 2 | 4 | 0 | 2 | 1 | 1 | 22 | 1594 |
| Purdue | 40 | 3-12 | 2-2 | 5 | 1 | 0 | 0 | 0 | 1 | 8 | 1572 |
| Illinois | 40 | 11-19 | 2-2 | 2 | 4 | 0 | 1 | 3 | 0 | 24 | 1564 |
| Ohio St. | 39 | 9-17 | 14-15 | 5 | 2 | 0 | 1 | 2 | 2 | 32 | 1540 |
| Northwestern | 36 | 9-18 | 3-4 | 0 | 1 | 0 | 6 | 0 | 0 | 21 | 1508 |
| Wisconsin | 40 | 10-15 | 3-5 | 3 | 1 | 0 | 1 | 2 | 1 | 23 | 1487 |
| Minnesota | 40 | 8-15 | 2-3 | 2 | 2 | 0 | 1 | 2 | 2 | 18 | 1464 |
| Iowa | 26 | 5-11 | 0-0 | 1 | 2 | 0 | 0 | 2 | 0 | 10 | 1446 |
| Illinois | 40 | 6-14 | 4-6 | 3 | 2 | 0 | 1 | 0 | 1 | 16 | 1436 |
| Purdue | 45 | 11-20 | 5-7 | 2 | 1 | 0 | 1 | 2 | 3 | 27 | 1420 |
| Ohio St. | 40 | 12-20 | 8-9 | 4 | 2 | 0 | 1 | 3 | 2 | 32 | 1393 |
| Wisconsin | 39 | 17-25 | 4-4 | 4 | 4 | 0 | 1 | 1 | 1 | 38 | 1361 |
| Northwestern | 34 | 8-15 | 3-3 | 5 | 2 | 0 | 3 | 5 | 3 | 19 | 1323 |
| Mich. St. | 40 | 9-19 | 5-5 | 0 | 3 | 0 | 3 | 2 | 2 | 23 | 1304 |
| Michigan | 37 | 9-15 | 2-4 | 2 | 1 | 0 | 1 | 2 | 3 | 20 | 1281 |
| Miss. St. | 32 | 5-11 | 4-5 | 1 | 2 | 0 | 2 | 1 | 2 | 14 | 1261 |
| Idaho | 33 | 11-20 | 2-2 | 3 | 4 | 0 | 5 | 2 | 0 | 24 | 1247 |
| Iowa St. | 35 | 12-19 | 0-0 | 6 | 5 | 0 | 1 | 1 | 2 | 24 | 1223 |
| Louisville | 40 | 11-16 | 5-6 | 4 | 5 | 0 | 2 | 3 | 3 | 27 | 1199 |
| Texas Tech | 33 | 5-12 | 0-0 | 4 | 4 | 0 | 0 | 0 | 3 | 10 | 1172 |
| La. Tech | 33 | 10-17 | 5-5 | 3 | 5 | 0 | 3 | 2 | 2 | 25 | 1162 |
| Kansas St. | 40 | 7-12 | 8-8 | 2 | 1 | 0 | 2 | 0 | 4 | 22 | 1137 |
| Kentucky | | | | | Did not play | | | | | | |
| Notre Dame | 39 | 13-23 | 6-7 | 2 | 3 | 0 | 2 | 3 | 3 | 32 | 1115 |
| Kent St. | 39 | 7-13 | 10-10 | 3 | 3 | 1 | 3 | 3 | 1 | 24 | 1083 |

### SOPHOMORE

| | M | FG | FT | R | A | BS | St | TO | PF | TP | Total |
|---|---|---|---|---|---|---|---|---|---|---|---|
| UCLA | 40 | 7-15 | 2-3 | 5 | 2 | 0 | 1 | 0 | 3 | 16 | 1059 |
| Tennessee | 40 | 9-14 | 5-6 | 2 | 3 | 0 | 1 | 1 | 3 | 23 | 1043 |
| Marquette | 50 | 10-16 | 9-10 | 4 | 1 | 0 | 0 | 3 | 2 | 29 | 1020 |
| Richmond | 37 | 7-13 | 0-0 | 1 | 4 | 0 | 2 | 1 | 2 | 14 | 991 |
| Butler | 39 | 11-16 | 4-4 | 4 | 2 | 0 | 8 | 3 | 0 | 26 | 977 |
| Michigan | 38 | 11-16 | 0-0 | 6 | 4 | 0 | 1 | 1 | 0 | 22 | 951 |
| Mich. St. | 40 | 2-12 | 4-5 | 1 | 2 | 0 | 0 | 1 | 3 | 8 | 929 |
| Iowa | 37 | 4-10 | 4-4 | 4 | 3 | 0 | 1 | 1 | 2 | 12 | 921 |
| Minnesota | 20 | 3-6 | 4-4 | 1 | 0 | 0 | 1 | 1 | 2 | 10 | 909 |
| Purdue | 40 | 3-12 | 2-2 | 2 | 2 | 0 | 1 | 2 | 4 | 8 | 899 |
| Illinois | 33 | 3-14 | 0-0 | 3 | 3 | 0 | 1 | 1 | 1 | 6 | 891 |
| Ohio St. | 40 | 2-9 | 3-4 | 0 | 2 | 0 | 0 | 0 | 0 | 7 | 885 |
| Northwestern | 39 | 9-17 | 3-4 | 4 | 3 | 0 | 2 | 1 | 0 | 21 | 878 |
| Wisconsin | 40 | 10-18 | 10-10 | 7 | 1 | 0 | 5 | 1 | 1 | 30 | 857 |
| Minnesota | 30 | 9-12 | 6-6 | 2 | 5 | 0 | 1 | 1 | 0 | 24 | 827 |
| Iowa | 39 | 6-18 | 0-0 | 3 | 0 | 0 | 0 | 0 | 4 | 12 | 803 |
| Purdue | 39 | 4-11 | 10-10 | 2 | 2 | 0 | 1 | 1 | 2 | 18 | 791 |
| Illinois | | | | | Did not play | | | | | | |
| Ohio St. | 40 | 8-15 | 2-2 | 0 | 3 | 0 | 0 | 4 | 3 | 18 | 773 |
| Wisconsin | 33 | 8-14 | 4-5 | 2 | 2 | 0 | 1 | 2 | 1 | 20 | 755 |
| Northwestern | 22 | 6-8 | 2-2 | 0 | 3 | 0 | 2 | 0 | 2 | 14 | 735 |
| Mich. St. | 35 | 6-16 | 1-1 | 4 | 1 | 0 | 1 | 0 | 0 | 13 | 721 |
| Michigan | 36 | 8-14 | 3-3 | 4 | 4 | 0 | 4 | 2 | 1 | 19 | 708 |
| Florida | 37 | 12-19 | 3-4 | 2 | 1 | 0 | 1 | 3 | 1 | 27 | 689 |
| Miami | 39 | 10-16 | 4-4 | 6 | 4 | 0 | 2 | 1 | 2 | 24 | 662 |
| Kansas St. | 40 | 11-17 | 10-12 | 6 | 5 | 0 | 1 | 2 | 2 | 32 | 638 |
| St.Joseph's | 30 | 10-12 | 2-2 | 7 | 3 | 0 | 0 | 1 | 0 | 22 | 606 |
| W.Kentucky | 31 | 6-8 | 2-2 | 1 | 4 | 0 | 1 | 3 | 2 | 14 | 584 |
| Iowa St. | 40 | 10-16 | 2-2 | 5 | 2 | 0 | 0 | 0 | 3 | 22 | 570 |
| Kentucky | 39 | 11-14 | 2-2 | 6 | 7 | 0 | 1 | 3 | 2 | 24 | 548 |
| Notre Dame | 34 | 1-6 | 2-2 | 2 | 2 | 0 | 1 | 3 | 4 | 4 | 524 |
| Ohio | 31 | 8-11 | 7-7 | 2 | 4 | 0 | 1 | 2 | 0 | 23 | 520 |
| Louisville | 40 | 7-16 | 4-4 | 3 | 1 | 0 | 2 | 3 | 0 | 18 | 497 |

### FRESHMAN

| | M | FG | FT | R | A | BS | St | TO | PF | TP | Total |
|---|---|---|---|---|---|---|---|---|---|---|---|
| Virginia | 38 | 2-7 | 2-2 | 1 | 2 | 0 | 1 | 4 | 2 | 6 | 479 |
| N.Carolina | 40 | 9-13 | 9-10 | 6 | 3 | 0 | 2 | 3 | 2 | 27 | 473 |
| Richmond | 40 | 6-12 | 10-10 | 3 | 4 | 0 | 1 | 3 | 1 | 22 | 446 |
| Ohio St. | 40 | 8-11 | 1-3 | 3 | 2 | 0 | 0 | 2 | 1 | 17 | 424 |
| Illinois | 35 | 7-11 | 0-0 | 1 | 1 | 0 | 1 | 4 | 2 | 14 | 407 |
| Purdue | 39 | 2-7 | 8-9 | 3 | 3 | 0 | 1 | 1 | 2 | 12 | 393 |
| Mich. St. | 40 | 12-18 | 6-6 | 2 | 5 | 0 | 2 | 1 | 2 | 30 | 381 |
| Michigan | 38 | 5-6 | 8-8 | 4 | 6 | 0 | 0 | 1 | 0 | 18 | 351 |
| Northwestern | 40 | 4-10 | 0-0 | 3 | 2 | 0 | 0 | 1 | 4 | 8 | 333 |
| Iowa | 40 | 3-9 | 3-4 | 2 | 3 | 0 | 3 | 1 | 0 | 9 | 325 |
| Minnesota | 44 | 10-14 | 3-3 | 3 | 1 | 0 | 4 | 1 | 3 | 23 | 316 |
| Wisconsin | 40 | 6-9 | 6-7 | 2 | 3 | 0 | 1 | 0 | 1 | 18 | 293 |
| Wisconsin | 39 | 4-7 | 4-4 | 2 | 5 | 0 | 1 | 2 | 2 | 12 | 275 |
| Minnesota | 34 | 8-10 | 4-4 | 5 | 3 | 0 | 2 | 4 | 1 | 20 | 263 |
| Iowa | 40 | 7-8 | 4-4 | 4 | 4 | 1 | 3 | 0 | 0 | 18 | 243 |
| Northwestern | 39 | 6-10 | 3-3 | 3 | 6 | 0 | 1 | 3 | 3 | 15 | 225 |
| Michigan | 37 | 5-11 | 2-2 | 1 | 0 | 0 | 1 | 0 | 2 | 12 | 210 |
| Mich. St. | 42 | 10-15 | 1-2 | 0 | 2 | 0 | 0 | 1 | 3 | 21 | 198 |
| Purdue | 36 | 1-4 | 2-2 | 2 | 2 | 1 | 1 | 4 | 3 | 4 | 177 |
| Illinois | 45 | 7-13 | 15-16 | 2 | 3 | 0 | 5 | 3 | 1 | 29 | 173 |
| Ohio St. | 30 | 9-15 | 6-7 | 7 | 2 | 0 | 0 | 3 | 3 | 24 | 144 |
| Boston Coll. | 35 | 3-5 | 13-14 | 3 | 4 | 0 | 0 | 5 | 2 | 19 | 120 |
| Ball St. | 27 | 1-6 | 0-0 | 8 | 5 | 0 | 2 | 0 | 2 | 2 | 101 |
| Kansas St. | 25 | 4-4 | 0-0 | 0 | 1 | 0 | 0 | 3 | 3 | 8 | 99 |
| Illinois St. | 21 | 4-5 | 2-2 | 0 | 3 | 0 | 0 | 1 | 0 | 10 | 91 |
| Texas A&M | 23 | 3-4 | 2-2 | 4 | 2 | 0 | 2 | 2 | 1 | 8 | 81 |
| Texas E.P. | 33 | 2-5 | 0-0 | 0 | 3 | 0 | 0 | 0 | 1 | 4 | 73 |
| Tenn. Tech | 38 | 9-15 | 8-11 | 5 | 3 | 0 | 3 | 0 | 3 | 26 | 69 |
| Kentucky | 39 | 6-10 | 5-5 | 2 | 4 | 0 | 3 | 3 | 5 | 17 | 43 |
| Notre Dame | 40 | 3-7 | 8-8 | 3 | 7 | 1 | 4 | 5 | 1 | 14 | 26 |
| Miami | 31 | 5-8 | 2-2 | 1 | 2 | 0 | 1 | 1 | 3 | 12 | 12 |

### ALL GAMES

| | G | S | Min | Hi | 40 | FG | Pct. | FT | Pct. | R | Av. | Hi | A | Hi | BS | Hi | St | Hi | TO | Hi | PF-FO | Pts. | Av. | Hi |
|---|---|---|---|---|---|---|---|---|---|---|---|---|---|---|---|---|---|---|---|---|---|---|---|---|
| Freshman | 31 | 27 | 1167 | 45 | 10 | 171-289 | .592 | 137-150 | .913 | 82 | 2.7 | 8 | 98 | 7 | 3 | 1 | 45 | 5 | 63 | 5 | 60-1 | 479 | 15.5 | 30 |
| Sophomore | 32 | 31 | 1158 | 50 | 11 | 232-431 | .538 | 116-126 | .921 | 101 | 3.2 | 7 | 85 | 7 | 0 | 0 | 44 | 8 | 49 | 4 | 51-0 | 580 | 18.1 | 32 |
| Junior | 28 | 28 | 1038 | 45 | 11 | 254-457 | .556 | 122-140 | .871 | 75 | 2.7 | 6 | 79 | 7 | 1 | 1 | 50 | 6 | 50 | 5 | 46-0 | 630 | 22.5 | 38 |
| Senior | 34 | 34 | 1261 | 55 | 8 | 241-508 | .473 | 160-180 | .889 | 87 | 2.6 | 6 | 123 | 9 | 3 | 1 | 39 | 4 | 64 | 6 | 52-0 | 749 | 22.0 | 42 |
| Career | 125 | 120 | 4624 | 55 | 40 | 898-1685 | .533 | 535-596 | .898 | 346 | 2.8 | 8 | 385 | 9 | 7 | 1 | 178 | 8 | 226 | 6 | 209-1 | 2438 | 19.5 | 42 |

### BIG TEN

| | G | S | Min | Hi | 40 | FG | Pct. | FT | Pct. | R | Av. | Hi | A | Hi | BS | Hi | St | Hi | TO | Hi | PF-FO | Pts. | Av. | Hi |
|---|---|---|---|---|---|---|---|---|---|---|---|---|---|---|---|---|---|---|---|---|---|---|---|---|
| Freshman | 18 | 18 | 698 | 45 | 9 | 114-188 | .606 | 76-84 | .905 | 49 | 2.6 | 7 | 53 | 6 | 2 | 1 | 26 | 5 | 32 | 4 | 33-0 | 304 | 16.9 | 30 |
| Sophomore | 17 | 16 | 601 | 40 | 5 | 102-222 | .459 | 58-62 | .935 | 45 | 2.6 | 7 | 40 | 5 | 0 | 0 | 22 | 4 | 19 | 4 | 26-0 | 262 | 15.4 | 30 |
| Junior | 18 | 18 | 674 | 45 | 8 | 163-294 | .556 | 78-93 | .839 | 45 | 2.5 | 5 | 40 | 4 | 0 | 0 | 29 | 6 | 33 | 5 | 26-0 | 404 | 22.4 | 38 |
| Senior | 18 | 18 | 687 | 55 | 4 | 126-267 | .472 | 85-95 | .895 | 44 | 2.4 | 5 | 63 | 9 | 2 | 1 | 22 | 3 | 34 | 4 | 25-0 | 391 | 21.7 | 42 |
| Career | 71 | 70 | 2660 | 55 | 26 | 505-971 | .520 | 297-334 | .889 | 183 | 2.6 | 7 | 196 | 9 | 4 | 1 | 99 | 6 | 118 | 5 | 110-0 | 1361 | 19.2 | 42 |